# SUMMER IN THE SEED

Spode — June 1984
Fran Riches

# Summer in the Seed

AELRED SQUIRE

LONDON
SPCK

First published 1980
SPCK
Holy Trinity Church
Marylebone Road
London NW1 4DU

The design on the cover of this book
is based on a photograph of
*Landscape in Autumn Storm*
by Hsia Kuei (*c.*1180–1230).
The original is in a private collection
in Japan.

Filmset in Great Britain by
Northumberland Press Ltd, Gateshead, Tyne and Wear
and printed by
Richard Clay (The Chaucer Press) Ltd, Bungay, Suffolk


ISBN 0 281 03695 0

*For James
and
so many other friends
in one country
or another*

Long sleeps the summer in the seed
Tennyson, *In Memoriam*


A culture is not a treasure which the custodians of museums and libraries should keep scrupulously dusted in order to pass it on intact to coming generations. It is a living tradition which can only be kept alive at the cost of ceaseless renewal, tirelessly maintained.

Henri-Irenée Marrou

# CONTENTS

# ACKNOWLEDGEMENTS

Thanks are due to the following for permission to quote from copyright sources:

E. J. Brill, Leiden: *Studies in the Book of Job* by Alfred Guillaume.

Burns & Oates Ltd: *Spiritual Canticle* (of St John of the Cross), translated by E. Allison Peers, 1961.

Jonathan Cape Ltd and the Estate of Robert Frost: An excerpt from 'Kitty Hawk' from *The Poetry of Robert Frost*, edited by Edward Connery Latham. Copyright © 1956, 1962 by Robert Frost. Copyright © 1969 (USA) by Holt, Rinehart & Winston; reprinted by permission of Holt, Rinehart & Winston, Publishers, New York.

Chatto & Windus Ltd and Farrar, Straus & Giroux Inc.: An excerpt from 'Five Flights Up' from *Geography III* by Elizabeth Bishop. Copyright © 1974, 1979 by Elizabeth Bishop. Reprinted with the permission of Farrar, Straus & Giroux Inc. This poem appeared originally in the *New Yorker*.

Eyre & Spottiswoode (Publishers) Ltd: Thomas Aquinas' *Summa Theologiae*, volume 30: 'Gospel of Grace', edited by Cornelius Ernst OP.

Faber & Faber Ltd and Random House Inc.: 'Ultima Ratio Regum' from *Collected Poems* by Stephen Spender.

William Heinemann Ltd: *To Speed the Plough* by Ian Niall.

Hughes Massie Ltd: *St John of the Cross*, translated by Roy Campbell and published by Penguin Books Ltd.

Penguin Books Ltd: Excerpts from *Fathers and Sons* by Ivan Turgenev, translated by Rosemary Edmonds (Penguin Classics, 1965), pp. 11, 17, 19, 31–2, 39–45, 58, 60–1, 66–71, 92, 96, 102, 106, 114, 116, 125, 163, 196, 210–13, 225, 230–32, 237, © Rosemary Edmonds, 1965. Reprinted by permission of Penguin Books Ltd.

Routledge & Kegan Paul Ltd: *Oppression and Liberty* by Simone Weil. Reprinted by permission also of the University of Massachusetts, 1973 (copyright © 1958 by Routledge & Kegan Paul).

SCM Press Ltd and Abingdon Press, Nashville, Tennessee: *Wisdom in Israel* by G. von Rad.

SCM Press Ltd and Harper & Row, Publishers, Inc., New York: *Old Testament Theology* by G. von Rad.

Sheed & Ward Ltd: *A Treasury of Russian Spirituality*, edited by G. P. Fedotov.

The Society of Authors as the literary representative of the Estate of A. E. Housman; and Jonathan Cape Ltd, publishers of *The Collected Poems of A. E. Housman*. An excerpt from 'Tell it not here, it needs not saying' from *The Collected Poems of A. E. Housman* copyright 1922 (USA) by Holt, Rinehart & Winston; copyright 1950 by Barclays Bank Ltd; reprinted by permission of Holt, Rinehart & Winston, Publishers, New York.

# FOREWORD

Newman and many of his generation in the nineteenth century began to talk about being old when they were still only in their thirties. There are, of course, still those who disappear sooner than they or anyone could have guessed. But longevity has probably become so much more normal for the physically and mentally active in our day that it is sometimes with an irrational regret that those whose views one would have liked to hear are no longer there to ask. *Some* are old teachers: one, in a very proud line, now in his eighties told me recently that his doctor had jestingly said that he would probably have to be shot in the end. Of those who went down without any shooting long ago I should in many ways most have liked Fr Victor White to see this book. For it was he who, with a wry smile, gave me on the day of my ordination as a priest my now much-thumbed copy of the *I Ching* in Richard Wilhelm's translation. Others are friends, like Doris Layard or Jytte Munthe-Kaas, as she was when I first knew her, who would have communicated a very personal pleasure at things they liked, and thrown up eyes and hands at anything they thought too mysterious or 'just going too far'.

My debts to the living are too numerous and too varied to be specified in much detail. Monks and nuns who have supported me with their interest and prayers will accept the book itself as a sufficient sign that they are not forgotten. Among Dominicans I must mention three particularly. Fergus Kerr has, I believe, never failed to answer with the utmost promptness any query or request for the loan of a book over the long period since I left the incomparable resources of Oxford in 1965. Over a more recent period Aidan Nichols has not only tried to keep me in touch with some of the things a young man should know, but also allowed me to read a thesis on the subject of the incarnation which will, I hope, some day be revised for publication. It shows a convergence in ways of thinking of which it was good to know. Gérard-Marie Ketterer of my own community in Oslo has helped to keep me *au courant* with some of the reviews of books coming from France.

But I owe a still more immediate debt to many Norwegian friends. Petter Maus has shared his interests and enthusiasms ever since the early days when we could talk only an odd mixture of his language and mine. He will know the kind of thing to expect here and be tolerant of it. Olav Vaalund gave me a long and decisively encouraging morning when the project was taking a more definite shape. With Noralv and Unni Veggeland I have discussed aspects of two specific chapters while they were in the writing, and their loyalty to an odd stranger has long been a support. Elisabeth and Willy Ruud and their children will guess why their friendship and many brief stays at the hidden house among the trees at Lia has meant something out of all proportion to the pleasant hours we have spent together in the last few years. None of these has any responsibility for the views expressed in this book, and all will perhaps disapprove of some of it.

I cannot, however, altogether absolve two people in England from some kind of continuing responsibility. Without my bookseller Katherine Watson I, like many small collectors, would probably never have laid hands on some of the books I quote. It is notorious that even people in cities wait for years for books that *should* be available, and that luckier friends sometimes get. And then my editor David Craig has made me feel his warm and generous encouragement, with many a word by return of post, when I felt the whole task was perhaps impossibly beyond me.

I thank in advance anyone who finds the result even a little useful. They will see that I offer them no ready answers: only, perhaps, a few seeds for further development. Summer is, in any case, a gift for which one can only prepare.

*Mariakirken, Lillehammer*                                        A.S.

# ABBREVIATIONS

*AF*    Aelred Squire, *Asking the Fathers* (London/New York, 1973)

*PG*    Migne, *Patrologia Graeca*

*PL*    Migne, *Patrologia Latina*

*RB*    Rule of St Benedict

*RSV*    Revised Standard Version

*SC*    Sources chrétiennes

*TLS*    *Times Literary Supplement*

Wand    J. W. C. Wand, *The New Testament Letters* (Oxford, 1946)

# 1

## THE DEMANDS OF LOVE

With some honourable exceptions it has become usual for the prophets of our times to proclaim a message of woe. The plausibility of these messages is only too evident to anyone alive to the mass of information on the human predicament daily made available to us. The enemies of mankind, whoever they may be, have got well beyond 'bending the bow and fitting their arrow to the string'. It remains, however, true that they tend to 'shoot in the dark', their shafts arriving from a wide variety of directions. Their arrows more surely reach the heart when their poison is introduced by the apparent realism which asks: 'If the foundations are destroyed, what can the upright man do?' David, afterwards to be the ideal king in Israel, embodies all these thoughts and suggestions in a little psalm of quiet confidence:

> In the Lord I take refuge;
> how can you say to me,
> 'Flee to your mountain, O bird'? [1]

The psalm reaffirms the need to take risks in certain clearly indicated circumstances, rather than to rush off to one's mountain hideouts. It expresses the belief that what cannot for the moment be understood or explained is not beyond either the comprehension or the control of an unpredictable God. He first brought David to prominence with the aid of the inadequate-looking equipment of a stone and a sling. David's psalm must have been much used by those going through similar experiences and with as little convincing chance of success. And history has not proved *all* these acts of courage wrong.

Dorotheus, a disciple of the 'great old men' of the deserts of Gaza, prolongs this tradition of faith, when he says on recovering from a painful and incapacitating illness:

It is good, brothers, as I never stop telling you, to refer everything to God, and to say that nothing happens outside him. One must not, then, be disturbed by what happens but, as I have said, refer everything to God's providence and preserve one's peace.

I

Some people are so upset by what happens to them that they renounce life itself, and count it good to die as a way of escape. People like this are moved by littleness of spirit and a great deal of ignorance. It is the memory of God that comforts the soul. But the passions no longer allow it even this memory.[2]

It is possible that an opening of this kind will be enough to confuse and discourage some readers but, if they have come thus far, they will perhaps have the greatness of spirit to go a little further. In a previous book, *Asking the Fathers*, I attempted, as authentically as I could, to communicate a sense of an indivisible tradition of doctrine and life which I genuinely believed was not my own. It is a tradition which tends to be born again wherever the desires which inspired primitive monasticism are awakened in the hearts of those who, as St Benedict says of suitable novices, 'truly seek God'.[3] The earlier book was addressed not, primarily, to monks in any technical sense but to all those who, in whatever walk of life, had reached a point where the need to change or be changed, to be 'renovated in their innermost self',[4] had assumed the urgency which drove seekers out to visit the desert solitaries in the early Christian centuries. These seekers went in the hope of receiving at least one appropriate word of life-giving help, rather than a mass of complicated and lifeless instructions. Not all those who at that time took this kind of trouble were necessarily motivated either by orthodoxy of faith or stability of purpose. But if they were prepared to listen to what was said to them, and act on it, they generally found both the one and the other. Understanding came in the wake of experience and stability rooted itself in co-operation with the stimulus and demands of the forces of life. Many such people exist today, as hidden from any kind of notoriety as they have normally tended to be. *Some* of these people have read and re-read *Asking the Fathers* as often as it was intended it should be bearable, and even necessary, to read it. They have perceived that its message as it had emerged in response to my own needs, and those of a few others, had presented itself as a fairly closely integrated whole. They have also seen that it consciously resisted looking at certain questions at all, and confined the discussion of others within carefully chosen limits. Many of its silences, like the book's many quotations from spiritual masters of various periods, were determined by a conviction which has recently been admirably expressed. A gifted translator of an anonymous series of sayings of the Desert Fathers says that 'the essence of the spirituality of the desert is that it was not taught but caught'.[5] It has been helpful to know that a number of people have found my own distillation of elements in this tradition concentrated enough to enable them to be 'caught' by something of whose existence they had hitherto been virtually unaware.

This new book is concerned, at least in part, with hidden riches of a related kind. In some cases these may come as a supplement to what has been offered earlier. In others they are riches of other times, other places and other traditions, whose value and meaning seems to be enhanced or revealed in a new light by an explicit contact with the tradition of the undivided Church. The spirit of this book was, I believe, clearly enough at work in its predecessor. There it seemed right at various points to suggest that insights even of people who felt little or no sympathy for Christianity as they happened to have met it were, in fact, the most natural introduction for anyone of our own day to some of the forgotten convictions of undivided Christianity. Over and above the experience common to the rest of humanity, the bulk of writers within the orbit of western culture have in any case often been, at least unconsciously, influenced by the underground life of that earlier undivided tradition. It has always been more vital than any of its desiccated derivatives. But, through all kinds of factors, traditions of different origin now present themselves for assimilation by the mainstream of a new culture. For two factors must convince even the most unshakably orthodox Christian that, if the world is not actually facing imminent destruction – a topic on which it does not seem useful to add another book – it must be on the brink of the evolution of a new culture never before seen in human history.[6] 'For better or worse, the die is now cast, the world is one. The citizen of the world has to live with his fellow citizens, at the ever-narrowing range of the aerofoil and the radio-wave.'[7] But the fact that information can be rapidly disseminated over the entire globe and that journeys between capitals can be calculated in a matter of hours will deceive no one of experience into supposing that these things *in themselves* constitute communication. It is, in fact, no longer necessary completely to arrive anywhere, and many travellers seem never to do so. The journeys of a few Europeans to India or Tibet or other hitherto remote places, in search of something they could not find at home, seem generally to have done little to remedy this state of affairs. The reason for this is not far to seek. It is from the fruitful labour now possible at the point of departure that most travellers recoil. We are surrounded by a wealth of unused equipment and invitations to unlived experience. If Christians of professedly traditional belief do not grasp these facts and rediscover the meaning of their faith under the impact of them, others will have to do so. Someone must bring back the news that something of universal significance did happen on the first Easter morning, and that it is useless to seek the living among the dead. Neither those coming from outside, nor those fighting their way forward from within organized Christianity will be likely to reach these convictions if they yield to 'littleness of spirit'. The going seems, on the whole, likely to be hard in the immediately foreseeable future. The reason for this is, as Gregory Nazianzen observed in the fourth century, sometimes clearer to non-Christians than it is to the kind of Christians who try never to look over the fences they have constructed around themselves.[8]

In the second place, the state of suspended animation in regard even to their own origins, in which many Christians appear to have remained encapsulated seems certain to ensure that, as the last structures of the post-Constantinian Church everywhere collapse, those who live their faith will have the advantage of rediscovering it under something like the conditions of the earliest centuries. When it came to distinctive forms of expression, early Christianity had virtually everything to make from the ground up. It is, of course, to these centuries that monastic life has constantly looked back and been revitalized, finding ever-changing forms for old convictions that do not require Gothic dress, and did not originally have it.

It is one of this book's subsidiary beliefs that *some* of what it has to discuss ought thus to interest even non-Christians. This is because it shares the view of T. S. Eliot that 'while we believe that the same religion may inform a variety of cultures, we may ask whether any culture can come into being, or maintain itself, without a religious basis'. It is possible to take a more optimistic view of the capacity of orthodox Christianity to undergo the radical culture-change through which it is now passing than that which emerges from T. S. Eliot's not always lucid or persuasive talks on this subject. This book does so because it holds a view of tradition – as opposed to mere traditionalism – which determined the very shape of the teaching presented in *Asking the Fathers*. On the other hand, it has a greater respect for Eliot's insistence upon the 'vital importance for a society of friction between its parts' than it has for the many self-conscious and generally rootless contemporary attempts at ecclesiastical adaptation. These can never, as T. S. Eliot repeatedly argues, amount to that mysteriously life-fostering thing, a 'culture', which is 'the one thing we cannot deliberately aim at'. As he says, in what is something like a conclusion, though it does not come at the end: 'When we consider the quality of integration required for the full cultivation of the spiritual life, we must keep in mind the possibility of grace and the exemplars of sanctity in order not to sink into despair.'[9]

Thus it is that this book is concerned once again with tradition as something alive, and with the inheritors of the spirit of the desert Fathers, wherever they happen to appear. 'For them, tradition is not the dead hand of the past, but the living wisdom of a master who himself responds authentically to the spiritual fullness of his immediate situation and helps others, who wish it, to do the same.'[10] In living with this sense of immediacy the true possibilities of integration lie. It is perhaps no accident that a theologian from a country where orthodox faith looks as though it has been revitalized under the friction of communism seems often to have said some of the more convincing things on these matters. In the course of a talk given in connection with the study of the sayings of the desert Fathers, Fr Dumitru Staniloae says that 'tradition is the transmission from one generation to another of revealed teaching in its concrete application to the life of the faithful'. He dwells at some length on this point, saying: 'Tradition is thus more than a remembrance of specific acts of Christ and specific words of his; it is continuous life with him through the Holy Spirit, who renders us apt for this kind of life'. He adds of the gospels that they are 'only a document of the tradition, but the tradition itself is revelation; it is Christ the Saviour in his saving action as it continues through the centuries.' It will be immediately comprehensible why Father Staniloae assigns a special role to the monastic life in the transmission and practice of the spiritual life and he repeats the conviction which has, again and again, blossomed in monastic renewal, when he says: 'The tradition of this spiritual life as the most conscious life in Christ, as the fullest accomplishment of the commands of Christ, as the deepest application of the revealed teachings, goes back to Christian life at the time of the apostles.'[11] At the same time it is valuable and relevant to note that an impressive monk, Fr Silouan, who died on Mount Athos in 1938, 'very rarely' advised those drawn to these ideals to try to live them out in a

monastery since, in his view, the day was drawing near when many
would live in the world and at the same time lead a monastic life. It
would be difficult to believe that a simple Russian, of peasant stock,
who entered his monastery in 1892, had reached this conclusion
had we not been told it by a qualified disciple, who adds that Father
Silouan 'thought that circumstances in general were becoming
unpropitious for the form of monastic life that existed in ancient
times but that the vocation and yearning for monasticism would
always exist'.[12]

It is somewhere in this area, where unwavering principles of life
find themselves undergoing the deeply disturbing processes of
change in the already crystallized outward forms, that people who
may hitherto scarcely have realized they had anything in common
find themselves meeting. Doubt and confusion so prevail that both
the man who has said in his heart 'there is no God', and the man
who has never doubted that there is, may find their hearts condemning them in a common sense of foolishness and helplessness.
It is then that it will be no false comfort to remember the Johannine
word that 'God is greater than our hearts',[13] and that our disturbance is not his. It will be no false comfort, since the business of
'truly seeking God' has always proved a sufficiently mysterious
affair in practice. Not only has the conscious seeker found himself
having to give up today the image of the divine with which he was
in love yesterday; he has also to believe that, whether they will it or
not, everyone is involved in this search, though repeated disillusion-
ment does not always appear to teach them this lesson. No one
interested in the viability of tradition – understood as the theologian and Fr Silouan understand it – can fail to be struck by the
fact that when a well-known ethologist, who has never held any
special brief for religion, comes to list the root causes of our
contemporary discomforts, he names among his chosen eight 'the
break with tradition'. On this, among other things, he has this to
say:

> The erroneous belief that only the rationally comprehensible
> or the scientifically provable belongs to the fixed knowledge of
> mankind produces disastrous effects. It encourages 'scientifi-
> cally enlightened' youth to throw overboard the enormous fund
> of knowledge and wisdom contained in the traditions of every
> old civilization and in the teaching of the great world religions.
> Anyone who believes that all this is null and void is harbouring

another illusion, just as disastrous, namely that science can create, from nothing and by reason alone, a whole culture with everything pertaining to it. This notion is only slightly less stupid than the opinion that our knowledge can 'better' mankind by interference with human genes.[14]

One may wonder, as T. S. Eliot wondered about Matthew Arnold, whether for Konrad Lorenz 'culture' is not the ultimate value which the presence of religion merely colours and underpins. If this is so, one understands why the overwhelmingly negative attitude to youth in what he has to say seems to go well beyond the undoubtedly distressing evidence he quotes to substantiate it. After all, it must seem to some of us involved in teaching to do too little justice to the role played by the middle-aged in the evolution of these problems. When all is said, it cannot be denied that many of the deeper problems of those now growing up in the world are of a kind with which their parents could not have been more ill-equipped to help them to deal. Commonly they had only the dead husk of traditionalism to hand on. Few had any notion of the living continuity of a spiritual tradition commensurate with the urgent need to breathe life into forms which, naturally, no one can be blamed for not having anticipated. It is perhaps for those for whom culture, as the bearer of tradition, is in fact the ultimate value that the feeling that the foundations have been destroyed will seem to inhibit all possibility of a favourable issue. This is one of the suggestions of the tempter. When the theologian and the man of prayer coincide, as the undivided Church believed they must, this thought must be resisted in the spirit of faith which it is still appropriate to express with the confidence of David's little psalm. At the same time, it will not be forgotten that, of the three whom tradition has honoured with the title of 'theologian' in the sense just referred to, Gregory Nazianzen is a striking example of a man convinced that the believer would be at fault to express indifference about or denigration of the cultural resources he finds to hand.

Be that as it may, it may seem something of a quirk of the imagination to place an investigation of the kind this book promises to be under the patronage of a poet whom, for all his eminent qualities, no one would claim for theological orthodoxy. Tennyson's intuitions and his sensibility were peculiarly alert to the currents already at work in his own day, and it is his sensibility that this book primarily invokes. In a recent essay on the relation between his poems and Tennyson's lifelong interest in science, it has been noted that 'many years before Darwin published his *Origin of Species* Tennyson had recognized the crucial questions raised',[15] and that some of the agonizing that goes on in the pre-Darwinian *In Memoriam* is precisely about these issues. It would be a mistake to make this just observation of fact bear more weight than it can. Again, it does Tennyson's religion no particular discredit that he was unable to reconcile himself to many of the features of the Christian faith as understood and expounded by some of his contemporaries. In brief, it would be an exaggeration to suppose that he ever reached a position on these matters which was anything like so coherent and articulate as that of Matthew Arnold.[16] Sir Charles Tennyson is shrewd enough to imply more than he is prepared openly to say, when he writes of one of the most familiar of all his grandfather's poems, *Crossing the Bar*, that probably few realize the real meaning of the last two lines

> I hope to see my pilot face to face
> When I have crossed the bar.

Sir Charles notes: 'When making them Tennyson had in mind a passenger sailing out of harbour through difficult waters, who does not know that a pilot has been at the wheel, until the ship is out of danger and the pilot comes on deck.'[17]

It is, of course, true that this thought would have seemed less agnostic to generations of Christians who genuinely believed that God is an unsearchable mystery than it must to anyone who reads it today. It is even with this very same image of a ship at sea that the passage from Dorotheus of Gaza, quoted earlier, begins. All that it is right to question is whether the 'not-knowing' involved in both cases is really substantially the same in kind, even though *as an experience* it may justly be described as having something of the same quality. Christopher Ricks is naturally right to warn us that 'we should heed Tennyson's complaint that: They are always speaking of me as if I were a writer of philosophical treatises.'[18] If *In Memoriam* haunts the memory as a gathering of the problems of a compassionate mind constellated about the very real difficulties of a great love, it also does so for a reason suggested by T. S. Eliot, which Ricks cites with evident respect: 'It is not religious because of the quality of its faith, but because of the quality of its doubt.' In his previous paragraph in the original, T. S. Eliot has said of Tennyson that 'his feelings were more honest than his mind'. This suggests what Eliot means when he insists that to qualify the poem's 'despair with the adjective "religious" is to elevate it above most of its derivatives'.[19]

Speaking in another context on the social function of poetry, T. S. Eliot says that 'not so much notice has been taken of the decline of religious sensibility. The trouble of the modern age is not merely the inability to believe certain things about God and man which our forefathers believed, but the inability to *feel* towards God and man as they did.'[20] This present book, in its title and occasionally in its course, takes the risk of supposing that at least religious *feeling* has not yet so far disappeared as T. S. Eliot obviously feared it might.[21] But it does not ask Tennyson's memorable allusions to the processes of natural growth to carry more than they have been traditionally asked to carry in many parables and allegories. The possibility cannot be overlooked that, in the very section from which the phrase 'summer in the seed' is taken, Tennyson means to include Christianity among the passing forms of which he asks 'who would keep an ancient form/through which the spirit breathes no more?' It is certain that in later life he was peculiarly enamoured of the poem he wrote under the impact of reading the Chinese texts which he and Jowett referred to as Laotsee. Quoting his own first line, Tennyson told his son that it was 'what I might have believed about the deeper problems of life a thousand summers 'ere the birth of Christ'.[22] Here is a matter on which both Tennyson's sensibility and his hesitations of mind unquestionably touch a much larger number of people in the western world today than ever they can have done while he was alive. It will therefore be necessary as this book goes on to look rather seriously at some of the ways in which alternatives to Christian belief are both enlisting the sensibility and at least modifying the ways in which even Christians of orthodox belief will wish to express themselves. Anyone who wishes to conduct polemics on these subjects must do so as best he can. But it may be said with some confidence that any lasting reconciliation of the mind to the realities of the situation in which we find ourselves is unlikely to occur without a very thorough harrowing of the house of a dead sensibility. It is one of the ironies of history that only a couple of years before the tragic drowning that released the flow of poetry collected in *In Memoriam*, a young woman living in a country house in Herefordshire was both reading and coveting the Benedictine edition of Gregory Nazianzen, a beautiful copy of which she had been privileged to use on condition of 'not leaning my arm on any part of the page'![23] She was afterwards to be well-known as the wife of a poet and a poet in her own right. But who would look among the bleak expressions of sombre puritan piety in Elizabeth Barrett Browning's poetry for the living religious sensibility that meets us in Tennyson's struggles to be true to a searching experience in his?

As we have already seen, this book does not believe that a new culture adequate to our future religious needs can be consciously constructed. But that it can be prepared for by an openness to messages coming from apparently quite different directions cannot be in doubt. Gregory Nazianzen was not alone in believing this kind of thing. The communication of a tradition that is both alive and true necessarily involves *in itself* a testing of the spirits to see whether they be of God.[24] The command to do this – which no man can ever fulfil alone – is specifically given in St John's First Letter in connection with the role of prophecy within Christianity as a faith centred on the incarnation of the Son of God. Thus the function of prophecy which tradition can accept confirms this faith, and helps to clarify its practical consequences for us here and now. As a major Russian theological study of ministry within the Church, recently made available in translation, has said: 'The age of the spirit, which is already the age of the Church, is not the age of a new revelation.'[25] But this in no way reduces the function of authentically prophetic voices in reawakening us to a sense of what the faith is, and what it requires of us here and now. It would be impossible either to write or to read this book without being willing to attend to some of these voices when they sound like articulations of recognizable tradition. Thus elements of Fr Zossima's discourse in Dostoevsky's *Brothers Karamazov* have a much more potent tradition behind them than that of the novelist himself. They sound as though they are speaking directly to the world in which we are now living. Take for instance:

Let not men's sins trouble you in your work. Fear not that it will obliterate your work and prevent it from being accomplished. Do not say: Sin is powerful, wickedness is powerful, bad environment is powerful, while we are lonely and helpless. Bad environment will destroy us and prevent our good work from being done. Fly from that despondency, children. You have only one means of salvation; take hold of yourself and make yourself responsible for all men's sins. My friend, believe me, that really is so, for the moment you make yourself responsible in all sincerity for everyone and everything, you will see that it really is so and that you are in fact responsible for everyone and everything. And by throwing your own impotence and indolence on to others, you will end up by sharing Satan's pride and murmuring against God.[26]

It is perhaps particularly the last sentence in this passage that needs to be taken very seriously. It is the note of not evading humble, human responsibility in these matters, the conviction of something to be done, even if it is only a preparation of heart, that also gives the message of Patriarch Athenagoras to a group of Italian journalists in January 1969 the character of something much more profound than a facile optimism:

The world today has reached a moment when every value is being put to the test. The new discoveries and the immense progress of technology . . . are leading to a confusion never before known. And this confusion often constitutes a temptation to discouragement and pessimism. But we should not yield to this temptation, not even for a moment, or abandon ourselves to despair. The situation of the world at present is a condition of birth, and a birth is always accompanied by hope. We regard the present situation with an immense Christian hope and with a profound conviction of responsibility for the kind of world which will emerge from today's travail.

This conviction of a bishop who could be very ironical about theologians of any other kind than those who might anciently have been given that title, was rooted in another which underlies the present book and gives it its sense of direction. 'Of all the events of history, the Resurrection is the only one which is ultimate, the only one which embraces in a certain sense the entire human and the entire cosmic reality. It is the Resurrection which gives meaning to history. All we have loved, all we have made, all the joy and all the beauty, will find their place in the kingdom.'[27]

These words taken out of the context of a life might suggest only the visionary about an immensely practical man whose supreme joy it was to be, with Pope Paul VI, instrumental in giving public expression in October 1967 to the need to reunite the Eastern and Western tradition of the undivided Church. It will therefore be appropriate to go at once to the witness of an equally practical-minded Latin pope of whose notions on our relations with our fellow human beings Athenagoras made it constantly clear he would have approved.

Leo the Great in the fifth century, like Athenagoras in the twentieth, was essentially a man whose ideas had been formed in the common teaching and practice of his local church and had been hardly seriously touched by anything like professional theology. Of more recent centuries Leo has been remembered almost exclusively in connection with one theme, and one theme only – the special consequences, whatever they may be, of the fact that the bishop of Rome is also successor of St Peter, spokesman of the apostles. Leo's intervention at the Council of Chalcedon, over which his legates presided, is also held in honour. It is perhaps time to bring back into the light an element in Leo's teaching, as recorded in his sermons, that bulks certainly much larger than that of the universal responsibility of the successors of St Peter. It is rather rarely that the recurring subject of universal responsibility for all men is explicitly linked with that aspect of the Christmas mystery which the undivided Church believes restores our human dignity. But Leo does say in one of his Christmas sermons that 'if it is a matter for human praise that the good qualities of a father should appear in his child, how much more splendid is it that the likeness of their maker should appear in those who are born of God'.[28] In thus connecting the restoration of the image of God in man with a way of living which mirrors God's own attitude towards the world, Leo is hinting at a matter to which he returns innumerable times. Leo's doctrine of the nature of the image of God in man is a very simple and unsophisticated one, but it is quite firmly the basis for his belief that all men have a claim on our compassion, simply on the ground of their being men.

'If we rightly understand our original condition, beloved, we find that man was made to the image of God that he might actually be an imitator of his maker. And this is the natural dignity of our kind that in us, as in a mirror, the character of the divine likeness should be resplendent.' This, Leo is careful to say, is not an attitude which includes only our friends, 'but absolutely all men, with whom we share a common nature, whether they be hostile or friendly . . . For one maker formed us, one creator gave us life.' Leo carries his conviction to its logical conclusion by saying explicitly that it includes even atheists. 'We must love God and our neighbour in such a way that we take the form of loving our neighbour from the love with which God loves us. For he is good even to the evil, and fosters with the gifts of his kindness not only those who worship him, but even those who deny him.' Thus it is both because of what God is, and what man is, that our compassion must be universal. It is naturally in the beatitude of the merciful that this conviction comes to life: 'For mercy wants you to be merciful and justice, just; so that in his creature the creator may appear, and in the mirror of the human heart the clear image of God may shine through the features of his resemblance.' This defines for Leo the specifically Christian way of living. 'For by those very ways by which our Saviour came to save us, those who are saved should approach their Saviour, so that the mercy of God may make us merciful and his truth true.' In thus insisting, as he does, on the connection between sound doctrine and sound living, and on the fact that this connection ought not to remain theoretical, Leo suggests the qualifications of a true mediator who is at once compassionate and straight, rather than merely clever at compromising. That Archbishop Athenagoras could, if he felt himself over-praised, say that he was 'just an old bureaucrat',[29] should lead no one to think that he was in reality merely trained in compromises. Of Leo, a man who in his time had succeeded in bringing off even trickier feats of diplomacy, such an accusation would be much less likely to be made. Whatever the theoretical limitations of either man, the substantially beneficent results of their efforts to bring their vision to bear upon life would be difficult to deny. Neither they, nor any of the great writers and saints to be cited in the pages that follow, are offered as an excuse for attempting a task by which much bolder and better-equipped men than the author might will be daunted. But they do in their different ways articulate something of the spirit which inspires this book.

Such qualifications as I have to offer are human rather than academic, though I hope that what follows will show some signs that I have not spent all my days in idleness. Like many of my generation, born not long after the end of the First World War and educated in the England of the 1930s, it has never been possible for me to pursue my progressive discovery of the tradition of Christian orthodoxy in isolation from the concern with social change and upheaval into which so much of the spiritual energies of friends I admired and books I read were almost exclusively poured. I was too young to belong to 'the Auden generation', on which the Professor of English at Princeton has recently written such an

uncommonly good book. But mine was the generation of school-
boys that read what the Auden generation was writing, passed
through its phases and shared some of its poses. War and politics
overshadowed us, largely as they were filtered through the literary
imagination, but also as the rumour of them reached us through the
curiously protective shell England had around it before 1939. My
first conscious memory of newspaper headlines is of those on the
morning after the Reichstag fire. But until the Second World War
involved us all it was, I believe, true of a much larger circle than
that of literary intellectuals in England that 'it was totally unaware
of economic and political realities in the public world outside'.[30]
The information was often there, but somehow it did not impinge.
For those of us who survived, it would never again be possible
wholly to keep the information out. Whatever we may make of
them now, it would for some of us be an unpardonable failure to
write as though the Marxism and socialism we first learned about
largely as heady theory did not deserve to be taken seriously as
views that might, after all, shape the future of the world.

In any case, the technological advances which the Second World
War speeded up have also been, mostly unwittingly, aiding another
kind of shaping that begins to occur of itself when very different
cultures meet. By an accident of personal history I happened to be
involved in the beginnings of some of this slowly accelerating
fusion, long before political theories were known to me even by
name. At the house of an aunt, I saw as a child many fine collector's
pieces of Chinese porcelain, drying before the fire, where she
repaired them. By the age of eleven China was my major enthusiasm, and the great Burlington House exhibition of Chinese art
in 1935–6 was one of the unforgettable events of my schooldays. By
that time I was regularly dipping into Arthur Waley's translations
from the Chinese. The first impulse to co-ordinate what these
vague suggestions of another world might mean to me was probably my meeting with the late Dr William Cohn, at that time
Keeper of the Department of Eastern Art at Oxford. At his invitation I became his pupil, and still feel for him that affection
which others who were privileged to examine an art object with
him certainly retain. He taught us not only to look, but to see. It
was through his kindness that, at the same time as I was trying to
deepen my acquaintance with eleventh- and twelfth-century
Christian writers and their sources, I was able to spend many of my
afternoons learning from the eloquent works of their Chinese near

contemporaries. How often I took a full hour with one of the versions of the great scroll of Hsia Kuei (*c.* 1180–1230), depicting a journey down the Yangtze. This scroll is, as Sirén says, like a symphonic poem, and I shall no more attempt to describe it than he does.[31] A more theoretical aspect of this line of development was my introduction to the work and thought of Carl Jung through two or three people then in Oxford who had known and worked with him personally. It was thus that, for rather different reasons and with a good deal less reading behind me, I found myself, like Jung on opening *The Secret of the Golden Flower*, looking into something that was already familiar. For that matter, my dwelling with Cistercian writers had already prepared me for the literature of hesychasm[32] before I knew it existed. In this way an unconscious preparation for that explosion of interest in Oriental religions and practices, which often now characterizes those who are for the most part in flight from political bewilderment, had been made in me many years before it became a social fact to be reckoned with. It is thus, too, with other eyes that I now read Jung saying that 'it cannot be sufficiently strongly emphasized that we are not Orientals, and therefore have an entirely different point of departure in these things'. I also notice him quoting a Chinese sentence to the effect that 'indolence of which a man is conscious and indolence of which he is unconscious are a thousand miles apart'.[33] It would be conscious indolence on my part, and perhaps in many cases on the part of my reader, to refuse to take seriously the impact of so many forces competing for spiritual allegiance in our contemporary world.

On account of my own limitations, and also for reasons of principle, I hope to persuade my reader to examine with me some, and only some, of these forces in as concrete a manner as possible. A personal distrust of the vague and general gives me a conscious sympathy with the postscript by Francis Jeanson to a modest and generous book on the human situation by a priest working at Notre Dame in Paris. Jeanson expresses the view that the one defence against mere mystification is a true effort of understanding. 'To acknowledge the other person is to take the trouble to know his situation and measure what constrains it . . . The human sciences have a role to play here which seems to me to be of first importance . . . Faith without learning is a kind of hell of good intentions.'[34] Yet he closes with a plea for a continual refreshing of these activities by the demands of love. What he means by this is more extensively explained in his own book, *The Faith of an Unbeliever*, where he insists on the concrete character of real love as opposed to the vague and disincarnate sentiments which many Christians unfortunately accept as being true charity.[35]

Monks accustomed to saying the psalter daily will not easily forget that 'there is a river whose streams make glad the city of God',[36] and that these streams of life do not wash around in a vacuum. In those same monastic circles in which the conviction grew that 'if you are a theologian you will really pray, and if you really pray you are a theologian', there grew up another which is in a certain way its fruit: 'A monk is a man who considers himself one with all men by the habit of seeing himself in every man.'[37] This suggests a sufficiently exigent view of the demands of love, whether one lives in the cloister or not. But it is safer to return to that and other matters after making the effort to understand what it is that really constrains both us and, to a greater or lesser extent, everyone around us in a world where every dream of freedom is daily called in doubt by determinism of one kind or another.

# 2
## DETERMINED LIVES

' "What'll y'ave? Lovin' mem'ry or deepest sympathy?" the woman in the shop asked when I went to buy a mourning card for one
of the office cleaners.' Enough survived into the 1920s for the nose,
the eye, and the ear of a man more than twenty years his junior to
vouch for the pungent accuracy of V. S. Pritchett. His sharp senses
took in an authentic London in which, as a teenager, he got his first
job. A younger man who happens to have belonged to any of the
Christian Churches will also, alas, probably understand what
Victor's dishevelled and likeable mother meant when she explained
of his grandfather, a non-conformist minister, that 'he was one to
whom hatred and the love of truth were very much the same thing'.
Not that this unattractive alliance of emotions is confined to people
with consciously-held religious beliefs. It is just as common among
those for whom politics has become the opium that religion may
once have been against the graver stresses of life. This hint of a
phrase of Karl Marx is likely to bring some ill-defined emotion to
the surface even in people who have the most unreliable information about what Marx may really have said. V. S. Pritchett
seems first consciously to have heard the name from a young
Cockney he met in the course of his daily work. From the little
reported of the conversation, this young man had obviously got
himself steeped in the kind of talk with which political Marxism is
not too unjustly associated. As Marx's latest large-scale biographer
says, Marx's views on some of the subsequent applications of his
theories may be gauged from his comment on certain French
Marxists: 'As for me, I am not a Marxist!' [1] This is a comment that
would still be appropriate as a retort to some snide remarks of a
contemporary French intellectual that Marxism 'swims in the
thought of the nineteenth century like a fish in the sea; that is to
say, everywhere else it ceases to breathe.' [2]
    But, smart talk apart, the thought of Marx continues to live and
breathe not only because it is often shrewder, sounder, and more
penetrating than any form of political Marxism. It survives also
because, in forms he could hardly have envisaged, the aspects of

human existence which engaged his interest and study have now assumed global dimensions. People of the most diverse political persuasions have been compelled to recognize this. The young Pritchett, without any specific political initiation, had been observing these things for himself, as he worked daily until 7.0 in the evening, and on Saturdays left between 2.0 and 4.0. 'My work was dull. The terrible thing was that it was simple and mechanical; far, far less difficult than work at school. This was humiliation ... Most people seemed to me, then, and even now [1968], chained to a dulling routine of systematised and tolerated carelessness and error. Whatever was going to happen to me, I knew I must escape from this easy, unthinking world ... In difficulty lay the only escape, from what seemed to me to be deterioration of faculty.' [3]

The final sentence in this paragraph implies the reason why something on the rather different topics of Marx and the political movements which theoretically derive their inspiration from him had to find a place in this book. The problem to which V. S. Pritchett found a personal solution without challenging the structure of society as it was is very much more difficult to solve today than it was, say, forty years ago. It can, indeed, become almost impossible even for someone with an enormous appetite for difficulty either to choose to move somewhere different, or even to decide to stay where they already are. The obstacles with which either choice is confronted are not always simply legal. Nor are they wilfully planned by the conscious malice of the modern equivalents of fairytale barons of unbelievable cruelty. No one has directly decreed the departure of the young and vigorous from many places in Norway where for centuries it has been possible to make an adequate if precarious living by fishing or farming. Yet this tendency can be demonstrated statistically, as it can for regions in the south of France and other areas of Europe, where a population in their sixties and seventies is left to run to seed amid rural beauties for which only tourism has a use. [4] It was to the remoter beginnings of this situation in the nineteenth century that the young Marx turned his attention.

It may, in any case, at once be said that nothing could be more opposed to a proper understanding of the doctrine of divine providence spoken of in the opening paragraph of this book – on which there will be a good deal more to say later – than to suppose that it absolves us from our duty to reflect about man's own problems and to make decisions about them as we can and see we should. There must have been many natively intelligent children whose problems about religion began with the difficulty of swallowing a verse in an enormously influential nineteenth-century hymn by a Mrs Alexander:

> The rich man in his castle,
> The poor man at his gate, .
> God made them, high or lowly,
> And order'd their estate.[5]

But did he really 'order their estate'? This was among the questions Karl Marx also asked himself. The theological and philosophical antecedents of the views of Marx would have been meaningless to the home-bred critics of a society of which Mrs Alexander's hymn offered so insidiously pious a defence. They still are to most people outside intellectual circles. But of the social circumstances Marx found himself compelled to study, working people had a direct and often acutely painful experience.

For us today a sense of perspective about these circumstances is necessary if we are to make anything sensible of what Marx had to say. Yet, as George Lichtheim writes in his immensely stimulating *Short History of Socialism*:

> The problem for the historian of socialism is this: industrial capitalism was born in Britain, but the socialist protest against it found its first coherent expression in France, a country that was slow to absorb the impact of the new mode of production. And the doctrine which pulled all these strands together – namely Marxism – was worked out in the 1840s by a theorist who obtained his philosophical training in his native Germany, his political education in France and Belgium, and his understanding of economics in England.

In other words, as Lichtheim adds later, 'Marx was a genuine European in the fullest sense'.[6] It is as just such a uniquely gifted interpreter of European problems, now evidently working themselves out on a world scale, that Marx cannot be dismissed.

'Men make their own history, but they do not make it just as they please; they do not make it under circumstances chosen by themselves, but under circumstances directly encountered, given, and transmitted from the past.'[7] The words of Marx occur near the beginning of a spirited piece of writing on political developments in France, short enough for anyone who wishes to get a glimpse of him as a writer to read in a comparatively few minutes. For the moment it is enough to notice the hint these words contain that the preoccupation of Marx with the element of determinism in history was not so naive as some accounts of it, including those of his followers, often lead us to suppose. The literary surface of the piece as a whole is, in any case, shot through with the wide range of humane study and reading which determined Marx's own way of thinking.[8] But in the England of the nineteenth century he met determinism in a very cruel and fundamental form. The picture of ageless stability, of ordered hierarchy, which Mrs Alexander's hymn somehow calls up was, in fact, a strange way of accounting for how at least *some* of the rich men had got into their not-always-very-old castles, and how the poor men had come to be standing at the gate. Between 1750 and 1850 the Industrial Revolution had not only transformed the world position of England, it had brought about a change in the social conditions of the masses of its people of a kind never before seen.

> Before the process had advanced very far, the labouring people had been crowded together in new places of desolation, the so-called industrial towns of England; the country folk had been dehumanized into slum dwellers; the family was on the road to perdition; and large parts of the country were rapidly disappearing under the slack and scrap-heaps vomited forth from the 'satanic mills'. Writers of all views and parties, conservatives and liberals, capitalists and socialists, invariably referred to social conditions under the Industrial Revolution as a veritable abyss of human degradation.[9]

How had all this come about? As Lichtheim says: 'It was only after Marx had intervened, that socialists began to understand how capitalism actually worked . . . He realized that the historical process had a logic of its own which could not be ignored.' To say this is, of course, to imply a deterministic view of history, which 'is not to be understood as signifying that there are historical determinants in the sense of physical or natural causation which men can do nothing about. The historical process is not something that goes on regardless of human wishes.'[10] Men make their own history, as we have just seen Marx saying, but they do not make it just as they please. Merleau-Ponty explains in what, for its length, must surely be one of the most brilliant short essays ever written on Marx, that 'it is a matter of understanding that the bond which attaches man to the world is at the same time his way of freedom; of seeing how man, in contact with nature, projects the instruments of his liberation around himself, not by destroying necessity but, on the contrary, by utilizing it.'[11] This is not, in other words, a fatalist doctrine, but it does lay bare the limitations of utopian voluntarism. The emphasis on sheer will is a topic to which it will be necessary to return when we come to look at political voluntarism in a supposed disciple of Marx, like Lenin. Marx himself was constantly at work on a critique of capitalism, revising and modifying and, in fact, never completing it. An essential part of this work was to see and to show not only what the world created by the Industrial Revolution did to human beings, but what it did to their thinking. In the short work just quoted Marx says in a few memorable sentences something which we shall have to bear in mind both in this chapter and later in this book.

> The social revolution of the nineteenth century cannot draw its poetry from the past, but only from the future. It cannot begin with itself before it has stripped off all superstitions in regard to the past. Earlier revolutions required recollections of past world history in order to drug themselves concerning their own content. In order to arrive at its own content, the revolution of the nineteenth century must let the dead bury their dead. There the phrase went beyond the content; here the content goes beyond the phrase.[12]

This is one of the many ways Marx has of saying that it is necessary to do something more than philosophize about the situation created by the Industrial Revolution. Something must be *done*. Anyone who takes the trouble to read him will see that it was not Marx's view that action should be a substitute for sound thinking. So conscientious a student and philosopher would have had no patience with such nonsense, as his break with the anarchist Bakunin sufficiently shows. But like many other things Marx says, a striking phrase such as 'you cannot do away with philosophy without fulfilling it'[13] could so easily be used as an excuse for forgetting completely the stringent argument that leads up to it. A similar warning about the materialism associated with the name of Marx is given by George Lichtheim:

> One must not make the mistake of identifying the historical materialism of Marx with the dialectical materialism later put

forward by Engels. Unlike his friend, Marx never proposed a
theory of the universe. And secondly, even if he had done so, it
would not necessarily affect one's judgement of the contribution
he made to the understanding of history.[14]

Confining ourselves for the moment to Marx's understanding of
capitalism and the way it functioned, it can be said that what
seemed to emerge from the social situation created by the
Industrial Revolution was that men's working power had become a
commodity to be bought and sold within a system that, of itself,
operated to keep a mechanism going. This mechanism subordi-
nated human needs and the distinctively human dimensions of life
to the interests of production. This was, and is, a very terrible state
of affairs, and Marx explains this again and again in substantially
the same terms. Why does the man who works for a wage sell his
work-capacity under this system? He does so, of course, in order to
live. But the danger, as Marx saw, was and is that he may in fact sell
*himself*, as though he were one of the commodities he produces. As
Marx says in *Capital*:

> The seller of labour power and the owner of money meet in the
> market and enter into mutual relations as commodity owners
> having equal rights, distinguished only by this, that one of them
> is a buyer and the other a seller; so that they are equal persons in
> the eye of the law. Such a relation can only persist on the
> understanding that the owner of labour power sells that labour
> power for a definite time and no longer; for if he should sell it
> once and for all, he would sell himself, would change himself
> from a free man into a slave, from an owner of a commodity into
> a commodity.[15]

This was a thought that had been with Marx from his early days
and he had often observed that feeling of remoteness from one of
his chief means of self-fulfilment which the man who works for a
wage experiences.[16] The further development of technological
processes has often vastly increased this alienation, even where it
has lessened the sheer physical labour of the worker in more recent
times.

To understand that Marx was first and foremost establishing a
criticism of a *system*, it is important to note what he himself
explicitly says about this in his preface to the only volume of his
great work *Capital*, which he himself lived to complete. There he
says:

To prevent possible misunderstanding, a word. I paint the capitalist and the landlord in no sense *couleur de rose*. But here individuals are dealt with only in so far as they are the personifications of economic categories, embodiments of particular class relations and class interests. My standpoint, from which the evolution of the economic formation of society is viewed as a process of natural history, can less than any other make the individual responsible for relations whose creature he socially remains, however much he may subjectively raise himself above them.[17]

Marx remains of interest as a thinker because he sees so clearly that it is not just any one group in the community that is the victim of the system which evolved with industrialism. Everyone is. His was one of those rare minds that, within their chosen terms of reference, can perceive things as a functioning whole. This is very cogently argued in the product of a lifetime's study of economic analysis by Joseph Schumpeter, who was certainly no political Marxist. As he insists: 'Marx's theory of history is a working hypothesis *by nature*. It is compatible with any philosophy or creed and should therefore not be linked up with any particular one – neither Hegelianism nor materialism is necessary or sufficient for it.' Aware that this firm assertion may cause surprise, he adds in a note that, as such, 'the economic interpretation implies neither absence of the individual's moral responsibility for his acts nor refusal to admit the possibility of supermundane influence upon these data themselves and the ways in which they work out. Marxists, it is true, will not admit this.' This clarity of judgement enables Schumpeter to say of Marx's work that 'the achievement is of first-rate importance although the elements that enter into it are of very unequal value, or rather, unequally impaired by obvious ideological bias.' His final conclusion is that 'the Marxist analysis is the only genuinely evolutionary economic theory that the period (1790–1870) produced. Neither its assumptions nor its techniques are above serious objections ... But the grand vision of an immanent evolution of the economic process ... remains after the most vigorous criticism has done its worst. It is this fact, and this fact alone, that constitutes Marx's claim to greatness as an economic analyst.' And this is also, of course, the ultimate reason why 'Marx's influence must be listed among the factors of the scientific situation today.'[18]

That much being said with regard to Marx's general frame of
thought, readers of this book will want to know how the most
frequently quoted phrase of Marx on religion fits into it. 'Religious
distress is at the same time the expression of real distress and also
the protest against real distress. Religion is the sigh of the oppressed creature, the heart of a heartless world, just as it is the spirit
of spiritless conditions. It is the opium of the people.' Anyone who
knows only the final phrase of this passage out of its context, in a
work Marx wrote in 1843, is likely to be surprised by what a short
leap Marx advances to saying that 'the criticism of heaven turns
into the criticism of earth'.[19] But having read so far, he is likely to
be fascinated by the lively commentary on these words written by a
Czech philosopher who – like many other Marxists in this chapter
– if not actually 'liquidated', disappeared from public view at the
behest of political Marxism not long after his disturbing study was
written. Gardavsky says in some paragraphs which keep Marx's
own text very closely in view:

> Marx's concept of religious suffering had nothing in common
> with the view that religion is primitive and obscure. Admittedly,
> Marx was aware that there are religious ideas abroad which are
> both childishly naive and obscurely fanciful. But . . . what he
> means to say is that as long as the material, economic, and social
> relationships which keep men apart persist, the only way the
> oppressed man can live under such conditions is to create his
> own realm of relationships which transcend his wretched situ-
> ation . . . One runs the risk of misunderstanding Marxist
> atheism entirely, and vulgarizing it, if one picks out no more
> than the need for a criticism of religion and sets aside all other
> forms of fictitious escape, simply because they are not specifi-
> cally religious.

Contemporary religiosity tends, Gardavsky continues, to be a very
primitive and passive phenomenon.

> Marx therefore differentiates between religion as the expression
> of suffering and religion as a protest against suffering; this is
> exceedingly important from the point of view of methodology
> . . . Marx's criticism of religion cannot therefore end up either
> by having man overruling religion in the realm of acts of the pure
> consciousness, for himself alone, nor with his doing this with the
> help of administrative methods . . . One must simply note that

criticism of religion is not an end in itself, as far as Marx is concerned: it is not anti-theistic, not directed against God.[20]

This is writing that demands reflection. It is easy enough to see why Czech administrators would not welcome such a writer. What is he, in fact, going on to say? Consistently with a *possible* atheistic position, he will say that religion must be studied because it is intimately connected with real human needs. These must be understood. And this is the reason why Gardavsky believes, as Marx certainly also believed,[21] that the problems raised by religion cannot be solved administratively. Unless they can be solved humanly, they cannot be solved at all, and are bound to persist.

After all, we do not blame the barometer if it shows bad weather, so there is no reason why the spread of religion should lead us to suppress it by artificial means. We must ask ourselves the following question: which are the places in our practical schemes, where a citizen of our state cannot translate his needs into reality as a man?[22]

This is, of course, also the kind of question it would be appropriate for politically responsible Christians to ask themselves, if they are genuinely worried about the repeated irruption of political movements under the banner of Marxism. Unfortunately, too many prefer to attempt the administrative solution rather than the more exacting business of trying to dig down to the roots of which Marx, according to his lights, made so proud a boast.

For Marx, as settled an atheist as Gardavsky, and generally much more acerbic, 'the root is man himself'.[23] Anyone reading Marx in the spirit of the foregoing attempt to suggest why he focuses attention upon problems that are still acute, cannot fail to see that the underlying inspiration is a form of humanism, an authentic concern for man. It is a bitter irony that of all the attempts to formulate a non-Christian humanism none has been made the excuse for more extensive crimes against untold thousands. Their extent already equals the horrors of hundreds of years of organized Christianity, which so scandalized Marx, as they have scandalized thinking people before and since. Indeed, it may require a Christian who admits the truth of much that Marx had to say, to help us to clear away the mental obstacles to any soundly-based reassessment of the theology of man. It is therefore unfortunate that Nicolas Berdyaev, who was expelled from Russia in the summer of 1922, should have tended since the 1930s to receive a rather bad press from communists and liberals alike. There may be truth in the remark that he can, when writing as a philosopher, be 'obscure and paradoxical'.[24] But his studies of Christianity and Marxism as it has worked itself out in Russia are neither obscure nor contemptible. They deserve the reprinting they have enjoyed in France in the 1970s. This book chooses to concentrate chiefly on another Russian in whose life the currents of Christian piety and communist unbelief cross. But one or two remarks of Berdyaev can usefully serve to introduce political Marxism in its Russian form. For this was the first considerable and lasting revolution which was ostensibly Marxist in inspiration. Its fortunes have inevitably influenced the reputation Marx enjoys outside Russia more than anything Marx himself ever wrote or would have approved.

Berdyaev writes:

> Revolution is like a judgement on historical Christianity, on Christians, on their denial of primary precepts, on the caricature they have made of Christianity. It is precisely for Christians that revolution has a meaning; it is they above all who ought to understand it. It is for them a summons, an appeal to that justice which they have failed to realize . . . Perhaps more than any other, the Russian revolution bears the marks of an apocalypse.[25]

The remarks follow a study of nineteenth-century Russian writers in which Berdyaev has been insisting how full they are of intimations of a coming upheaval. To these more general reflections about communism Berdyaev frequently returned. Nor did the way the revolution had affected his own life prevent him from writing: 'The greater part of the truth lies on the side of socialism.' Not, he explains, socialism as a substitute religion or a version of utopianism, but as a witness to an historical reality. It is for him 'a judgement pronounced on a lying humanity which betrayed Christianity . . . on a human civilization founded on mystification. In this way can be shown, in all its complexity, the connection between Christianity and Marxism and its view of history. Marxism exposes the idols and strips bare a Christianity which has not realized its truth. In this its religious and prophetic vocation lies.'[26]

It is too large a question to discuss here what Marx himself might have thought of the fittingness of the achievements of 1917 under the resolute leadership of Lenin. Both Marx and Engels were, in any case, often mistaken about what could and should happen in their own day. What is of supreme interest is what did in fact happen, and perhaps especially what it did to those who carried through and afterwards maintained the revolution in Russia. The revolution was, as Berdyaev says – and no one will dispute this – the work of Lenin and Bolshevism. It seems tolerably certain to anyone not already politically committed to some other view that Berdyaev is also right in saying that it was not a revolution of the people, but rather a revolution carried out in the people's name; a revolution 'in the name of Marx but not *according to* Marx'. And this meant, in the social and intellectual condition of Russia at the time, that the revolution needed a new myth.

> The myth of the peasant people had to be changed into the myth of the proletariat . . . But in this myth of the proletariat it is still the myth of the Russian people that comes to life again in a new form. A sort of identification is produced between the Russian people and the proletariat, between Russian messianism and proletarian messianism . . . Lenin returned to the old tradition of Russian revolutionary thought. He declared that Russia's industrial backwardness, the embryonic state of its capitalism, constituted a marked advantage in favour of social revolution.

Berdyaev is certainly correct in thinking that this is exactly the point Marx might have disputed, and it is somewhere in this area that classical Marxism and Russian Marxism begin to diverge.

What was the cost? 'The revolution was accomplished under the colours of internationalism,' says Berdyaev, 'although it was profoundly national. It becomes ever more national in its results.' [27] These words were written as early as 1935 and subsequent events seem only to have shown how justified they were. A recent study, *Russia under the Old Régime*, which nowhere mentions Berdyaev, makes an impressively documented case for believing what was already Berdyaev's intuition forty years previously. There seems to be a substantial continuity in Russian history which the upheaval of the revolution only served to ensure. Professor Pipes points out that

> the criminal code of 1927 contained provisions against anti-State crimes which neither in breadth of definition nor in the severity of the punishments differed substantially from those instituted by the imperial régime . . . Lenin and his fellow-revolutionaries,

who so quickly on taking power began the reconstruction of the police state, certainly regarded these moves as emergency measures, exactly as in its day did the imperial government . . . But the same fate befell communist 'temporary' repressive measures as their predecessors: regularly renewed, the indiscriminate application of their violence came to overshadow the order they were meant to protect. Had they read more history and fewer polemical tracts the Bolshevik leaders might have been able to foresee this outcome.[28]

In a moment we shall look at the case of a man who could, at least from time to time, see too clearly for his comfort what was going on in the state whose existence Lenin had made possible. Lenin himself was, at one level of his being, one of its first victims. Maxim Gorky was foolish enough to say this and as Gorky's is the more interesting case for our present purposes, it is only possible to glance at Berdyaev's singularly level-headed estimate of Lenin. The main contrasts it establishes are sufficiently contained in three sentences which may be gathered in the course of several pages.

> Of a detached nature, totally devoted to ideas, he had no ambition or any real taste for power, for he thought little of himself . . . Lenin was a revolutionary to the marrow of his bones precisely because he had defended all his life an all-embracing conception without permitting the least fissure in it . . . Dictatorship was the natural result of the views of Lenin, or rather, he had built up a conception of the world which was only compatible with dictatorship.[29]

It was left to Stalin who, as George Lichtheim says, 'lacked any sort of theoretical capacity' to draw practical conclusions from the Russian experience which Lenin would probably never have countenanced. By deciding on a state revolution ruthlessly directed from above, he created a dictatorship of a kind never before seen. 'It was only after Stalin had destroyed Lenin's party in the purges of 1934-8 that totalitarian communism became a serious rival of totalitarian fascism.'[30]

The reality and extent of the purges no one now denies, and it was exactly in the middle of this period, in 1936, that Maxim Gorky died. On the matter of his death it is virtually impossible to accept the view of the otherwise reliable recent English translator of two of the volumes of Gorky's absorbing autobiography. That this death

was only 'at first' mysterious is very hard to admit.[31] The presence
of Stalin at the funeral and the arrest of someone else as the culprit
probably only compounds the crime. Unlike Lenin, Gorky was no
monolith. He was, one could almost say, split right down the
middle; and it was a crack that he was, probably to his lasting
honour, never quite able to mend. Two years older than Lenin, he
had genuinely risen from the lower depths, a subject on which he
wrote a rather shapeless play. Its première took place in Moscow
not long after the first production there of Tolstoy's *The Power of
Darkness*, in September 1902. The theatregoing public may well
have been right to see in Gorky's pious pilgrim Luka a conscious
polemic against a character in the play by Tolstoy, who produced a
similarly wordy combination of moralizing and consolation. There
was an inevitable tension between Gorky, the populist from the
people, who knew what he knew by experience, and Tolstoy the
populist from the aristocracy. Tolstoy's knowledge came largely
from an effort of the imagination and, as Kenneth Clark recalls,
among his last words was the question: 'How do peasants die?' It
may be true that Gorky wished 'to reproduce what he saw as
Tolstoy's fundamental lack of concern for people, which he concealed behind constant readiness to give them moral advice'.[32] But
it is difficult to dismiss the feeling that Luka also carries some of
Gorky's own unresolved nostalgia for an authentic alternative or
complement to that side of himself that was instinctively drawn to
revolution. For his revolutionary leanings he was arrested in both
1901 and 1905. The latter imprisonment terminated, on the intervention of western writers, with an ill-starred journey to
America. Here he wrote a hostile tract on New York as the city of
the god of gold. Kenneth Clark, with an urbane detachment, chose
the same motif to open the final lecture in his television series
*Civilisation*. It was a lecture he called *Heroic Materialism*, in direct
allusion to the thrust of technological achievement since the Industrial Revolution, but also obliquely implying the social significance
of Marx and Engels. Theirs are specifically mentioned among the
voices of protest in the nineteenth century, and the next but last
sentence of the lecture unmistakably expresses the profound disappointment of even the least radical at the way the idealism that
wanted to turn the flank of the Industrial Revolution has in practice
worked out. It says quite simply: 'The moral and intellectual
failure of Marxism has left us with no alternative to heroic materialism, and that isn't enough.'[33] But before we look at the weak-

nesses that practical, untheoretical materialism is apt to foster, the Russian dilemma remains the centre of our interest. The voices of its victims cannot go unheard.

The American episode over, Maxim Gorky's life and activities continuously express his ambivalence towards what was going on in Russia. Living mostly in Capri until 1913, he had written among other things an attempt to reconcile Christianity and Marxism which earned Lenin's disapproval. But he was back in Russia in 1913, where he succeeded in getting himself disliked by everyone, liberal or communist. After the revolution, he could not and would not keep silence about what politicians thought they should do in the public interest, and about the kind of people they, Lenin among them, were themselves thereby unknowingly becoming. Nevertheless he strove to organize the dream of a boy who from childhood had been a voracious reader of anything and everything. A project for Russian translations of literature of an international scope remained his interest and concern even after 1921 when, on Lenin's advice, he left Russia for Italy again. In these years he also saved a great number of Russian writers from fates that might have been very unpleasant. It was in Sorrento that he completed the final volume of his autobiography. Near the end there is a conversation about a murdered man which prophetically airs the issues of which Gorky's own fate is almost certainly another illustration. This had been finished in 1923. Irresistibly drawn in life as in writing to see for himself what was really happening, Gorky visited Russia several times, and finally settled there in 1931. Since he had been born in 1868, he was by then a man in his early sixties. His three-decker autobiography apart, he had up to that time produced a mass of pretty turgid writing. But these last years witness an unprecedented attempt to say what was expected of him, and perhaps even what he expected of himself. It is almost unbelievable to find the lively-minded author of the first volume of the autobiography of 1913 writing in 1933 on themes in books for children that 'children should be brought up in such a way as to preclude, even in their games, any conscious or unconscious attraction to the past'. He had earlier excused his own obvious involvement with the past by saying that he must tell 'the loathsome truth' so that it might be forgotten. But how could he manage to forget what he certainly knew of more recent loathsomeness so as to be able to say in a vacuous address to the first All-Union Congress of Soviet Writers in 1934: 'In our country, God is rapidly and easily falling into

disuse precisely because the reason for his existence has disappeared – the need to justify the power of man over man, since in
our country any man is the collaborator of his fellow-men but never
lord over their minds and wills.' Were there, in spite of these public
utterances, moments when Gorky also remembered the present as
accurately as he had once shown himself capable of remembering
the past? In any case the damage was already done. He had, in his
time, written enough and done enough to make those who prefer a
world without even a shadow of grey feel uncomfortable as long as
he was around. If a great new literature could be created by will
and work alone, as Gorky's lecture virtually implies, Stalin believed that so could a monolithic state. Possibly Gorky had decided to yield to the weakness he mentions in the final sentence of a
kindly sketch of conversations with Chekhov which he had written
some years earlier: 'We all hunger for the love of our fellow-
creatures and, when one is hungry, even a half-baked loaf tastes
sweet.'³⁴ The loaf Gorky got was not enough to keep him alive for
very long.

Of greater length than his conversations with Chekhov are the
notes Gorky kept of meetings with the aged Tolstoy. These notes
are full of the life that an encounter with a striking human being
always seems to have awakened in Gorky. He was doubtless right to
feel that when Tolstoy spoke of Christ or of Buddha there was in
his words 'not a spark of the heart's fire'. Nor has one any difficulty
in believing how tedious it must have been to listen to one of
Tolstoy's monologues, whether on God or on women, of which
Gorky probably spares us the worst. It is therefore greatly to his
credit that he records with obvious honesty two shrewd things that
Tolstoy, for all his own confusions, said about Gorky himself. One
day, after a pause in some ribaldry about women, Tolstoy said:
'You're a queer chap. Don't be offended. You're very queer. And
the funny thing is that you are good-natured, though you have a
perfect right to be vindictive . . . I don't understand your mind. It's
a very confused mind, but your heart is wise . . . yes, you have a
wise heart.' More than halfway through his notes Gorky says: 'I
observed Tolstoy very closely, for I have always sought, and shall
seek to the day of my death, for a man of real, living faith.' At the
end Tolstoy turned the tables on him by suddenly saying: 'Why
don't you believe in God?' To which Gorky replied: 'I have no faith.'
Whereupon Tolstoy retorted: 'That's not true. You're a believer by
nature, you can't get on without God. You'll soon begin to feel

that. You don't believe because you are obstinate, and because you are annoyed – the world isn't made the way you'd like it to be.'[35]

It is difficult not to feel that Tolstoy was right in both these observations and that they were brought to the surface in different ways in Gorky's encounters with the most unanswerable person he ever knew, his own grandmother. For those who can still meet her through the pages of Gorky's autobiography, she is also likely to become one of the most vital characters they have ever met in a book. Her presence links the three volumes together. Gorky was never to see her again after the farewell with which the final volume opens. Then he believed – in vain – that he was setting out to get himself a university education. His universities were, in fact, to be a continuance of that hard school of life and work which had been his chief educator since his childhood. At this parting, his grandmother said to him a very few words not unlike those of Tolstoy in their import about Gorky's character, but impregnated with that deep Christian piety which, however unorthodox its verbal expression might be, was unmistakably authentic. 'In parting, Granny told me: "Don't you be cross with people. You're always so cross. Stern you're getting to be and too demanding. That comes down from your grandfather . . . You keep one thing in mind: It's not God that judges men. That's the Devil's pastime . . . We won't meet again. You'll be moving further and further off, restless soul, and I'll be dying . . ."' Gorky continues: 'Now it came to me with sudden pain that I would never again meet a friend so close, so much a part of me. From the stern of the boat I looked back to where she stood, at the edge of the pier – crossing herself and, with the corner of her worn old shawl, drying her face and her dark eyes, bright with the inextinguishable love of man.'[36]

It was from this astonishing old lady, tough and practical enough to organize the extinguishing of a dangerous fire while the men panicked and the horses jibbed, that Gorky derived that part of himself which gave him the wise and compassionate heart that Tolstoy discerned in him. Gorky tells us that in the confusion of his boyish emotions on getting a job as a washer-up on a steamship, 'particularly when I recalled Grandmother, everything nasty and offensive vanished, and changed into something more interesting and pleasant and everyone became better and kinder.' It was thus, on parting with a chef who had, in his strange way, been genuinely kind to him, Gorky could note: 'Afterwards I met so many people who were just like him, people who were kind and lonely, and

whom life had left behind.' It was also very like his grandmother to
comment: 'Sounds like a good man, may the Blessed Virgin preserve him! Don't ever forget him! You should always make sure
that you remember the good things and forget the bad.'[37] As
Gorky looked back on his childhood he felt compelled to write: 'It
was her unselfish love of the world that enriched me and nourished
me with the strength I would need for the hard life that lay
ahead.'[38]

It might be easy to dismiss this quality as merely natural in the
old lady, of whom Gorky says that 'in the forest she seemed just
like the mistress of the house, and was familiar with every part of it.
She looked like a great bear as she walked along, seeing, praising,
and blessing everything.'[39] But as a child who had slept near her
constantly, Gorky knew that his grandmother's love was nourished
by her prayer. Night after night she finished the day in prayer
before the icons. 'She always prayed for a long time after a day of
quarrels and aggravation,' he writes. 'Her prayers made fascinating
listening. Grandmother told God about everything that had happened in the house, down to the last detail.' This was natural
enough for, as he tells us a little later, 'her God was with her all day,
and she even talked about him to animals.' When he also describes
how she took a terrible beating from his grandfather, he adds the
final touch to his estimate of her by bursting out: 'You're . . . like a
saint, you suffer and suffer and you never complain.' She characteristically caps this with the retort: 'What rubbish are you talking
now?'[40] Yet she must have taught him a very great deal more about
religion than Gorky ever fully admitted to himself. Thus, in the last
volume of the autobiography, seeing a little old man praying before
the icons in the corner of the room, it cannot be an accident that
Gorky spontaneously thinks: 'He reminded me of a portrait of
Seraphim, the Sarov hermit' (who had in fact been canonized by
the Russian Church in 1903). 'As I stood watching him, a sense of
something wrong came over me.' Gorky explains that this feeling
was due to the fact that he had been told that the old man was a
revolutionary 'and a revolutionary should not believe in God. The
devout old man seemed to me out of place in this house.'

This sense of contradiction certainly went deep in Gorky himself, battle against it as he would. It also suggests the weak side in
most revolutionary Marxism and even reflects the limitations of
Marx himself who, seeing quite correctly that religion has a social
and human dimension, excluded dogmatically that it might have

any other. At this stage it is enough to have tried to see what might have to be taken seriously in a deterministic view of the human condition based on a study of economics. It is also important to have caught a glimpse of what seems to happen once a large group of people, even a whole nation, tries to take this view as though it were in itself sufficient to solve the problems of life and happiness. Near the end of his autobiography Gorky describes how a man who had the awkward habit of seeing that there was more than one side to every question is found lying in a boat with his head split open. One of those who knew the man, musing over his tea after the event, says:

> It's such a pity, the way these folk kill off the best and finest among them. It looks as if the better a man is, the more they fear him. They've no use for him – he's in their way . . . I've come up against it time and time again – this fear of 'saints', this extermin-ation of the finest people. It's one of two things, when people have to do with a 'saint'; either they'll make away with him, by one means or another, when they get tired of baiting him; or – less frequently – they'll hang on his every word and look . . . But so far as learning from him, imitating his ways of life, is con-cerned – that's a different matter. They don't know how to go about it. Or – perhaps they've no desire to? . . . And still the truth is with those who say, Your life isn't right. The truth is on their side.[41]

It is with some deliberation that this chapter takes a final leap to a living Russian of impressive modesty whose witness for the inde-finable and inarticulate dimensions of life might easily be lost among the voices of the better reported. We have a Russian transcript of Andrei Sinyavsky's spontaneous defence before the court which sentenced him for publications abroad under the pseudonym of Abram Tertz. It is a spirited plea for common, human sense in the face of the inhuman nonsense that rigid adher-ence to an all-embracing theory normally produces. It deserves to be read as a whole, but at its close Sinyavsky says: 'The nature of an artistic image is complex, and often the author himself cannot explain it . . . But you who are jurists have to do with terms which are the more precise in direct correspondence to their narrowness. In contrast to legal terminology, the significance of an artistic image is the more precise in direct correspondence to its breadth.'[42] This is essentially the plea of a literary man, and a plea of a kind we shall need to bear in mind often in this book. But since leaving Russia Sinyavsky has once consented to speak about the problem of communication between the most ordinary, simple people as he experienced it in prison, where the possibilities of personal expression can be reduced to an unbearable minimum. The report of the discussion after this short talk reveals how understandably moved almost everyone was who heard it. Although he had to speak through an interpreter, one or two of Sinyavsky's measured answers deserve to be better known than a Geneva report is likely to make them. To the one man who got up and said, in effect: Why all this talk about Christianity and prayer? It isn't Christianity that has given an ideal to the world. It is communism, Sinyavsky replied:

> I have not come to speak to you in the name of a programme . . . I am a poor Christian. I do not claim to judge the Christian Church in the 2000 years of its existence; still less to predict the radiant future. Yes, you are right. Communism has given an ideal to many twentieth-century men; and I myself have been inflamed by that ideal: as a youth, without being a member of the communist party, I belonged to the Communist Youth. But Soviet communism has given us millions of corpses, innocent people who have been exterminated in the camps. This real premiss is my point of departure, and not the ideal. I am myself some kind of refuse spewed up by a Soviet camp.

This moderate tone, and the repeated insistence on confining himself to what he knows, characterizes all Sinyavsky's replies, and it is in the light of this attitude that we should doubtless understand his answer to a final question: Is communication between the languages of desperation possible?

> This simple question you ask me is perhaps the most complex of all. We are all, everywhere in the world, desperate, each in his fashion. And we have no common language between us – or we try to find one without success. For myself, I would say that there are two languages which could in the long run unite the various kinds of desperation. There is religion and there is poetry.[43]

It is impossible, hearing this, not to recall that Sinyavsky's plea before the court had been that language which is alive has many dimensions. There are in the world today many judgement seats, public and private, which would like to insist that it has only one.

# 3

## SMOKE

Of all the great writers of Russia it was, in the end, Tolstoy who proved to be the most accommodating for political Marxism. This is perhaps because his political and oddly individual religious thought moves largely in the realms of rationalistic theories. He was a great arranger of even his own life, as his staunchest admirers are compelled to admit.[1] He was, of course, far too intelligent not to see from time to time the weaker aspects of his own dearest convictions. As he notes in his journal of August 1898: 'Even if that which Marx predicted should happen, then the only thing that will happen is that despotism will be passed on. Now the capitalists rule, but then the directors of the working people will rule.' But asides of this kind are easily forgotten and, to Lenin, Tolstoy seemed to be 'a mirror of the Russian revolution'.[2] Dostoevsky, on the other hand, is a writer much more difficult to claim for any party line. Already in 1866 his first great novel, *Crime and Punishment*, incorporates extended criticisms of revolutionary aspirations, notably in the mouth of Razumikhin. 'Truth won't run away, but life can easily be boarded up' is probably a sufficiently direct expression of Dostoevsky's own reserves about intellectual theories, whether political or religious. 'I can show you their books,' says Razumikhin in the middle of a heated argument.

They reduce everything to one common cause – environment. Environment is the root of all evil – and nothing else! A favourite phrase. And the direct consequence of it is that if society is organized on normal lines, all crimes will vanish at once, for there will be nothing to protest against, and all men will become righteous in the twinkling of an eye. Human nature isn't taken into account at all . . . That's why they instinctively dislike history so much . . . That's why they dislike the living process of life so much! They don't want a *living soul*! A living soul makes demands, a living soul scoffs at mechanics, a living soul is suspicious, a living soul is retrograde! The sort of soul they want may smell of carrion, and it may even be possible to make it of rubber, but at least it is not alive, at least it has no will, at least it is servile and can be guaranteed not to rebel! And the result of this is that they reduce everything to bricklaying and the planning of corridors . . .[3]

Whatever one's ultimate verdict on an author of whom George Steiner says that 'no one, with the exception of Shakespeare, has more fully represented the complex energies of life',[4] Dostoevsky's stature as a writer can scarcely be denied. One is therefore impressed when in the early pages of *Crime and Punishment* he suddenly, with a writer's emulation, names Turgenev as 'a great artist'. He is bracketed with Pushkin as one capable of presenting a picture with 'all its details so delicately etched and unexpected, yet artistically consistent with everything else'. Gorky, a man of a very different temper of mind, expresses the same admiration for Turgenev's craftsmanship when speaking of that period of his life when he had earned the name of 'bookworm'. 'I greedily read Turgenev,' he says, 'and was amazed how he made the whole of life so easy to understand, so simple, as clear as the days in autumn.'[5]

Two Russian writers who both, for their own reasons, equally disapproved of Turgenev's involvement in the bourgeois European life of his day, are thus agreed on his unusual gifts as an artist. Those who have to content themselves with the best translations they can find may therefore feel confident they are not deceived about his felicities. There are, in fact, several reasons why Turgenev remains a uniquely interesting writer for those who are concerned with the problems it is a major part of the purpose of this book to discuss. He began as a miniaturist and, by comparison with the vast canvases of Tolstoy or Dostoevsky, even his most developed and intricate works are of very modest proportions. But Dostoevsky was right to notice their perfect articulation and Gorky their uncanny knack of establishing the spiritual weather. In Turgenev's hands not only had the Russian novel evolved from the short-story form several years before *Crime and Punishment* or *War and Peace* appeared on the scene. It had also been established as a vehicle for displaying the tension between theories and personal behaviour which thinkers of classical and medieval times would have thought it the business of 'philosophy' to discuss. Indeed it could be argued that it is primarily in the novel that in modern times the more interesting of the activities once associated with 'philosophy' have gradually found their safest retreat. At the same time it would be foolish and perverse to claim, at least for Turgenev, something he himself would probably have dismissed with saturnine distaste. His own declared aims and methods are, given his gifts, sufficient to explain why he continues to be intriguing. They also have the merit of being not too difficult to verify in relation to what he actually wrote. 'I have aspired', he writes in the introduction to his collected novels, 'conscientiously and impartially to depict and embody in suitable types both what Shakespeare calls "the body and pressure of time" and that rapidly changing physiognomy of Russians of the cultured stratum, which has been pre-eminently the object of my observations . . .'[6] It was this unusual sensitiveness to differences of time that gave Turgenev the idea of writing what was in effect to be a pioneer novel on what is now called 'the generation gap'. It was an idea that took long to form itself. But, like many other creative writers, he found his imagination being constantly invaded by characters who insisted on his attention. He told Henry James, whose admiration for Turgenev was unbounded, that 'the first form in which a tale appeared to him was as the figure of an individual or a combination of individuals whom he wished to see in action'.[7] These characters became so real that they demanded the right to live their own lives. It is rarely that Turgenev does not succeed in making us feel that we should know them if they walked into the room.

In a chapter on the 'intelligentsia' in Russia before 1900 Richard Pipes cites Turgenev to illustrate the original broad sense of this term. Turgenev's writings are also named as illustrating the typical westernized intellectuals' reaction to the quandary created by an infinitesimally small number of radical activists in Russia from 1840 onwards. Even the conservative Dostoevsky can be quoted as having limits, in practice, to his anti-radical convictions.[8] There are many parallels between this historical situation and that which prevailed in the much more complex world of England after the First World War. For someone who lived through the 1930s in Britain it is difficult not to feel the almost archetypal quality of Turgenev's efforts for a whole century of European experience. They combine a sense of 'the body and pressure of time' with compassion for and interest in the human beings submitted to period impulses. There are signs enough that, although the forms it takes and the people it involves have changed a great deal, the political dilemma remains, after more than another thirty years since the Second World War. Now it would be to falsify our perspective to suggest that these political concerns are ever entirely central to Turgenev's true interests, even when he possibly meant them to be so. But they fascinate and distract him only to a slightly lesser extent than other problems of a more timeless character. It would be easy to trivialize or sentimentalize these by exceeding the reticence with which Turgenev normally implies their presence. Theoretical and political issues preoccupy his intellectuals in their conscious lives. But these lives are also determined by other forces they do not discuss, though they may sooner or later have to submit to them. These forces, love and death, so nearly related and sometimes so very much alike, have acquired a special bitterness in the yawning gap created by a faith that is simply absent though never explicitly denied. Their lurking presence suggests a compelling argument for supposing that human beings are the victims of illusions more deceptive and more cruel than those purveyed by even the most perverse of religions. This is a conclusion Turgenev himself never explicitly draws – at least in his novels. He merely confronts us with the problem. He thus remains an essentially more contemporary writer than many who came after him and who lacked his supreme artistic tact.

The way Turgenev's instincts functioned may well be illustrated by *Rudin*, the first of his stories of novel length, which we happen to know was more than once reworked. Yet, in the form in which we now have it, it has an internal consistency that results from an authentic struggle with an intuition that is sure and convincing. Rudin, the intriguing visitor who arrives one evening as dinner begins at a country house surrounded by fragrant old lime trees, is very largely a portrait of Michael Bakunin. Turgenev had shared lodgings with Bakunin when they were both students in Berlin in 1840 and their relationship was a mutually warm one.[9] No one questions now that the memory of it and Turgenev's later ambivalence about it are built into the novel *Rudin*. In assessing how just is the likeness, it is not entirely relevant to recall that Bakunin was 'not at that time occupied in politics', as Turgenev tells us in a carefully-worded autobiographical note.[10] For now that what survives of the written output of a man who was capable of producing twenty-four letters a day is being systematically edited, it is possible to see that Bakunin must always have been a prolific talker, pouring out theories as his active brain conceived them. Anyone who wonders whether Turgenev has seriously misrepresented him may care to ponder a letter written to his sisters in 1836, which

deservedly comes first in the latest English selection of Bakunin.[11]
What it is like to have to live with someone who is constantly
insisting upon how much we all love each other, those with experience of anything of the kind can best judge.

But that such a man as Rudin is represented to be was also a
gripping if sometimes overwhelming guest the first time one met
him, there is no reason to doubt. As the conversation proceeds,
Turgenev warms to his task. The setting as he depicts it is, as
always, part of what he wishes to say:

> A fragrant misty twilight lay like a soft shroud over the garden;
> the nearby trees breathed a dreamy freshness. Stars gleamed
> calmly. The summer night both basked and soothed. Rudin
> looked into the darkened garden – and turned round. The music
> and the night, he said, reminded me of my time as a student in
> Germany . . .

Rudin was not, Turgenev tells us, a storyteller but he 'possessed
what is almost the highest secret – the music of eloquence'.

> By striking certain heartstrings he could set all the others ob-
> scurely quivering and ringing. A listener might not understand
> precisely what was being talked about; but he would catch his
> breath, curtains would open wide before his eyes, something
> resplendent would burn dazzlingly ahead of him . . . The very
> sound of his voice, quiet and intense, heightened the
> enchantment.[12]

The company, with one resistant exception, retires mentally in-
toxicated. But before they do so Turgenev permits his hero to voice
some sentiments that are really his own. Rudin's story of the
warriors who witness a bird flying through the darkened hall and
out again into the night is not implausibly called 'a Scandinavian
legend'. For Bede, who first tells it, certainly means it to originate
in a pre-Christian setting. Turgenev, in remembering it, trans-
forms the original's agnostic point into something very recognizably post-Christian on the fleetingness of life and the finality of
death.[13] We are back nearer the true Bakunin when we are told
later that 'Rudin talked readily and frequently about love'. It is
Lezhnev who makes the comment on the man who fails to recognize the effect he is producing on Natalya by doing this. 'He has a
fondness for living off people, acting a part and so on . . . That's all
in the order of things. But what's bad is that he is as cold as ice.'

This is a shrewdly devastating observation and the development of the story does very little to dispel it. Yet some justice is already done to Rudin when, in his letter of explanation and excuse to Natalya, he is made to write: 'I will end by sacrificing myself for some nonsense in which I won't even believe . . .' It is, in a way, Turgenev himself who receives the letter, when he tells us that on reading it, 'Natalya remembered her childhood and the times when, out for an evening walk, she always tried to go in the direction of the bright edge of the sky, where the sunset glowed, and not to the dark. But it was the dark of life that now faced her, and her back was turned to the light . . .' [14]

It cannot be just external pressures on Turgenev that explain why in the final form of the story this tragic note of disappointment is not allowed to stand as the ultimate verdict on Rudin himself. Taken together, chapter 12 and the epilogue cannot be read merely as a belated attempt to retrieve a too negative portrait of the hero. Turgenev's own honesty to one of the characters who appeared to invade his imagination makes him put the right words into the appropriate mouth. Lezhnev's reappraisal of Rudin is thoroughly consistent with what has gone before. After an interval of four years, several of the characters who had been present on that memorable first evening are sitting together on a balcony, and the name of Rudin comes up. Lezhnev proposes that they drink his health and explains that he wants to talk, not about Rudin's defects but 'about what is good and rare in him. He has enthusiasm; and that, believe me . . . is a most precious quality in our time. We have all become intolerably rational, indifferent, and effete; we have gone to sleep, we have grown cold, and we should be grateful to anyone who rouses and warms us, if only for a moment! It's time to wake up!' Lezhnev goes on to say how important this man had been to him when he was young and 'not so blasé'. Basistov, who had spent the whole night writing to a friend after his first meeting with Rudin, is thus given his chance to say: 'How right he is! So far as Rudin's influence is concerned, I swear to you that this man not only has the power to shake you up, he could make you get up and go; he never let you grow settled in your ways, he turned the very foundation of things upside down, he set light to you!' Lezhnev confirms his toast: 'I drink to the health of a comrade of my best years, I drink to youth, its hopes, its strivings, its truthfulness, its honesty to everything that made our hearts beat fast at twenty and which was better than anything else we've ever known.' [15]

After several more years, the epilogue describes a chance meeting at an hotel on a cold autumn day. Lezhnev, in a last conversation with Rudin, is given an opportunity to pay his tribute personally and with less conscious nostalgia. Rudin, his eyes and his entire being expressing 'an ultimate exhaustion of spirit', repeats the catalogue of his failures to achieve anything he had hoped and expected. Lezhnev jumps up:

> What sort of a judge of things would I be, what sort of a man would I be if, at the sight of your sunken cheeks and your wrinkles the word 'phrase-mongering' could enter my head? You want to know what I think of you? – I rouse your compassion – No, you're wrong. You rouse my respect – that's what . . . Why is it that you couldn't fit in with things at the high school, why is it that you – strange chap that you are – no matter with what grand idea you embark on a project, end it every time without exception by sacrificing your own personal interests, by not putting your roots down in unfriendly soil no matter how rich it might be? . . . It's not a worm that gnaws you, not a spirit of empty restlessness, it's the fire of the love of truth that burns within you, and evidently it burns, despite all your tribulations, more strongly in you than in many who do not even consider themselves egoists and who would no doubt call you an intriguer. I would have been the first in your place to have silenced that worm long ago and to have made peace with the world.[16]

This is, all in all, a very round amends and the voice of a very genuine admiration for someone who still might 'start once again on a new project just like any young man'. Was it not qualities of this very kind that made an ambivalent figure like Lawrence of Arabia the natural hero of the young poets of the 1930s in England? Even a communist critic saw this at the time of Lawrence's death, and the conservative Winston Churchill found himself having to try to say something about it:

> The world naturally looks with some awe upon a man who appears unconcernedly indifferent to home, money, comfort, rank, or even power and fame. The world feels, not without a certain apprehension, that here is someone outside its jurisdiction; someone before whom its allurements may be spread in vain . . . a being readily capable of violent revolt or supreme sacrifice.[17]

It is, of course, with violent revolt that the name of the real-life
Bakunin is normally associated and he had many more years of
political activity to run. At least in Spain he left a memory and a
tradition which still shows signs of life.[18] But, in his incarnation as
Rudin, Turgenev makes him die waving a red flag in one hand and
a blunt curved sword in the other, on one of the barricades in Paris
in June 1848. In view of what Turgenev, no less than Marx, had
hoped from the abortive events of that particular summer, to
connect Rudin's death with them was a handsome crowning com-
pliment.[19] Hapless, irresistibly attractive idealist to the end, when
the bullet goes through his heart, one of the French insurgents calls
to another: 'Hey! They've just killed the Pole!' The fact that a
Russian radical volunteer thus dies unrecognized, like some unknown warrior, gives the novel its final ironical twist. Not only does
this touch set the book firmly in the context of Turgenev's deeper
and more constant preoccupations; it also sets a seal on its timeless
and representative quality.

Even had Turgenev never known Bakunin, there would be no
need to look for the inspiration of *Rudin* in books.[20] Turgenev
stood close enough to the thinking generation of the 1840s in
Russia to have shared with them a European awareness that was to
make itself first effectively felt in France. It was an awareness that
looks somewhat old-fashioned after the later developments of socialist theory and in the light of the critical work of Marx. But there
is a feature of this awareness which remains a constant through
every social change down to our own day. It was not necessary to
agree with the changing and often tentative practical judgements of
Marx to agree that the nineteenth century had witnessed the
growth of a world that could not be allowed to continue as it was.
It was a world that had to be interpreted and changed. But the
question was, and is, how? And what kind of sacrifices are the
appropriate price of change? *Rudin* is a first attempt at depicting an
embodiment of aspirations to which people of very different political sympathies have felt themselves called to respond. These
quixotic figures, who at least attempt to break the fetters by which
more and more people feel themselves to be bound, have tended on
the whole to be increasingly identified with leftwing politics.
Camillo Torres or Che Guevara die, like Rudin, by the bullets of
those in whom a faceless power is vested. They seldom die alone.
There are always some, with a poorer grasp of the issues involved,
and harder to identify with any particular cause, who fall beside

them. Professor Hynes, as so often in a brilliantly sure book, is entirely right to cite the lines that some of us who lived in England during the Spanish Civil War could have repeated without any prompting. They come from a poem by Stephen Spender that first appeared in the *New Statesman* in May 1937:

> The guns spell money's ultimate reason
> In letters of lead on the spring hillside.
> But the boy lying dead under the olive trees
> Was too young and too silly
> To have been notable to their important eye,
> He was a better target for a kiss.

As Samuel Hynes notes, it is impossible to tell which side of the battle the boy was on, or even whether he was Spanish. Spender is not taking sides. His compassion is at once unmistakably genuine and yet that of an observer.[21] That, in very much older terms, is also the position of Turgenev. His struggle to see the truth of his character as it presents itself to him leads him to make two reserves when Lezhnev calls for his toast: 'You remember, Sasha, I was once talking to you about him and I reproached Rudin for his coldness. I am both correct and incorrect in saying that. This coldness is in his blood – through no fault of his own – but not in his head.' Lezhnev is saying that Rudin's failure to respond to Natalya's love and take responsibility for it is not the sign that he is incapable of real commitment in other ways. Later heroes in Turgenev novels are not going to have 'coldness in the blood' as part of their fate. But it is perhaps natural that the first in a line of radicals should have been portrayed as more obsessed by the allurements of ideas than of relationships. He is not a lover but, contrary to his last protests, neither is he 'words, all words'.[22] Rudin is, like those of whom he is in many ways the prototype, essentially a man of action rather than a thinker. So was the real-life Bakunin. Unlike Marx, he left behind him no coherent body of thought, but neither did he, like the elderly Marx 'attend continental spas for his health or even boast of gambling on the stock exchange'.[23] Moreover, his guess as to how Marx's theories might work out when applied by those who tried to put them into practice has, it may be thought, been largely vindicated by history. 'They affirm that only dictatorship, *theirs* of course, can create a popular will. We reply that no dictatorship can have any other aim except to perpetuate itself, and that it is capable of instilling and fostering only slavery in the masses that endure it.' [24] It may be that many of Bakunin's words are not too difficult for the big guns to demolish, and Turgenev's novel about a radical-in-the-making may be dismissed as even lighter weight. Yet both give a glimpse of something it is the whole point of any theory of political determinism to explore, and no amount of argument can put it out of court. Human history cannot remain human if it can no longer make room for people who do not readily fit in with anyone else's theories. How this need is to be defended, even as a necessary instrument in any true social change, may not be very clear. Indeed the problems presented by defending this necessity on any widely acceptable grounds may be so great that some people – and Turgenev may have been among them – may be thrown back upon a determinism much more terrible than any political theory and from which they seek in vain for a satisfactory escape. It is enough for the moment to notice that Lezhnev's second revision of detail in his character sketch of Rudin is a plea of innocence before any of the more obvious charges that might be brought against him: 'He is not an actor, as I called him previously, not a swindler, not a scoundrel; he lives at someone else's expense not like a sponger, but like a child . . .' [25] This is a plea much less sentimental than it can be made to sound, and it would be an inept and inexperienced advocate who tried to fill the eloquent pause these words create.

It looks as though Turgenev had conceived of a novel to be called *Two Generations* as early as March 1853, but wrestled with it in vain. [26] *Rudin* and two other fine novels followed before *Fathers and Sons* in 1862. Whether it was an indirect fruit of earlier efforts is not clear. It is certainly a novel about a man of the 1860s seen through the eyes of a man who belongs essentially to the 1840s, yet has already anticipated in many of his attitudes the thoughts the younger generation have turned into absolutes. This book depicted a clash of generations in Russia 'in a manner which the protagonists at once recognized as accurate'. [27] This small masterpiece, which in Russia disturbed conservatives and radicals alike, was apparently conceived amid the breezes of Ventnor on the Isle of Wight. It began, it would seem, in the manner to which Turgenev was accustomed. 'I was out for a walk and thinking about death . . . Immediately there rose before me the picture of a dying man. This was Bazarov.' [28] 'I dreamed', Turgenev wrote in a letter, 'of a sombre, savage, and great figure, only half emerged from bar-

barism, strong, méchant and honest, but nevertheless doomed to perish because always in advance of the future.'[29] With consummate art Turgenev contrived to set him against an appropriate foil.

The novel opens with a sketch of a father, Nicholai Petrovich, a man in his early forties, who is awaiting the return home of his son Arkady. Arkady, like his father a little more than twenty years before, has just taken his degree at the University of St Petersburg. Turgenev depicts the comfort and quiet of the country life in which Arkady had grown up. The young man's parents 'read together, sang and played duets together at the piano; she grew flowers and looked after the chickens, while he went hunting now and again and busied himself with the estate.' Although greater composers are mentioned in the book's many references to music, the atmosphere must have been essentially that which is evoked for us today by the music of John Field, who had died in Russia in 1837. But in Nicholai's case these calm waters had not been unruffled. In flight from the grief occasioned by his wife's death, he has heard the 'noises off' from Paris in 1848 and has returned to make the kind of changes he can understand. Thus, at the time of Arkady's return, his land is now let out to his former serfs. His manservant contents himself with a perfunctory bow to the son instead of kissing his hand, which would once have been required. But it is upon Arkady's unexpected student companion Bazarov that our attention is at once riveted. His face, when he throws back his coat-collar, is 'animated by a tranquil smile betokening self-assurance and intelligence ... His light brown hair, which was long and thick, failed to hide the bulging temples of his broad head.' On the journey to the house we already become aware of the tensions which the presence of this young man, whom Arkady so much admires, will inevitably create. It is the contrast between the elegant bachelor uncle, Pavel, and 'that long-haired creature' which is clearly going to make the sparks fly. Bazarov says little during supper, confining himself to eating heartily. But afterwards he says to Arkady: 'All that foppery in the country – just fancy! And his nails, his nails – they ought to be shown at an exhibition!' Meanwhile Uncle Pavel has changed his patent-leather shoes for a pair of heel-less red Chinese slippers.[30]

Next morning Bazarov is up and out collecting frogs with the help of two farmboys, who ask for an explanation of this curious interest: 'I shall cut the frog open to see what goes on inside him and then, since you and I are much the same as frogs except that we walk about on our hind legs, I shall know what's going on inside us too,' explains Bazarov. He adds that he is going to be a doctor. Challenged by Uncle Pavel over the morning tea, Bazarov declares that physics is his special subject; and natural science in general. 'A decent chemist is twenty times more useful than any poet.' As Nicholai and his brother eventually rise from the table, Pavel says without looking at anyone: 'What a calamity it is to have spent five years in the country like this, far from mighty intellects. One becomes a complete fool. You struggle not to forget what you have learned – and then one fine day it all turns out to be rubbish, and they tell you that sensible men no longer have anything to do with such nonsense, and that you, if you please, are an antiquated old fogey. What is to be done? Obviously the younger generation are more intelligent than we are.' Behind this waspish reaction to the younger man there is also something pathetic, for Pavel 'was just entering on that indefinite twilight period of regrets that are akin to hope, and hopes which are akin to regrets, when youth is over and old age has not yet come'. It is an experience that is not to be Bazarov's. Arkady at least realizes that his uncle is profoundly unhappy and tries to defend him. Bazarov prefers to insist that 'what is important is that two and two make four, and the rest is just trivial . . . Nature too is trivial, in the sense *you* give to it. Nature is not a temple, but a workshop, and man is the workman in it.'[31]

Just as he says this, the two friends hear from the house the sound of Nicholai playing the cello. Bazarov roars with laughter at what strikes him as the incongruity of it all. 'Your father's a good man,' he says, 'but he's old-fashioned, he's had his day.' Nicholai is, in fact, a far more hesitant character than his brother and will not allow that Bazarov is a fool, despite his obvious conceit: 'Only there is one thing I cannot make out. I thought I was doing everything to keep up with the times: I have done well by the peasants, set up a model farm, so that all over the province I am known as a *radical*. I read, I study, I try in every way to keep abreast of the requirements of the age – and yet here they are saying I am over and done with. And, Pavel, I really begin to think they are right . . . Yes, Pavel. It seems the time has come to order our coffins and cross our hands upon our breasts.' Pavel's comeback in a subsequent discussion proceeds along not unfamiliar lines: 'In the old days young people had to study. If they did not want to be thought ignorant they had to work hard whether they liked it or not. But now they need only say, "Everything in the world is rubbish!" and the trick's done. The young men are simply delighted, whereas they were sheep's heads before, now they have blossomed out as nihilists.' To which Bazarov retorts: 'I shall be prepared to agree with you when you can show me a single institution of contemporary life, private or public, which does not call for ruthless repudiation.' As the two brothers are left alone, speechless, Nicholai again attempts to mediate between the contenders. He reminds Pavel that they are really only hearing what he himself had once thought when trying in vain to explain himself to their mother.[32] Pavel remains convinced that his brother is much too good-natured and modest. Apart from a ludicrous duel which Uncle Pavel insists on fighting with Bazarov later in the novel, this scene is the final trial of strength between the two. At Bazarov's instigation the two friends set out for visits in the country, each to meet a fate of a rather different kind.

'I am very curious to meet a man who has the courage not to believe in anything,' says Madame Odintsov, after dancing with the enchanted Arkady. When the first meeting occurs, Arkady notices to his secret astonishment that Bazarov appears to be embarrassed before the self-possessed Anna Sergeyevna. Bazarov is annoyed too at what he finds himself beginning to feel. The impassive Anna recovers from her initial distaste for Bazarov's behaviour for, as Turgenev observes, 'only the commonplace was repulsive to her, and no one could have accused Bazarov of being commonplace'. Three days later, at Madame Odintsov's country house, Bazarov fences with his usual weapons: 'People are like trees in a forest: no botanist would dream of studying each individual birch tree.' But this time he senses an opponent who is a match for him, and she too is intrigued. 'His total lack of affectation and the downright severity of his views appealed to her.' He, on his side, finds himself progressively caught by something more than physical attraction, something which, according to all his theories, he has always hitherto scorned. A message from his parents gives him the excuse to leave. But the evening before he goes he is alone with Anna while Arkady, in another room, listens to her sister Katya playing the piano. Near the beginning of what is going to be a very intense conversation, Madame Odintsov asks Bazarov to open the window. 'The mild dark night looked into the room with its almost black sky, its faintly rustling trees and the fresh fragrance of the

pure untrammelled air.' It is like a symbol of the detachment which
is no longer Bazarov's. As she accepts the simultaneous departure
of the two friends, Anna Sergeyevna recognizes that the encounter
with Bazarov was 'not something to trifle with'.[33]

It is not to be their last meeting. Bazarov is frankly bored at the
home of his father, a country doctor with a wife Arina 'who ought
to have lived a couple of centuries earlier in the days of Muscovy'.
They have so longed to see their son, and the old couple are broken
by his decision to go again so soon, being only too well aware why
he is going. There is a moment after the tarantass leaves when
Arina, pressing her grey head to her husband's grey head, says: 'It
can't be helped, Vasya. A son is an independent person. He's like a
falcon that comes when he wills and flies off when he lists; but you
and I are like the funguses growing in a hollow tree; here we sit side
by side, not budging an inch.' Bazarov will be back sooner than
they expect, for developments make him decide to break entirely
with the world to which Arkady has introduced him. But he does
not leave it without taking a last look at it all. As Arkady is
proposing to Katya in Madame Odintsov's garden, a snatch of the
conversation with Bazarov is overheard as the two go past. Anna
Sergeyevna is saying: 'You know I am afraid of you . . . and at the
same time I trust you, because you are a fundamentally good man.'
Bazarov refuses to be drawn. 'Talking to you is like walking on the
edge of a precipice. At first one is frightened, then one picks up
courage. Do stay.' Arkady catches Bazarov packing. 'You see what
I am doing: there happened to be an empty space in my trunk, and
I'm stuffing it with hay; it's the same with the trunk which is our
life: we fill it with anything that comes to hand rather than leave a
void . . . you have acted sensibly: you were not made for our bitter,
harsh, lonely existence . . . You are a nice lad, but you're too soft, a
good little liberal gentleman.'[34]

For a moment the joy of Bazarov's parents is rekindled at his
unexpected return. But it is not long before he contracts typhus,
after carrying out an autopsy on a peasant who has died of that
disease. 'Well, if Christianity is no help, be a philosopher, a Stoic
maybe!', he says to his distracted father. In his final fever Bazarov
sends for Madame Odintsov who, in an appropriately grand ges-
ture, comes. Before she kisses him, at his request, he has time to
beg that she will be kind to his parents: 'You won't find people like
them in your great world even if you search for them by daylight
and with the help of a lamp.' And it is with them kneeling at the

well-kept grave of their son that the book closes. 'However passionate, sinful, and rebellious the heart hidden in the tomb, the
flowers growing over it peep at us serenely with their innocent eyes;
they speak to us not only of eternal peace, of the vast repose of
"indifferent" nature; they tell us, too, of everlasting reconciliation
and of life which has no end.'[35]

Having made us believe in characters whose substantial truth to
life is compelling, Turgenev leaves us with these final words in no
serious doubt that he himself knows of no comfort to offer us that
will not reveal itself to be a cruel mockery. Although the setting is
now so remote, and so many details are nineteenth-century, there
are few who will not feel that they have heard phrases out of some
of the book's conversations only the day before yesterday. Its
greatness is that it is neither a political pamphlet nor does it argue a
case. It has all the allusive directness of a fine poem. Sometimes,
when savouring Turgenev's subtle skill, one calls to mind an
English poet who, like many since Turgenev, had suffered similar
torments:

> Tell me not here, it needs not saying,
>     What tune the enchantress plays
> In aftermaths of soft September
>     Or under blanching mays,
> For she and I were long acquainted
>     And I knew all her ways.
>
> On russet floors, by waters idle,
>     The pine lets fall its cone;[36]

– lines, with their simple aural and visual perfection, that anyone
who loves his language would have given a great deal to have
written. In an ingenious defence of what he rightly calls 'one of
Housman's best poems', Christopher Ricks points out that not only
were Housman's 'eye and ear never more alert. But this straightforward, respectable, and explicit feeling is entwined with a remarkable erotic force . . . Housman is taking seriously two conventions
that are usually trifled with; that nature is a mistress, and that
loving a mistress is like loving nature.'[37] Do we not find something
of the same entwining of painful feeling in Turgenev? And is not its
cause quite independent of the special, and different, emotional
problems of Turgenev and Housman in their personal lives?

> For nature, heartless, witless nature,
>     Will neither care nor know . . .

What these and a few writers like them over the last 150 years
voice specially, and often memorably, is not just the ancient themes
of the brevity of life and beauty, and the pain and uncertainty of
love, but they do so in an atmosphere of thought and feeling of
which Darwin's *Origin of Species* (1859) and Marx's *Capital* (1867)
are only different symptoms. At least from Turgenev's time onwards more and more people, intellectual and simple alike, are
going to be persuaded, generally without the help of philosophical
argument, of some kind of determinism that rides roughshod over
warm and breathing men. With what matchless ingenuity
Turgenev describes the feelings of an adolescent boy, to whom the
mysteries of adult love are still obscure, in his story *First Love*,
written in 1860. Even though he seems to have admitted to this
story's autobiographical foundation, it is a rare man who can put
himself so accurately back where he once was, remembering to
forget what he was afterwards compelled to recall. For it is certainly the adult man of our period who writes the last sentence: 'I
felt aghast for Zinaida, and *longed to pray for her, for my father –
and for myself.*' [38]

This is clearly the expression of what Turgenev takes to be a vain
wish, as it would be also for a host of people a century later. There
were far fewer when Turgenev was writing, and Gorky's grandmother was still a comparatively young woman. But their numbers
were growing, and neither the new theories of the scientists nor the
propaganda of political philosophers were very evidently the *direct*
cause. For most of the period, popular information on the views of
scientists about man and nature have seldom been much less than
fifty years behind the times. And G. D. H. Cole would still be as
safe to guess as he was in 1957 that 'only a small minority of those
who regard themselves as Marxists have read *Capital* at all'. [39] Like
that older book, after which Engels said that *Capital* was being
called 'the Bible of the working class', [40] it was better known by
report than by reading. But throughout the period something had
begun to be missing that Gorky had seen alive and central in the
life of his grandmother, and it was neither reading nor philosophy.
It was prayer. Not at all the same thing as the *saying of prayers*, as
Gorky observed when he formed the impression that his grandfather and grandmother worshipped two different gods. His
grandfather's God had been on his deathbed for some time then.
And his confidently expected demise may have had something to
do with the fact that already by the middle of the nineteenth

century a few were beginning to regard the matter as so settled that they did not even feel the anguish of not being able to pray. Perhaps, like Arkady in *Fathers and Sons* on his first night home again, the *thought* of what others might have wished and prayed may have crossed their minds in their beds. But, as Turgenev notes, 'for himself he said no prayer'.[41] And they will not do so either.

Only one little door remains, for some, slightly ajar. 'Tell me,' says Madame Odintsov in her second conversation with Bazarov, 'why is it that even when we are enjoying music, for instance, or a beautiful evening, or a conversation in agreeable company, it all seems no more than a hint of some infinite felicity existing apart somewhere, rather than actual happiness – such, I mean, as we ourselves can really possess.' Bazarov replies that such ideas never enter his head. Reason has firmly shut *that* door. Anna Sergeyevna, in her turn, equally firmly shuts in Bazarov's face a door he had never thought would open for him. 'After all, a quiet life is better than anything else in the world,' she reflects when the deed is done.[42]

Yet experience seems to show that, where what is believed to be 'reason' rules, where everything has been rationalized as far as possible, the irrational returns by its own routes, and often with a power with which no one has reckoned. Prevailing over the imposing theories with a force which is not that of argument, the incalculable gets through locked doors and guarded gates. By keeping *people* rather than politics or some form of impressive philosophy in the foreground, Turgenev continues to remind us of the problems of securing 'a quiet life' on one's own terms. Both political and philosophical theories of any merit will generally have tried to allow for this; but seldom adequately. In the over-rational West, some enchantress generally has her way. The list of Turgenev enchantresses is a long one. In *Torrents of Spring* (1872) the full machinery comes into operation and she rides on a horse in the middle of a storm. In whatever guise, the 'old enchantress' comes back. Were this present book primarily a literary study, it would perhaps be necessary to discuss *Smoke* (1867) at greater length. It is generally regarded as a failure. Yet it probably succeeds better as a work of the imagination than as the thinly disguised political pamphlet Turgenev may have intended it to be. In defending what he had done in *Fathers and Sons*, Turgenev had complained, like other writers before and since, that 'the artist is frequently not a

free man in his own creations'. And in a letter to Tolstoy he had
said: 'Systems are only dear to those who cannot take the whole
truth into their hands, who want to catch it by the tail; a system is
just like the tail of truth, but truth is like a lizard; it will leave its tail
in your hand and then escape you; it knows that within a short time
it will grow another.'[43] In *Smoke* Turgenev has depicted the world
of Russian émigrés in Baden-Baden, which he knew so well. He has
probably tried to say of conservatives and radicals alike, 'a plague
on both your houses!' But the frame is again the personal dilemma
in whose ramifications Turgenev was so well-versed. Litvinov,
awaiting the arrival of his betrothed in Baden-Baden, meets an old
flame, Irina. The fires are fanned strongly enough for him ruthlessly to break his engagement. But when Irina decides that she is
too attached to the world of Baden-Baden to elope with the man
she has bewitched, he takes the train back to Russia and to his first
love.

> He was alone in the compartment; there was no one to disturb
> him. Smoke, smoke, he repeated several times; and it suddenly
> seemed to him that everything was smoke. He thought: all seems
> to change continuously, everywhere new forms appear, events
> follow upon events, but at bottom all is the same; everything
> hurries, hastens somewhere – and everything disappears without
> a trace, attaining nothing; the wind changes and everything
> rushes in the opposite direction, and there the same unceasing,
> ruthless, and futile game begins again.[44]

Litvinov, and the author of *Smoke*, were quite correct to assume
that within five or six years no one would be listening to the words
of the more fashionable university professors of the day. But philosophical temptations of the kind implicit in Turgenev's work have
continued to persuade more modern people of their truth than any
single scientific or philosophical theory, however cogently argued.
*Either* the course of the world and of life is determined in some way
which can, with more or less accuracy, be calculated – *or* the
kaleidoscope of change is merely the outward display of some vast
illusion. In the one case, one must find a way of being as happy as
possible despite the circumstances. In the other, one must systematically cure oneself of the deceptions of the world of illusion.
Perhaps either view has something to be said for it, and neither
commands the monopoly of the truth.

# 4
## WATCHMEN

Whatever they may have been reading during the day, whatever thoughts may have entered their minds, the monks of the West have long been accustomed to hearing the reader begin the final prayers with a warning of eminent Christian antiquity. As they gather in the dormitory, the chapter room, or in the darkened church, the voice says: *Fratres, sobrii estote et vigilate*. 'Be sober and watch,' read the classical translations. The phrase is, in any case, no more than a snatch from the conclusion of a letter it is still possible to believe was written by St Peter.[1] The two sentences referred to may usefully be quoted in full, since they are a reminder of that awareness of the surrounding world which marks the thought of the entire letter. In what he was modest enough to call a paraphrase, though it is often tighter and nearer the Greek than many versions that pass for translations, the late Bishop Wand gave us:

> Don't get excited, but be continually on the watch, for the Devil like a roaring lion is continually on the prowl to see of whom he can make a meal. Against him stand steadfast in your faith, remembering that the same tribute of suffering is being paid by the rest of the brotherhood throughout the world ...[2]

Never since early Christian times has the solidarity of the monastic vocation with the common Christian life been clearer than it is today. It is therefore hardly necessary to insist upon the universal significance of the tradition about the importance of examining one's thoughts. It has seemed necessary for the purposes of this book to see to it that we have some concretely formulated thoughts to examine. Thoughts too shallow and moods too cheap to disturb any thinking person would hardly do; though these too have their effect. For it is simply not possible for anyone alive today to be unaffected by the states of mind which the current forms of determinism or fatalism easily engender. There are many over whose heads the winds of Marxism have so far blown without ruffling their hair. But they will often, half-consciously, have formulated in their hearts convictions like those which led Turgenev, a year before his painful death, to write with conscious and tragic logic: 'A blue sky, light fleecy clouds, the scent of flowers, the sweet notes of a young voice . . . What is the good of it, what is the good of it all? A spoonful of nauseating, ineffective medicine every two hours – that's all that's needed.' [3]

As Gorky's grandmother told him on parting, it is not our business to stand in judgement over another man's life and sufferings. That really is the Devil's business and unlike the God who, until the last, 'sends his rain on saint and sinner'.[4] But if we are to be like him, it is very much our business to see what our own thoughts do to us. The monastic tradition is often presented as impatiently anti-philosophical. That, perhaps in concrete instances, it has sometimes thoughtlessly been. Yet it remains true that a philosophical argument *as such* is no answer to life, and it is not normally the most consistently thought-out positions that lead men to action. It is to the importance of this area where thought is translated into action that the monastic tradition bears witness. Unreflective that tradition certainly is not. But it is concerned with the whole man, the one who becomes, and the one who acts from that living centre of his being to which it is not misleading to refer as his 'heart'. For it is not in reflection alone that 'thoughts', as the monastic tradition understands them, are accepted or rejected. It is rather in that less readily accessible area of our being to which the word 'heart' satisfactorily refers, when understood in no superficial or primarily emotional sense. It is here, where all our powers meet, that the real battles take place.[5] And so we come to that place of battle of which Gregory the Great, a monk sitting on Peter's chair, says:

The place of battle is the heart of the one who hears the word of God. It is called a place of battle because there the word which is received makes war on well-worn ways of life. The heavenly things it hears begin to have their attraction, but long-standing habit arises and suggests that the message should be despised. The struggle then gets worse because what the teacher commends, the evil spirits cry down by dissuasion. Like warriors they rise up against God's holy ones, destroying in conflict whatever the teacher has been saying. What does it mean, then, to come to the place of battle if not by the approach of acute discernment to come to the very depths of the heart of the listener, where the enemies may most quickly be found and most

ruthlessly cut to pieces? For those who do not know how to wage
an internal conflict can never come to the true battlefield.[6]

The representative character of this passage needs no argument
for those who steep themselves in the literature which it instinctively receives and transmits. William of St Thierry, a twelfth-
century monk and another great transmitter, is as clear as his
predecessors that what Gregory is saying about the battle with the
notions our thoughts openly or covertly suggest is no facile affair of
simply dismissing them as though they did not exist. As William
says:

> Those temptations are easily overcome and readily met by rea-
> son which are evidently suspect, or which declare themselves
> for evil at first brush. But those which insinuate themselves
> under the cover of good are both more difficult to discern and
> more dangerous to let in – just as it is very hard to be moderate in
> what is believed to be good. Not every desire for the good is
> invariably prudent.[7]

It is with considerations of this sort that this inner discipline is
brought down to the personal level. Going back still earlier in time,
to a writer like Barsanuphius the Great in the sixth-century desert
of Gaza, we find a letter of direction opening with words which
experienced spiritual masters will tend to repeat wherever this
recognizably consistent tradition is alive: 'The business of examining thoughts is this, that, when a thought comes, you pay attention
to what it gives birth.'[8]

From how many troubles even many non-Christians would be
spared if there were rather more informed voices to remind them
of these fundamentally human and life-saving principles. Even in
modern times these voices have not been lacking. They come,
generally, not from seats of authority but from those fighting their
way towards their own integrity amid the problems of an ever
more ruthlessly oppressive world. For that reason these voices have
easily been drowned or have gone altogether unheard. No one,
for instance, could rightly accuse Simone Weil of not having felt
the fascination of Marx, or of not being shrewd or honest enough
to have understood what he was saying. Pages of her essays and
notes are there to bear witness to the trouble she took to be fair
to him through the accretions of subsequent events and theories.
Therefore one sits up when, in fragments she left in London at
the time of her death in 1943, we find her suddenly saying:

It was left to our own age to make the maximum use of Marx's works. The idealistic utopian doctrine contained therein is immensely valuable for stirring up the masses, making them carry a political party to power, keeping youth in that state of permanent enthusiasm necessary to every totalitarian regime. At the same time the other doctrine, the materialist doctrine which freezes all human aspirations under the cold metallic touch of force, provides a totalitarian State with a great number of excellent answers when faced with the timid aspirations of the people. Generally speaking, the mental juxtaposition of an idealism and a materialism, each equally superficial and vulgar, constitutes the spiritual character – if one may be permitted the term – of our time.

This paragraph already contains the hint of how her argument will develop, and it is one which no Christian who recognizes that Marx cannot be dismissed with a wave of the hand can fail to ponder with care. Simone Weil continues:

In omitting spiritual factors, Marx ran no risk of being greatly mistaken in his analysis of a society which, all in all, allotted them no place. At bottom, Marx's materialism only expressed the influence of society upon him; his weakness lay in becoming himself the best instance of his own thesis concerning the subordination of thought to economic circumstances. But in his best moments he rose above this weakness. At such times materialism horrified him, and he would stigmatize it in the society of his time. He discovered a formula impossible to surpass when he said that the essence of capitalism lies in the subordination of subject to object, of man to thing. The analysis which he made of this point of view is of an incomparable vigour and depth; today still, today especially, it is an infinitely valuable theme for meditation. But the general method is of still greater value. The idea of working out a mechanics of social relationships had been adumbrated by many lucid minds. It was doubtless this that inspired Machiavelli. As in ordinary mechanics, the fundamental notion would be that of force. The great difficulty is to grasp this notion.[9]

At this point Simone Weil's intuitive and unresting mind proceeds to a sustained and richly suggestive meditation on the simi-

larity between the image of society as a great beast, which occurs in
Book VI of Plato's *Republic*,[10] and the same image which is also
found in the last book of the New Testament. The passage in Plato,
which could not possibly be more apt for our times than it is, well
deserves a close reading if one is to get all one should out of what
Simone Weil is saying. The beast in either literary tradition stands
for mass constraint, what Simone Weil calls 'force'. She notices
how the *kenosis* or 'self-emptying' of God in the incarnation, in
Paul's letter to the Philippians[11] is the very reversal of the way the
beast operates. Nevertheless, to all appearances, the beast is supreme on earth. To Christ in the desert the Devil says: 'To you I will
give all this authority and their glory; for it has been delivered to
me, and I give it to whom I will.' This, as Simone Weil says,
'accounts for almost everything'. 'Almost', but not quite, for it
leaves out the hidden presence and intervention of God, whose
absence from the picture of the world generated by socialist and
capitalist societies alike we have been noticing in our previous two
chapters. The reason for this absence, even in a view of the world
which is not always consciously or systematically atheistic, is accurately diagnosed by Simone Weil:

> The share of the supernatural here below is secret, silent, almost
> invisible, infinitely small. But it is decisive ... The decisive
> operation of the infinitely small is a paradox which the human
> intelligence finds it difficult to acknowledge. Through this para-
> dox is accomplished the wise persuasion that Plato speaks of,
> that persuasion by means of which divine providence induces
> necessity to direct most things towards the good. Nature, which
> is a mirror of the divine truths, offers us everywhere an image of
> this paradox.

Later in this chapter and the next we must see how a venerable
tradition of Chinese wisdom reached a conclusion not very different from this.

Whether we decide to put it in Simone Weil's way or not, it is
simply necessary to note in passing that the omission of God,
combined with a devastating criticism of the effects of organized
religion, can only be seen as a systematic atheism in Marx by those
who have their own reasons for going very much further than he
himself did. It is certainly not his rediscovery of some form of
Christianity which justifies Roger Garaudy in writing: 'Marx

criticizes religion, not metaphysically but historically. For him, religion is not only a reflection of man's real distress, but a protest against it . . . His atheism is not metaphysical but methodological.' [12] Many who will not otherwise feel able to follow Garaudy in the rest of what is really an extended political pamphlet will readily admit the justice of his observations on this subject. They will also be able to see that Gardavsky is speaking as an entirely honest modern disciple when he says that Marx's criticism of religion is 'not directed against God'. He genuinely believes, as Marx believed, that religion is a social phenomenon which will only persist so long as certain types of social problem remain unsolved. Probably rather fewer who appreciate these points correctly will be likely to recall that a medieval thinker like Thomas Aquinas also rejected the idea that religion is a virtue which has God for its immediate object. For Aquinas it is very clearly a moral virtue which is much concerned with the human condition, and exists not for God's sake but for ours. As such it is subject to many human abuses. [13] But to pursue this point further would take us into another world of discourse.

It is more urgent for the moment to get clearer about a phenomenon which cuts right across contemporary life in countries which may be classified as socialist or capitalist indifferently. This phenomenon was already being described by Simone Weil in 1934 with a vividness that must have been, at that time, a terrible test to tolerate:

> Never has the individual been so completely delivered up to a blind collectivity, and never have men been less capable, not only of subordinating their actions to their thoughts, but even of thinking. Such terms as oppressors and oppressed, the idea of classes – all that sort of thing is near to losing all meaning, so obvious are the impotence and distress of all men in face of the social machine . . . We are living in a world in which nothing is made to man's measure; there exists a monstrous discrepancy between man's body, man's mind and the things which at present constitute the elements of human existence; everything is disequilibrium.

She does not leave these distressing thoughts hanging in the air. She continues:

> This disequilibrium is essentially a matter of quantity. Quantity

is changing into quality, as Hegel said, and in particular a mere
difference in quantity is sufficient to change what is human into
what is inhuman . . . Now everything that the individual becomes powerless to control is seized upon by the collectivity.
Thus science has now been for a long time – and to an ever-
increasing extent – a collective enterprise. Actually, new results
are always, in fact, the work of specific individuals; but, save
perhaps for rare exceptions, the value of any result depends on
such a complex set of interrelations with past discoveries and
possible future researches that even the mind of the inventor
cannot embrace the whole. Consequently, new discoveries, as
they go on accumulating, take on the appearance of enigmas,
after the style of too thick a glass which ceases to be
transparent.[14]

These forceful paragraphs on a world over which 'science is
king' convey in concentrated form that sense of an opaque, brood-
ing mystery of nature which is all many artists have left, as the
changing views and probing questions of the natural scientists filter
through to the non-specialist. Imaginative writers and thinkers
pick up more quickly and express more memorably the shocks that
everyone will soon be receiving. Darwin's *Origin of Species* was not
published until 1859. Perhaps it would not have been published
then, had not another English naturalist, Alfred Russel Wallace,
independently reached the same conclusions about the same time.
These conclusions were reached roughly mid-way in the writing
career of Turgenev. In their different manner men intellectually
and personally very unalike thus register the same phase of human
development in ways which have some affinity. Tennyson, too, as
we have seen, had early been preoccupied with the question: What
is nature doing? Dr J. Bronowski, in his television series *The Ascent
of Man*, now published as a book, plausibly suggested that Darwin
was himself 'to some extent' shocked by his own theory.[15] Even for
him it took time to assimilate. It would indeed be interesting to
know how far, in spite of the impressive advantages of the mass
media, many subsequent theories of comparable importance have
yet been in any serious way widely assimilated. Bronowski's ingenious pictorial explanation of Einstein's principle of relativity
was, for instance, something of a *tour de force*. But how many viewers
will have seen it as much more than high-class entertainment? To
pose this question is not to belittle Bronowski's achievement or to

demean its value. But, as Simone Weil was seeing long before most people were experiencing the world that way, shocks can come so fast and frequent and involve readjustments so vast that many people stop thinking altogether.

It probably matters a good deal less that individual theories are not popularly understood than that the reserves and general perspectives of the specialists are hardly appreciated at all. For these are of major importance. Popular Marxism, like popular science, both of them fairly remote from their generating origins, have doubtless done much to reinforce the sense of a fate-bound world which the encroaching collectivity would in any case have tended to produce. Yet for those who will listen, reporters of integrity are constantly trying to prevent this situation arising. Let us notice, for instance, what Bronowski has to say on the significance of the conclusions to which Darwin and Wallace had come:

> The theory of evolution by natural selection was certainly the most important single scientific innovation in the nineteenth century. When all the foolish wind and wit that it raised had blown away, the living world was different because it was seen to be a world in movement. The creation is not static but changes in time in a way that physical processes do not ... Unlike physics, every generalization about biology is a slice in time; and it is evolution which is the real creator of originality and novelty in the universe.

Alas, how many people see the world since Darwin in a way which is really so dynamic? If they fail to do so, this is partly because the overall vision is difficult to get, save with the help of a teacher like Bronowski. As he says:

> Nature works by steps ... Evolution is the climbing of a ladder from simple to complex by steps, each of which is stable in itself ... I call it *stratified stability*. That is what has brought life by slow steps but constantly up a ladder of increasing complexity – which is the central progress and problem in evolution. And now we know that that is true not only of life but of matter.

The background to these remarks must be seen as the statement of Niels Bohr mentioned by Bronowski earlier in the lecture just cited: 'Every sentence that I utter should be regarded by you not as an assertion but as a question.' Appropriately enough, Bronowski

called the following lecture 'Knowledge of Certainty', and began it
by saying:

> One aim of the physical sciences has been to give an exact picture
> of the material world. The achievement of physics in the twen-
> tieth century has been to prove that that aim is unattainable . . .
> There is no absolute knowledge. And those who claim it, whe-
> ther they are scientists or dogmatists, open the door to tragedy.
> All information is imperfect. We have to treat it with
> humility.[16]

It would, of course, be a false humility, and at this stage of
human development a dangerous error, to suppose that we can
safely close our books and go back to nature by some other way
than that which brought us where we are. There are many who feel
this temptation today, but it must be recognized as an impossible
wish. Knowledge is not so easily sloughed off. But this is not to say
that the views and approaches with which we are most familiar may
not need complementing by others that are either unknown or
forgotten. Bronowski's final lecture in *The Ascent of Man* may
probably be forgiven its easy swipe at Zen, but not entirely its own
vague moralizing and above all its European insularity. It is, after
all, a very long time now since Joseph Needham, in the preface to
his great enterprise on science in China, said of the temptation of
Europeans to conclude that wisdom was born with us: 'A salutary
correction of perspective is necessary.'[17]

Perhaps, for the moment, a doctor nurtured in the European
tradition but not unmindful of others, may make the issues sharper
for us. Jean Hamburger, an eminent French specialist, opens
his recent book *L'Homme et les hommes* (*Man and Men*) with a
conversation with the Tempter on the credentials of medicine to
intervene in so weighty a matter. Taking as his point of departure
the problems of grafting, on which he is an expert, Professor
Hamburger presents in a modest and engaging way the issues for
the survival of all that we value in man as recent developments in
biology suggest them to be. The problems of grafting reveal that,
with the exception of authentic twins, no two individuals are
exactly alike even within the same animal species, as their living
tissues are able to recognize at once. Individuality is so marked that
it appears to have a built-in defence mechanism, though there are
still many unsolved problems about tolerance and immunity. Jean

Hamburger asserts, with apparently good reason, that there are still some doubts about the extent to which we can really explain the evolution of a species. But there are almost none about the fact that *within* a given species factors are at work which ensure an evolution adapted to hostile conditions. He supports this statement with two examples from the recent biology of animal life and one from that of man. It is, however, the latter section of his book which is of most interest for our present purposes. For it is there that he discusses how far what we know of the mechanism of life can throw light on what we regard as distinctively human. It has been established earlier in the book that the maintenance of a sufficient diversity of individuals is necessary to the survival of the species as a whole, within a given group. The really fascinating question is to know how far there is a spiritual equivalent of the polymorphic genetics which determine the individuality of our bodies. There seems to be no indisputable answer to this question as yet, but the evidence looks as though it favours an affirmative reply in some form. There may also be, as Professor Hamburger suggests, a field of conflict here which exists as a result of a false analysis of what we actually know. Even supposing the brain is the instrument of thought, it would be false to suppose that this implies that a day will ever come when it will be possible to show that we can predict what thoughts will come on a purely physico-chemical basis. For the psychological and neuro-biological fields of investigation are different in kind. Having ventilated a little the eternal disputes about what genuine freedom might mean, Jean Hamburger concludes by saying:

> Let us leave these gentlemen with their divergent views to continue their debates without us. What the one side and the other will have to admit is that the latest child of the marionettes, human thought, unquestionably takes an independent flight. By which I mean a flight capable of being in its turn the source of an action. This birth of freedom − whatever be the sense one chooses to give that word − is the birth of an attitude of potential resistance. The freer the thought is, the more capable it is of resisting the established order. It becomes capable of creation, that is, of revolt. And everything happens as though, thanks to his brain, man acquired the means of siring incalculable flash-back effects on the world in which we live − effects which can be so many breaches of the natural rules of life. Flash-backs of fire.[18]

In brief it is Professor Hamburger's plea that men are capable of creating unthought-of situations, a quite new state of affairs in the natural world, as all kinds of evidence daily confirms. As he says, this is a moral question and quite unlike that which arises in the animal kingdom, where a species appears to be programmed primarily for survival. The passionate concern of men for other things than mere survival is the cause of man's problems. But it is also the salt and nobility of the human adventure which refuses to be simply passive to the laws of evolution and survival as they otherwise obtain in the animal kingdom. Naturally, this refusal to accept the insolubility of problems can take destructive forms. But it does not have to – and perhaps in the majority of cases it does not, and would not. This is exactly where the idea of the individual who carries the species to survival is so important. It throws, Jean Hamburger feels, a light on the problem of the man who is not-quite-the-same-as-others in a given field. Even judged on medical grounds alone, there are countless examples of men alive today who are not quite the same as others. From this point on we move into the world of hypothesis. But it is possible to do it with open eyes. 'In wars between men we have learned to our cost that there is never a victor, only victims. Let us take care that in the conflict between man and nature both do not emerge victims. That would be the most pointless of struggles.' It is possible that a new harmony between the spiritual desires of men and the world could be born. Its pre-condition is at least an awareness to which reflection alone can keep us alive. If Professor Hamburger's book closes with a statement of the need to recover, in a life too short, the arts of recollection and retreat,[19] it brings us by a circuitous but often necessary route back to where older traditions tend to begin.

As one reads modern writers concerned with these problems, or meets people who consciously share them, one hears so many echoes in what they say of the kind of thing the 'great old man' Barsanuphius was constantly saying so many centuries ago. In letters of direction, one of whose first preoccupations was to help his disciples to find their true spiritual liberty, he writes with some warmth. 'Brother, you are slowly burrowing deeper in pursuit of hidden things and I, ass that I am, believe that what you are asking of me no one can discern save he who has reached that measure . . . Talk to anyone as much as you will, what he needs more is a taste of experience.'[20]

It is probably part of the hidden logic of life that at about the same time in the same year as Professor Hamburger's book appeared, another French doctor published a study in which he compares most of the practices popularly associated with the contemporary pursuit of experiences with the alternative flight to drugs and other reliefs from the unbearable. Its title, *Les Techniques du bonheur* (*Techniques of Well-being*), makes it sound a good deal more catchpenny than it actually proves to be. For there is nothing dishonest in seeing that yoga, psychoanalysis, 'transcendental meditation', and Zen have *something* in common both in their appeal and, sometimes, in their results. Nor is it impossible to discuss them with openness and sympathy while retaining one's critical sense. Nevertheless, as this unassuming and worthwhile attempt at a global presentation shows, the practitioners of these aids to human equilibrium seem to be often less than sufficiently explicit about the status and role of the philosophical presuppositions to which their own books frequently refer. Dr Maurin does not allow this fact to fall out of view, though it is primarily through a medical man's eyes that he conducts his examination. It is, interestingly enough, precisely in this perspective that he makes one of his few very positive references to the oldest Christian tradition. He writes: 'In fact, anyone who fancies that a "guardian angel" guides part of his acts (counselling him to avoid the more glaring errors), this believer, in his simplicity, is nearer the truth than someone who supposes he can programme the substance of his life on the basis of scientifico-philosophic notions.'[21]

These two voices from the world of medicine are an important corrective to over-simplified views of what an all-discerning and almighty consciousness can do for us. To insist upon the limits of direct responsibility and upon a respect for what cannot be measured, is not necessarily to open the floodgates of fancy. In his *Portrait of Nature*, a portrait every bit as ingenious and readable as Bronowski's, Sir Alan Cottrell concludes by saying:

Broadly, there are three things portrayed in the picture: the world of the very *large*, the cosmos; that of the very *small*, the elementary particles; and that of the very *complex*, all the middle-sized things from the sun and the earth down to atoms and molecules, including man himself. If we probe deeply enough into each of these we find in the end that nature becomes so strange as to be almost incomprehensible. We meet the curvature of space and time, the curious circularity of matter making the geometry and geometry making the matter. We meet the mirage-like nature of elementary particles, some of which seem as incorporeal as the disembodied grin of the Cheshire cat. In the middle-sized world the strangest are the most intimate things of all, the self-awareness which each of us has, and the mysterious frontier along which the mental and physical worlds meet. At the world of the mind our scientific picture reaches its limits . . . If we wish to believe that God created the world – set it going, to find its own way along some indeterminate but physically lawful course – there is nothing in science to contradict this, nor can there be.[22]

This also needed saying by someone competent to say it.

For the portrait of nature, of which the developing natural sciences have been filling in more and more detail for well over a century, is necessarily in either the foreground or the background of the minds of those who consult one of the various kinds of doctors today. These people will be feeling either that *someone* knows enough to spot the missing information about which some expert can certainly put them on the track, or they will be hoping to find some way of escape from a world they fear to contemplate. If the latter kind do not consult a medical practitioner, then perhaps they will find an astrologer or, if they are not feeling too unwell, just 'trust to luck'. Both types would be wiser to listen to those doctors who will remind them that there are no infallible tricks of technology to make them more masterful than they already are. Nor are there any neat escape routes, quite inaccessible to the unpredictable forces of change. But there are, and for centuries have been, recommendable ways of preserving a truly human equilibrium which do not require for their practice that we sacrifice either our intelligence or our authentic feeling. They are concerned with our integration as a whole. No one can legitimately blame the two doctors we have quoted for not turning to a Christian tradition of meditation and prayer in making their point. If the thought of the one turns instinctively to the value of a Japanese meditation garden it is doubtless because, though he may be too polite to say so, he knows what a hubbub of excitement there has been in many western cloister gardens about competing with what they seem to know how to do better in other places and by other methods. The other doctor, not silencing his questions and reserves, tries to present what is humanly valuable and true from sources that are still culturally new to us: he likewise almost certainly because these are precisely the values that western Christianity in particular has often betrayed, first in practice and afterwards in vacuous theory. Its own oldest traditions ought to have reminded it of something rather different. By an irony appropriate to the sins of pride involved, it is usually the genuine men of science who inherit that fear of spiritual illusions which was once part of a view of the human condition that has become virtually inaccessible under the accretion of centuries of neglect. Pondering this situation in some days of recollection with a group of scientists, a modern theologian, to whose words we shall later return, has justly pointed out that the orthodox tradition of Christian thought has always asserted *in principle* the sort of thing modern science has made it necessary to reassert about the world we see and live in: 'But, paradoxical as it sounds, one must say that it has too little *lived* it.'[23]

In the autumn of the same year in which his book *Man and Men* appeared, Professor Hamburger was invited to give a talk on the social significance of modern biology for political life. This gave him the opportunity of briefly summarizing what he regarded as the message of his book. In the course of this paper he hit on a striking formulation of its theme. He cites the familiar phrase of Rousseau which appeared in 1762: Man is born free and everywhere he is in chains. 'The biologist of 1976', he continues, 'would be inclined to say exactly the opposite: Men are born the slaves of the genetic deal they receive and of the intractable biological laws which rule the world of living things; and the life of men represents a struggle to acquire a certain degree of liberty with regard to these initial constraints'.[24]

In that same year a young English ethologist, Richard Dawkins, published a brilliant book, *The Selfish Gene*, whose final message is essentially the same, though certainly more coherently integrated into its biological context. With the genius of a born teacher Dr Dawkins provides us with an intelligible and convincing model for interpreting what we know about the 'intractable' aspect of biological laws. The substance of his case is so tightly argued that it is difficult to quote from it without misrepresenting it. But he does say on an early page that 'if you would extract a moral from it, read it as a warning'. The warning, which he repeats several times in relation to specific definitions of his terms is that 'we must teach our children altruism, for we cannot expect it to be part of their biological nature'. Only in his last chapter does Dr Dawkins move into that realm of psycho-social speculation about the uniqueness of man, where his position is substantially the same as that of his French medical colleague, though rather more broadly conceived. In saying that 'most of what is unusual about man can be summed up in one word, "culture"', Dawkins explains that he uses this word 'as a scientist uses it'. He adds that 'cultural transmission is analogous to genetic transmission in that, although basically conservative, it can give rise to a form of evolution'.[25] He cites the case of language which seems to evolve by non-genetic means 'and at a rate which is orders of magnitude faster than genetic evolution'. Cautious of what he calls 'quite unnecessary mystical overtones' Dawkins takes advantage of the occasion to talk about 'the idea of God' as a congeries of notions that have continued to propagate themselves with enormous power. It will not be to our purpose to discuss what Dawkins has to say under this heading, except to note that its general tendency – which is almost certainly not specifically intended – is to argue like Marx or his modern disciple Gardavsky that the God idea is a social product, whose power is its psychological appeal under the circumstances which continue to prevail. Its disappearance could be expected if these circumstances substantially change. Here his French colleague has for once a slight edge on him in insisting both in his book and in his lecture on the fact that we cannot afford to neglect the role of the 'passions' in human conduct. In *Man and Men* Jean Hamburger cites the notable case of the campaign for the protection of the blue whale. In spite of all the efforts of competent naturalists to spread accurate information on the critical situation for this species, the campaign only became effective when in Stockholm it was taken up with emotional arguments not always too accurately based on the facts.[26] This example and others that could doubtless be assembled from political and social life is not, of course, any case for launching into what Dawkins calls 'unnecessary mystical overtones'. But it is an important reminder of just that complexity of factors which in unique and decisive cases determines what is likely to happen once we enter the realm where man is developing along lines 'analogous to those of genetic evolution'. Since biologists appear to be agreed that not just man as a species, but *each individual man* is a special case genetically considered, it is difficult to see why any of them should underestimate precisely those 'apparently trivial tiny influences on survival probability which can have a major impact on evolution', of which Dawkins speaks when talking of genes. Men being the complex creatures they are, these influences cannot be so exclusively intellectual as Dawkins's references to music and poetry would appear to envisage. The references are obviously spontaneous but have, somehow, too academic a ring. It is perhaps their commitment to the problems of individual patients that compels the two French doctors we have cited to recognize the need for *some* regular *practice*, rather than adventitious delights, in the fostering of what concerns them all. Such a practice would have to be favourable to the survival *in individuals* of just those factors that would seem to have made human evolution a distinct affair. Dawkins implies his awareness of this aspect of the problem about the distinctness of man when he chooses to reject the argument of some of his colleagues that the evolution of the human brain sufficiently explains everything. He defends his use of analogy to extend his theoretical model to the properly human area of life by saying: 'We biologists have assimilated the idea of genetic evolution so deeply that we tend to forget that it is only one of many possible kinds of evolution.' [27] He thus comes as near as he feels he can allow himself to a field of discussion which he rightly knows it is impossible to enter with the intellectual tools of the discipline to which he is accustomed, and which he prefers.

Yet Dawkins's concern for intellectual integrity is relevant to and, indeed, implied in the thought of those who feel they must go a little further, at least at the practical level. Only Dr Maurin has risked his reputation by describing as therapeutic techniques a number of systems whose theoretical basis he has decided not to examine more than superficially. [28] This is a defensible position. For it is morally certain that most of the practitioners of these techniques have a very imperfect grasp of the theories which are often built around them, or may be part of the tradition in which they originally developed. It is equally outside the purpose of this book to examine these philosophical and religious systems as such. One general remark alone seems to be necessary from a theological point of view. In so far as any practitioner of these techniques is seriously and systematically committed to some form of philosophical pantheism it would seem that, whatever the appearances to the contrary, there is a real danger of their limiting themselves to what is, in fact, an experience of themselves alone. Deliberately isolating themselves from the rest of differentiated existence they necessarily open themselves to the illusions to which such a state of mind would easily lead. There are, of course, no barriers through which God cannot and sometimes does break, especially when these are not wilfully and perversely erected. But possibly the root of that inner idolatry which constructs so many false images of God, of the kind which biologists and theologians must alike reject, is the temptation to believe that there is a substratum of 'being', in which what people have called 'God' and also all finite and changing beings, men among them, are really simply one and the same. Only the illusion of difference needs tearing away.

Those who wish to believe that the world is one vast illusion, rather than that we ourselves are subject to illusions about it, will no more be able to reconcile themselves to the findings of the natural scientists than they will to Christian belief and practice. For both will sooner or later have to insist that reality is resistant to such views, even if experience does not teach us this lesson the hard way. It is not always realized that orthodox Christianity is necessarily committed to taking the world, which it believes God created, entirely seriously. There is still, and often has been in the past, a kind of piety which in practice supposes that it honours God to demean what he has made, especially when it causes us some kind of spiritual difficulty. But, on reflection, this attitude is evidently incompatible *both* with what we believe about the nature of God, and what we are bound sooner or later to discover about things. Thus, long before many churchmen who should have known better had made so many blunders about the development of the sciences, St Thomas Aquinas had felt compelled to say that *some* people had understood God to be at work in the world in such a way that nothing really operates in virtue of its own internal causes; that it is not fire that warms us, but God in the fire. But this, he says, is a quite impossible view. For it makes the very conception of created things meaningless.[29] It is not necessary to agree either with Aquinas's, or Aristotle's, picture of the way things are caused to see that what is here being said *must* be right. It looks as though there has probably been only one long and ancient philosophical tradition which has been brave enough to recognize at one and the same time that there is something mysterious about the world *and* that the element of mystery should not be used to cover up a failure to explain things by observation and common sense. But the tradition of Taoism and certain other aspects of Chinese philosophy relevant to this book will require a chapter to themselves. It is enough for the moment to have seen that, within the limits of their discipline, the natural scientists today do not appear to be saying anything that should cause the believer to lose his balance or disturb his nights. Some of the things being said may have upset the more comfortable picture of the world which it was possible to have when less was known about it. But genuine belief has, in the long run, never been an easy or comfortable affair. The new knowledge is *in itself* in no way a serious threat to faith. Indeed it may be, rather, a summons to its purification. As Karl Rahner was saying to his natural scientists in the talk already mentioned:

> Because the world as a whole, while expressing *itself*, only speaks silently of God by leaving unsaid the ultimate word which is proper to it, it is possible to miss hearing this call of silence, it is possible to think that God cannot be found because one always encounters more of the world the further one's investigation penetrates into it. In reality, however, this experience is not the genesis of atheism, but the discovery that the world is not God.

He adds, consistently with the undoubted tenets of Christian orthodoxy, that 'wherever anything happens in the world which forms part of the "normal" make-up of the world, it is always possible to discover for it a cause which is not God himself'.[30] This is a point which so many charming and witty Taoist tales repeatedly make. And *if* – as appears to be the case – some natural scientists are saying this too, with less charm and in rather more strident tones of voice, there is no need to suppose that they are necessarily very dangerous lions. The watchmen have met them before.

> Set a man to watch all night,
> Dance over my lady Leigh,
> Set a man to watch all night,
>     My fair lady.

This idea of the watchman is common to all traditions. Only the one who stays awake can save a bridge or a falling world.[31]

# 5
## CHANGE

Of the many *biblical* watchmen, those who appear twice in the great
love poem of the *Song of Songs* either do not know the answer to
the seeker's question, or even treat roughly the one who sleeps with
a heart awake.[1] For there are different ways of being awake to the
world. They are not necessarily mutually exclusive. Up to this
point we have found it important to look rather carefully at two
enormously influential views of the world at which seekers after
truth have been working since the middle of the nineteenth century, the one political, the other scientific. Both are of an evolutionary character and these views as reported, and sometimes as
imperfectly understood at second hand, have tended to generate
moods and theories more ferociously and confidently deterministic
than either type of source would seriously seem to justify. The
political one is still largely strongest as an intuition which very few
people have had either the ability or the learning to follow up. The
task of mastering what is involved becomes daily more exacting as
what Marx began as the investigation of a European problem is
extended to the political economy of the entire globe.[2] The scientific one, which more easily crosses all political frontiers, has gathered to itself a much larger body of able workers and now stands
on an altogether more secure intellectual footing. Its inner vitality
is shown in the strength it has drawn from its continued self-
questioning stance – also the mark of the only kind of philosophical
activity that is likely to have a future before it. Political Marxism
has often been shockingly retrograde in this respect, and has itself
furnished us with some sharp reminders of how much the activities
of the natural scientists can be governed by political factors. But to
the extent to which the authentic intuitions of these very different
disciplines are being genuinely pursued and explored they may be
expected to furnish us with truths which command our respect. In
the face of all this activity a 'theologian' – in the oldest sense of that
word, and not just a professional intellectual under that name – will
feel a quiet confidence. Even though he may have his reserves
about the so-called Aristotelian synthesis of Thomas Aquinas, he

72

will necessarily share his view that since his faith is grounded in unfailing truth, it will be impossible to bring a conclusive demonstration against it. For all arguments which may appear to be contrary to faith must *in principle* be soluble.[3] This is, of course, a principle which stops a long way short of asserting that any specific person has some theoretical answer to every problem at any given time – a fact which some professional theologians would have done well to remember. In any case we do not seem to have met anyone of standing in either of the fields we have been considering, who seriously claims to be putting forward such an argument.[4] There are simply a few of them who reveal some desire to do so, if they could find it. For those who are capable of it, a direct confrontation with scientific disciplines is thus likely to be morally fortifying, provided they can keep their minds alert to what really seems to be the established fruits of investigation.

But intellectual effort alone is not likely to dispose of all the temptations against faith which the universal awareness of some kind of determining forces at work in the world awakens today. Even the most unreflecting people in a time of rapid and profound change are experiencing a frustrating sense of these encroaching factors, which seem to leave them little choice but passive submission and, in the end, personal defeat. The problems are, naturally, not altogether new, though they can seldom have been so intense or so universal since the Church's very earliest days. The Fathers also had to contend with the difficulties raised by people who, then as now, were oppressed by what they called 'fate'. The Fathers recognized, even then, the extreme difficulty of deciding satisfactorily what may well be determined about a given life, before the true search and battle for spiritual freedom begins. Because they also saw the dangers which a direct concern with so many uncertain matters may involve for those whose faith is weak, they often chose not to discuss them at length. However, these problems are frequently commented on, incidentally, in the course of other works. St Gregory of Nyssa's little book 'in the form of a letter', *Against Fate*, must be one of the few works by any major Father of the Church explicitly and wholly devoted to this subject.[5] It expresses a number of views which crop up with such unerring frequency in other writers that we shall find ourselves inevitably referring to them later. For developments in politics and the natural sciences, combined as they are with a decline in the supportive force of the typical social expressions of the great world religions, have made an explicit discussion of the entire concept of 'fate' an imperative need today. It is not necessary to be even tempted by some particular political theory to see that the lives of everyone everywhere are determined in more minutely detailed ways by politics and economics than ever before. A feeling of uncertainty also prevails about what the latest findings in biology and medicine are going to reveal on topics which have, hitherto, never seemed to be worrying ones. To this extent, the temptation to take a wholly fatalistic view of life is also greater than it has ever been. After all, the kind of postscripts doctors and biologists may wish to write on their researches are neither widely enough known nor sufficiently attended to. Indeed, without some change in habits of mind and living such as those to which several of the writers quoted in the previous chapter exhort us, it is difficult to see how larger and larger masses of the world population can escape massive manipulation by forces whose nature they do not understand or know how to resist. This phenomenon is daily reflected in the known, and apparently growing, number of people whose only hope and refuge is their horoscope.

Thus a very ancient temptation reappears under new conditions and, appropriately to the circumstances, often with the trappings of a pseudo-science. Anyone who looks around in the orthodox Christian tradition for formulated views on these matters will probably be struck by the fact that responsible writers and preachers are not concerned, first and foremost, to say that the predictions of the horoscopes are *untrue*. Their concern is rather with that element of truth in those predictions which is likely to be fastened on, *to the exclusion of every other possibility*. In an interesting articulation of the tradition as he understands it, Thomas Aquinas finds it useful to quote a remark of Augustine made in the course of his lengthy commentary on the Book of Genesis. There Augustine says that Christians ought to keep a proper reserve about predictions, 'especially when they tell the truth', since *then*, they may incline the soul to collude with the powers of evil.[6] Leaving aside for the moment the additional problem of the way hidden spiritual powers may be at work in these complexities, it is enough to notice the concern Aquinas expresses for the directly *human* dimension of an unreserved belief in prediction. Although his natural science may be very primitive (and often certainly wrong) we should still agree, as he does, with the observation of Aristotle that changes in weather and climate, and physical changes in general, do have an indirect effect on human choices, through the moods they tend to produce. But wherever we locate these forces, or however we investigate them, we can never achieve for human beings the reasonably predictive certainty of the men who make the weather charts. For with human beings factors other than purely physical ones *can* come into the picture. Someone at once objects that what the astrologers foretell is often true. Yes, replies Aquinas, but this is because men, by and large, yield to their bodily humours, and thus their actions are largely determined by the forces which operate on them. 'Only a few, those who are wise, temper their moods. And this is why astrologers foretell a lot of things that are true, especially public events which depend on the masses.'[7] In other words – and in this he is representative of his sources – Aquinas believes that one of the primary dangers of fortune-telling, even when it turns out to be true, lies in the temptation its practice presents to give up the exercise of the liberty we certainly have. For it tends to make us see only the ways in which we are *not* free. We should, incidentally, add that even those who would laugh at a horoscope but, nevertheless, believe that everything *of necessity* functions in terms of verifiable and ascertainable causes, ultimately fall into the same crippling position. This is why St Thomas in defending, in another context, his willingness to use the word 'fate' says that, in so far as 'fate' is understood to cover the area of events in which causes are allowed to produce their natural effect *unimpeded*, then *of course* fate exists. And so 'whatever is bound by causes of this kind is bound by fate'. To choose, in virtue of whatever persuasion, to live as though everything had about it a predetermined inevitability is in fact to allow oneself to be bound by such causes, instead of merely respecting them, taking them into account.[8] People who live like this will inevitably cease to pray – as we have seen the disciples of both the major kinds of modern determinism have tended to do. For that there could exist any cause whose action they cannot investigate or predict will seem to them to be an incredible illusion. And so, as Boethius saw, they will equally inevitably become daily 'involved more deeply in the meshes of fate'.[9] An attentive reading of Gregory of Nyssa's little discussion of the question of fate will reveal his substantial agreement with the points emphasized in these later views. He will not deny the presence of an *element* of truth in what the astrologers predict. But he is concerned that human beings should see that only some act of choice[10] – or, of course, its absence where it ought to have been – can make a fate truly binding.

It would indeed have been satisfactory to know what this traditional Christian attitude to fate and divination would have made of the fact that in China there existed from ancient times a philosophical tradition whose central interest was the pattern and workings of change. Elements in this Chinese tradition, which had originated in primitive divination, were eventually embodied in and used to interpret a classical collection of texts called the *I Ching* (*Book of Changes*)[11] which – contrary to what is often, apparently, made of it – is concerned precisely with the element of freedom in every fate-bound situation. Its emphasis falls on the situation as it already exists or is building up, rather than on predictions of the future. In spite of the difficulties involved – intrinsic to the many kinds of competence required for doing it satisfactorily – it would seem that some kind of evaluation in the light of the Christian tradition of this other tradition from the far side of the world cannot be indefinitely delayed. The obstacles to such an investigation being taken seriously are certainly of the kind to which Simone Weil refers when she says that the human intelligence finds it difficult to acknowledge the paradox of the decisive operation of the infinitely small, of which nature offers us everywhere an image. It might be as well to allow for the possibility that it was in this book of nature, which he said he had always with him, that Anthony the Great learned some of those lessons of humility and common sense which may be learned by any watcher of this open book whose heart is as awake as his intelligence.[12] When in China a very long time ago Hui Tzu said to Chuang Tzu, 'Your teachings are of no practical use', Chuang Tzu replied, 'Only those who already know the value of the useless can be talked to about the useful.'[13] No one uninterested in the value of the useless need read any further.

Anyone who has been reading around for a very long time among books that might throw light on the problems raised by the *I Ching* will be likely to agree with Joseph Needham that the small introduction by Helmut Wilhelm is still the best in a western language.[14] We shall save ourselves time and confusion if we begin with what Wilhelm has to say about the concept of change in Chinese philosophy. He points out that the Chinese word *I*, in the title *I Ching*, is a word of great antiquity in Chinese and, although it may now be satisfactorily rendered as 'change', it also retains the undertones of earlier usages. The first thing the character *I* yields us is 'the easy, the simple, the naturally given'. In other words, life takes its form from what is given in nature. The most immediate experience of what is given is, as the early Greek philosopher Heraclitus observed, the fact of constant change. In words which recall Heraclitus's aphorism, 'everything flows', Confucius is recorded as saying: 'Like this river, everything is flowing on cease-lessly, day and night.' But as Wilhelm points out, in Chinese philosophy change is not simply movement as such, for its opposite is also movement. This opposite is regression. Applied to the human condition, development is not a fate dictated from without, but rather a sign showing the direction that decisions take. 'To stand in the stream of this development is a datum of nature; to recognize it and follow it is responsibility and free choice.'[15]

This picture of change is never thought of as one-dimensional, and the western idea of the forward movement of 'progress' is quite foreign to it. As Wilhelm says: 'The attempt to exalt the new at the expense of the old, the future at the expense of the past, was alien to Chinese thought. The accent lies solely on the ability to keep within the flow of change. If earlier times have been superior to us in this respect, the fact is recognized without prejudice, and the lesson is drawn that we should feel obliged to do as well as the ancients did.'

Thus there is a third aspect of the old word *I*: 'the secure, the constant'. Probably it was at first associated with the hierarchy of relationships in society. But it also implies a certain inner dy-namism, such as the second aspect at the same time suggests. Change is not something that happens abruptly and irrationally. There is a channel along which things flow. In this respect *I* is already very close to the idea of *Tao*, a word and a notion which is, in fact, used in the later materials gathered round the *I Ching*. This latter is a conception we must soon discuss, but for the moment we can say that the aspect of *I* which suggests its nearness to the idea of Tao is the attribute of consistency and all-inclusiveness. Both heaven and earth have their Tao, for change is at work in all things great and small. Anyone whose heart is aware of these forces is able to act in harmony with them, and to do so with great fruitfulness. As Wilhelm says: 'Since every seed attains development in change, it must be possible to introduce into its flow a seed planted by man. And since knowledge of the laws of change teaches the right way of

placing such a seed, a highly effective influence becomes possible.'
This is an idea which both frees man from his subjection to nature
and confronts him with his own responsibility. 'Only by taking up a
counter position, by confronting events with live awareness, can
developments be guided into desired paths.'[16]

If we are to grasp the implications of Tao, in so far as they can be
explained in words at all, we shall do well to look closely at the
brilliant work of Marcel Granet on Chinese thought,[17] as well as at
that of his almost unqualified admirer Joseph Needham.[18] As
Granet says, in introducing his discussion of the fundamentals of
Chinese thought:

> There are no signs that any sage of ancient China felt the need of
> notions which could be compared to our abstract ideas of num-
> ber, time and space and cause . . . But instead it is with the help
> of concrete symbols (the Yin and the Yang) that the wise men of
> every school of thought attempted to capture that feeling of
> rhythm which the interplay between time, space and number
> sets up. The Tao is the symbol of a notion still more synthetic,
> entirely different from our idea of cause and more embracing:
> by it is evoked – I would not say, the unique Principle of
> universal order – but rather, in its totality and its unity, an order
> which is at once ideal and acting.[19]

Needham begins his analysis of these matters by saying that 'for
the Taoists, the Tao or Way was not the right way of life within
human society, but the way in which the universe worked; in other
words, the *Order of Nature*'. One of the great classics of this school,
the *Tao Tê Ching*, says this of the things which come into existence
as a result of the workings of Tao:

> Rear them, but not lay claim to them,
> Control them, but never lean upon them,
> Be chief among them, but not lord it over them;
> This is called the invisible Virtue.

It is in this way that nature gives the wise man his model. 'By
yielding, by not imposing his preconceptions on Nature, he will be
able to observe and understand, and so to govern and control.'[20]

Needham next quotes several texts from the collection of the
conversations of Chuang Tzu which, in their earliest strata, must
be from about the same period as the *Tao Tê Ching* – somewhere
around 300 B.C. He finds in them what he calls 'a naturalistic

pantheism'. But to say this is probably often to underestimate the importance of their extreme professions of ignorance about what is ultimate. The passages he himself quotes contain phrases like this: 'Those who study the Tao [know that] they cannot follow these changes to the ultimate end, nor search out their first beginnings – this is the place at which discussion has to stop.' Needham is perhaps wiser when he says a little later: 'The point is that at this early stage of development of thought in China we are standing at a point *before* the differentiation of religion and science.'[21] Thus it is that his emphasis on Taoist interest in the here and now, on really seeing the naturalness and structure in things, is closer to the real centre of concern of these texts, and of the way of life with which they are bound up. It must certainly be right to emphasize the notion that the original name for Taoist temples, generally found in places of wild natural beauty, was *kuan* – a word which originally meant 'to look', and then 'to look down' as from a watchtower. But is it not a little remote from the appreciation of the unexplicated spirit of Taoism to insist that the later use of this same word for the equivalent of what we might call 'contemplation' has *altogether* lost touch with the earlier sense of really looking?[22]

For this business of 'really looking' requires, in any case, rather different qualities of mind from those which are appropriate to organizing things, to 'lording it over them'. These qualities, whether concerned with very concrete or more spiritual things, the *Tao Tê Ching* connects with two symbols, of which water is probably the primary one:

> The highest good is like that of water. The goodness of water is that it benefits the ten thousand creatures, yet itself does not wrangle, but is content with the places that all men disdain. It is this that makes water so near to the Tao.

As a later chapter in the same book tells us, water finds its way everywhere, without apparent effort. Even rock is no obstacle to it:

> What is of all things most yielding
> Can overwhelm that which is of all things most hard.

This, says the wise man, is how he knows the value of seeming not to act:

> Value in action that is actionless,
> Few indeed can understand.[23]

Alternatively these qualities of the sage can be symbolized by the 'mysterious feminine' of other chapters of the *Tao Tê Ching*. Chapter 28 opens with the words:

> He who knows the male, yet cleaves to the female
> Becomes like a ravine, receiving all things under heaven . . .

And it concludes by saying: 'Truly, "The greatest carver does the least cutting".' As a whole the passage implies that very fundamental complementarity which underlies the Taoist picture of the way the world works – an interplay between male and female forces. Yet even on the masculine side, Taoism emphasizes, as Needham points out, 'yieldingness'. And he cannot refrain from noticing striking parallels from the Christian tradition to the conclusions drawn by those who follow the selflessness of heaven and earth:

> Therefore the sage
> Puts himself in the background; but is always to the fore.
> Remains outside; but is always there.
> Is it not just because he does not strive for any personal end
> That all his personal ends are fulfilled? [24]

Anyone who ponders the texts just quoted will see that, although to follow them in practice might lead to calmness of mind, it is a calmness not cheaply bought. They are certainly not 'quietist' in the technical sense which that word acquired in the course of certain Christian controversies. They are quite clear that even not-doing, when chosen, is a doing, an action, and maybe even a demanding one. As Joseph Needham is concerned to show, the characteristic Taoist virtue of *wu wei*, often translated as 'inactivity', really means 'refraining from activity contrary to nature', and he quotes two convincing and impressive texts to demonstrate his point. The *Huai Nan Tzu* says:

> What is meant, in my view, by *wu wei*, is that no personal prejudice interferes with the universal Tao, and that no desires and obsessions lead the true courses of techniques astray . . .

The *Kuan Tzu* book says:

> Heaven helps him who works according to [the sense of] Heaven, and opposes him who works in opposition to [the sense of] Heaven. [25]

We are, it is to be hoped, already glimpsing a very different notion of what adaptation to the workings of 'fate' might mean from that which has been familiar to western thought. And, if there is a mystical element in it – as indeed there certainly is – it is equally certainly not anti-rational, though it be very strongly opposed to that kind of intellectualism which is typical of academic and political life the deeper it buries itself in books and theories.

But an awareness of this danger cannot be used as an excuse for evading some of the problems of the scholars. These are especially complex when we try to investigate the origins of the idea of the yin and yang, which are so fundamental to understanding the sense of the *I Ching*. Dr Needham believes that there can be very little doubt that the philosophical use of these complementary terms began about the beginning of the fourth century B.C. As Granet insists, they express the interplay of groups of complementary aspects of things. The characters for them are connected with darkness and light as we perceive them passing over the sunny and the shady sides of a valley, the yin being the shady and the yang the sunny side. The yin, the shady, is associated with the feminine, and yang with the masculine aspect of a thing or situation. It is important not to suppose that they are themselves things, which are either masculine or feminine with a full stop. 'When the Great Appendix to the *I Ching* says, "One Yin and one Yang; that is the Tao!", the general sense must be that there are only these two fundamental forces or operations in the universe, now one dominating, now the other, in a wave-like succession,' writes Needham. 'The sage', adds Granet, 'knows how to adapt himself to an alternating régime made up of released activity and restorative retreat.'[26]

It is with this business of adaptation to the alternation of the forces of yin and yang that the *I Ching* is concerned. But as Needham points out, of the sixty-four oracles or pictures of situations which occur in the *I Ching* as we now have it, each is arranged so that the yin and yang elements never become fully separated. But at each stage, in any given fragment, only one of them is manifested. His comment is that this

> cannot but interest the scientific mind because the path of thought thus trodden was one to which we have become accustomed in modern scientific thinking, namely, it was the principle of segregation . . . In so far as the *I Ching* scholars intuited that no matter how long the purification of material substance might

be carried on, there would still remain the positive and negative combined together, even though in appearance one or the other might dominate, their thought was quite close, after all, to the perspectives of modern science. Indeed their thinking here was 'field' thinking.

Like Granet, Needham notes that the yin and yang involves no hint of the opposition between good and evil,[27] which seems so easily to obsess students of this philosophy in Europe. The process which absorbs and interests Chinese science and the philosophy of change is what Granet calls interdependence and Needham Order 'and above all Pattern'. As he says, 'in coordinative thinking conceptions are not subsumed under one another, but placed side by side in a pattern, and things influence one another not by acts of mechanical causation, but by a kind of "inductance"'. And perhaps one of his shortest and neatest statements of what is involved here is: 'In a way, the whole idea of the Tao was the idea of a field of force. All things orientated themselves according to it, without having to be instructed to do so, and without the application of mechanical compulsion.'[28]

In pursuance of this liberating notion Needham finds an appropriate Chinese conversation from the fifth century to introduce his more specific study of the *I Ching*. A Taoist monk is asked: 'What is really the fundamental idea of the *Book of Changes*?' The reply is: 'The fundamental idea of the *I Ching* can be expressed in one single word, Resonance.' Like many Chinese stories, and like the *I Ching* itself if one pursues it with over-eager curiosity about an answer that goes over one's head, the story ends with a benign refusal to go any further by way of explanation. This is indeed a very puzzling book, having, as Needham says, no close counterpart in the texts of any other civilization. As we have it now, the *I Ching* is a very complex book consisting of sixty-four changes, or patterns of typical situations, followed by commentaries which belong to a later date than the original material. The basic texts may be as old as the seventh or eighth century B.C., while the latest of the commentaries may be as late as the first century of the Christian era. In this way, what seems to have begun as a simple book of peasant omens acquired a cultural significance which makes it an education to use. In a general way, as Needham says: 'The more abstract the explanations become, the more the system as a whole assumed the character of a *repository of concepts*, to which all concrete phenomena in nature could be referred. It would be surprising, with no less than sixty-four of these, if a pseudo-explanation could not be found for almost any natural event.'[29] These two sentences sufficiently anticipate what his final verdict will be on the influence of the *I Ching* on the development of Chinese science which is, after all, his primary purpose in placing it where he does in his great study. To the extent to which this is *all* there is to be said about it, perhaps our verdict would have to be much the same.

But first let us follow Needham a little further. He goes on to cite a Han scholar of the third century saying: 'Things do not struggle among themselves at random. They flow of necessity from their principle of order. They are integrated by a root cause. They are gathered together by a single influence. Thus things are complex, but not chaotic. There is multiplicity of them but not confusion.' Needham must be right to comment that this is not necessarily to be read as a reference to something like an Aristotelian 'unmoved mover'. In their cultural context, the words certainly have rather in mind the immanent Tao. 'What he was trying to describe was perhaps a series of fields of force (as we might call them) contained in, but subsidiary to, the main field of the force of Tao, and each manifesting itself at different points in space and time. He believed that to each of these corresponded one of the hexagrams of the *I Ching*.' This interpretation is thoroughly consistent with the world view to which the book belongs. Needham next goes on to show how utterly disastrous could be the temptation to classify all phenomena in terms of a satisfying picture rather than to look at them in themselves.

It tempted those who were interested in Nature to rest in explanations which were no explanations at all. The *Book of Changes* was a system for *pigeon-holing novelty* and then doing nothing more about it. Its universal system of symbolism constituted a stupendous *filing-system*. It led to a stylisation of concepts almost analogous to the stylisations which have in some ages occurred in art forms, and which finally prevented painters from looking at Nature at all.[30]

Dr Needham finally suggests that this ancient book most probably continued to be influential for so long precisely because it fitted satisfactorily into the bureaucratic organization of ancient China. Whether it might ever conceivably have had for anyone any more commendable function than that of giving them the peace of mind

which comes from tidying up inconvenient and apparently dis-
parate things, he does not seriously consider; any more than in his
account of Taoism he considers the possibility, as Maspero does
that, here and there, in its earlier days this school perhaps produced
some mystics who had got beyond absorption with the physical
techniques at which even a medieval Chinese scholar could
laugh.[31] It would be an irony if, in translation into European
languages, the *I Ching* were perhaps sending a few people back to
take a more respectful look at Nature, and helping them to attend
to some of the eloquent messages that come from a world that really
does function as though it were an interdependent whole.

For those who have not already abandoned the pursuit of the
usefulness of the useless, it may be apt to return first to Chuang
Tzu:

> Hui Tzu said to Chuang Tzu, 'Can a man really become
> passionless?' Chuang Tzu said, 'He can.' Hui Tzu said, 'A man
> without passions cannot be called a man.' Chuang Tzu said,
> ' "Tao gave him substance, Heaven gave him form"; how is it
> possible not to call him a man?' Hui Tzu said, 'I would rather
> say, Granted that he is still a man, how is it possible for him to be
> passionless?' Chuang Tzu said, 'You do not understand what I
> mean when I say "passionless". When I say "passionless" I
> mean that a man does not let love or hate do damage within, that
> he falls in with the way in which things happen of themselves,
> and does not exploit life.'

This conversation, which I do not remember Dr Needham quoting,
concludes with a lesson which can sound hostile to knowledge:

> Neglecting your soul,
> Wearying your spirit,
> Propped up against a pile of books.[32]

Just as there is another, which he *does* quote from the same
source, which can sound hostile to technology. It concerns an old
man seen watering his garden by the laborious process of carrying
each jar from a well. A visitor looking on tells him about the time
saved by using the counter-balanced bailing bucket for raising
water. He laughed. 'I have heard from my master', he said, 'that
those who have cunning devices are cunning in their affairs, and
that those who are cunning in their affairs have cunning hearts.

Such cunning means the loss of pure simplicity. Such a loss leads to restlessness of spirit, and with such men the Tao will not dwell. I knew all about the bucket, but I would be ashamed to use it.'[33] Joseph Needham points out that this story has an added force when seen in relation to Taoist political opposition to the role of inventions in the running of feudal society, to which they so much objected.

Such stories are, of course, less concerned with books or inventions as such than with what these things may do to us personally here and now. And, as they also implicitly reveal, they are neither told about, nor told to, ignorant men. They would hardly make much impression on those who had never felt the fascination either of study or of ingenious devices. They are rather concerned to underline those special sorts of modesty which are always required of those who appreciate things intrinsically good. In this way they are expressions of that overall awareness of the limitations of what we can be and know, which are so characteristic of Taoist thinking. Joseph Needham mentions a social facet of this when he describes 'having seen scholars positively struggling for the least honourable places at a dinner-party' in China. 'The rest of the world', he notes, 'seems the poorer for the lack of a similar deep-rooted tradition.' As his impressive study has shown, this tradition is modest before the ways of Nature in ways which even he would sometimes find excessive. Nevertheless a Christian who remembers the gospel emphasis on humility will be likely to agree that 'all in all the Taoists have much to teach the world and ... perhaps the future belongs to their philosophy.'[34] If something like it does not prevail, we shall certainly be in a parlous condition.

But there is still more to be said about these two stories which is to the immediate purpose of the efforts of the first five chapters of this book. A strong and honest spiritual life in terms of the most authentic Christian tradition cannot be lived in a cultural and human vacuum. But it can be lived more honourably and more easily with those who can recognize their limitations in the way that Christians ought to recognize theirs. On every hand, of course, it cannot readily flourish with those whose noisy and argumentative belief must, when compared with the best of Taoism, seem like a kind of irreverence before God and man. Watchmen of this kind tend to be self-appointed intruders, wherever they come from. Within the living tradition of Christianity the true watchmen, the true spiritual fathers, emerge as those who, however hidden, have

not neglected to cultivate their minds, as they should, when they
should. But they have also noticed what even the best things do
to us in a world in which life is always lived in a context. Those
who have learned to respect the Taoist sages – and frequently
for the reasons which make them so appealing to a scholar like
Needham – will often think when reading a great director like
de Caussade how deeply in harmony his thought is with theirs,
though there is never a doubt about his faith or his orthodoxy.
'Apart from God,' he says, 'books are merely useless externals,
and being devoid for us of the life-giving power of God's plan,
they succeed only in emptying the heart by the very satisfaction
which they give to the mind.'[35] Here surely is, at a more sublime
level, the kind of thing the Chinese farmer was observing about
the disadvantages of an apparently helpful technology thoughtlessly
used. Why should it so readily be thought automatically better
to use everything we discover, rather than to go one step further
and decide that it would be better not to use it? Wiser because
a device, like a life, never exists out of a context. Here too is Chuang
Tzu's insistence on the priority of guarding the heart from those
kinds of meddling with the way things ought to be allowed to
go which inevitably leads to the 'exploitation of life'. We can say
of this book up to this point, as of any other, that if it is not the
right moment to read it, it will only empty the heart by any kind
of satisfaction it may happen to give to the mind. And the same
may be said of any activity which may be, in itself, compatible
with Christianity, but which is in fact being pursued as an exploitation of life.

The kind of advice which the Taoist philosophers gave their
disciples and the kind of advice which noted Christian directors
have given theirs is deliberately mentioned before discussing the
rather special case of the *I Ching* as a book of 'divination'. For this
advice is of the greatest relevance to the right use of this book, if
such a right use is conceivable at all. For all who have ever used this
book, whether Christian or otherwise, Chinese or western, insist
that it should only be used rarely. When they give a reason for
saying this, they all appear to give a reason not unlike that which
suggested that we should examine rather closely the various kinds
of deterministic theories prevalent today. For there is a danger that
any convincing picture of life's determining factors will dazzle us
into relinquishing that measure of liberty we genuinely have. Many
people would certainly be shocked if surprised into confessing how

frightened they are when confronted by freedom and how much they long to be offered any plausible excuse for giving it up! They are not likely to find excuses of that kind in the *I Ching*, unless they really want to. For we must note at once that the *I Ching* stands in a class apart among books that are referred to as books of 'divination'. I, like others who have held conversations from time to time with this remarkable old book, can simply say that over more than twenty years I have never found it to be a book of prediction, as that notion is ordinarily understood. I do not know whether this is because I have never expected this of it, and would indeed not have thought it proper for a Christian to ask for a prediction about the future. But I do not think this can be the reason. I think it must rather have some connection with the fact that while Dr Needham can show how, in the field of science, the *I Ching* has been used as an *alternative* to examining the problems of the real world, it does not invariably *have* to be used like this. I cannot be the only person who finds how, in weighing up a human situation surrounded by complexities, the *I Ching* helps one to picture that situation as it exists, and not to neglect aspects one would prefer not to see or could not articulate. I can certainly agree with Lama Govinda, who writes in a foreword to a recent translation that 'the *I Ching* uses divination not for determining the future, but for raising the hidden tendencies of the human mind into the light of conscious awareness, in order to give the individual a glimpse of the various possibilities before him and a chance to choose the best course of action, according to circumstances.'[36] This describes how the *I Ching* has always functioned for me. In other words it has always fulfilled the sort of role which is proper to a director, as that role was understood in the classical Christian tradition. There will be a little more to say on this subject later in this book. But briefly one can say that this function, whether the one who fulfils it is formally called a director or not, is to help one to be aware of those factors which ought not to be neglected about a situation involving moral choice. While speaking of my own experience with this book – which is inevitable in a field still so obscure – it seems right to add that I have never known the *I Ching* to fail to be firm and clear about a course of action which any wise adviser would have regarded as morally doubtful. No one should consult it who does not wish to know their own weakness. Nor can I quite understand how one modern promoter of its use can suggest that it may be an alternative way of finding out what many people learn by meditation and prayer. It is true that it *can* be used as an alternative to asking advice when one is in a situation where it is for some reason impossible to do this. And for many people these situations are not uncommon. Nor have wise directors at any time been particularly abundant. But not only does the *I Ching* itself frequently send one back to one's prayers or even at times suggest that submission to the ways of God is the only way through obscurity. It is hard for a Christian to imagine how *anything* can be used outside the context in which one is living a life with God. Any Christian who supposes that this is ever permissible lacks that respect for what we cannot know which even a Taoist philosopher would have. For what is impressive about Taoism is that it does not turn its back on God. It simply and steadily refuses to reduce him to our dimensions, or to let us off our human responsibilities. At its best it never excludes his hidden presence or influence, as one who asks for and believes in a prediction necessarily does. Christians should also be aware that even the wisest director can be used superstitiously. The *I Ching*, like a director rightly used, leaves us in the end alone with our freedom.

But to say this is not, of course, to recommend anyone who does not already know this book to use it. Even the best of directors is not necessarily the right man for everyone, though it can safely be said that we often need the advice of someone from whom we would prefer not to ask it. Those who suppose they never need advice from any quarter are frequently mistaken and may find themselves humbled by hearing it through instruments they despise. There is, however, probably one final word of warning that should be uttered in relation to the use of the *I Ching*, a word appropriate to any new thing whose relationship to the life of faith is still being explored. We have today largely forgotten a vice about the proper use of study which medieval writers called 'curiosity'. It is a vice which has probably been forgotten because a spontaneous interest in the unknown has, with the development of the natural sciences, come to be regarded as invariably and under all circumstances a virtue. In this matter medieval Christians had a sense of the appropriate akin to that of Taoism and posed a question which does not *have* to be the enemy of sound knowledge. They were concerned about that lack of mental temperance which leads to the attempted rape of knowledge by the wrong person, at the wrong time, and in the wrong way. This is what they meant by 'curiosity'. Aquinas connects it, in one of its manifestations, with meddling with the occult, whether good or evil,[37] which is precisely another of those attempts to exploit life of which we have already spoken.

Further, it does not seem for the moment possible to go. I do not know, any more than any reliable person I have ever read or met, why the *I Ching* appears to work as it undoubtedly does, not like a lucky dip, but like a shrewd teacher with often something strikingly apposite and unexpected to say. Simplicity, which according to a gospel paradox consists in being as wise as serpents and as innocent as doves, will not close its ear to a word of good advice, wherever it comes from. This attitude will, naturally, only be tenable for a Christian who shares something like de Caussade's convictions: 'Holy Scripture is the language of a still more mysterious God; the events of the world are the obscure sayings of this same God, so hidden and so unknown . . . All drops, all brooks of water have the savour of their source.'[38] For anyone who believes this, the right acceptance of change, however apparently confusing or violent, is necessarily life-bringing and a challenge to the discovery of that true liberty of which change is the mysterious bearer.

But, when all the counsel that may be obtained has been taken, the context of this way of living is, of course, a prayer which in the end knows no words and cannot be explained. It is only taught by that 'instructed ignorance', as Augustine once calls it,[39] that we can face the more searching tests of personal change such as we must consider in our next chapter. In any case, if in all we do, whether under the trials of thoughts or events, we are to resist the Devil so that he flees from us as St James assures us he will, it can only be because we begin and go through everything with that instant prayer which comes first in St Benedict's thoughts. Any director or book, however apparently wise, that guides us away from this heart of mystery can and must be left aside. In a single sentence of de Caussade: 'The whole essence of the spiritual life consists in recognizing the designs of God for us at the present moment.'[40]

# 6
## LEVIATHAN

Looking back in old age on his first schoolboy encounters with philosophers and theologians, Carl Jung was able to explain with convincing vividness why, as a class, they had from his youth puzzled and shocked him. For the philosophers 'had the curious notion that God was a kind of hypothesis that could be discussed'. Whereas, for this boy at any rate, God's existence was 'as plain as a brick that falls on your head'. The image he uses is as apt as it is deliberate and it is probable that many who have never entered any place of worship will, even today, find it appropriate. Alas, as the son of a clergyman, the young Carl could not escape what often goes on in churches, and of this he says something disarmingly honest which is likely to commend itself to many believers, especially perhaps as they reach their middle years.

> Church gradually became a place of torment to me. For there men dared to preach aloud – I am tempted to say, shamelessly – about God, about his intentions and actions . . . always on the assumption that revelation had made the will of God plain. To me, on the other hand, it seemed the most obscure and unknown thing of all. To me it seemed that one's duty was to explore daily the will of God . . . that religious precepts were being put in the place of the will of God for the sole purpose of sparing people the necessity of understanding God's will . . . Nobody had any responsibility for the world except God and, as I knew only too well, he could be terrible . . . Obviously we do not know the will of God at all, for if we did we would treat this central problem with awe.[1]

In these sentences, all of which are Jung's own words, only those words have been omitted which imply the theory he later developed to explain what, for believers and unbelievers alike, must always remain a problem. As a description of an encounter with forces which resist all logical explanation, and cannot ultimately be escaped down any avenue, they are admirable. The latent anger which also haunts them is still reserved for the facile explanations which try to whittle away the inherent difficulty of being truly and continuously alive to the world.

It is in this context of awe before the mystery of God as it is encountered in the unfolding of life that Jung mentions how a knowledge of the Book of Job might, even at that time, have helped him to get a glimpse of the dimensions of his problems. But things of this kind were never mentioned in confirmation classes. When, eventually, in 1952 he published his *Answer to Job*, it was greeted, especially by many professional theologians, with a good deal of the hostility he had anticipated.[2] This he had in certain ways – and not perhaps wholly unintentionally – provoked. The book discusses from his own evolved psychological point of view a number of rather different issues which, in a phrase he was fond of using, he would have agreed in other contexts were not 'just' psychological. The book's canvas is enormous, as would-be prophetic visions are apt to be, and in its wilder flights it loses that sense of awe to which in its final sentence he brings it back and with which, in explicit reference to the Book of Job, the last of Jung's *Late Thoughts* closes.[3] Yet not all the *cognoscenti* were exacerbated. In the year in which *Answer to Job* appeared, at least one able exegete could finish an admiring and lucidly critical review by saying that it was 'a generous book, abounding in magnificent insight. If it falls short of, and in many ways fantastically obscures, the biblical truth, in many ways also it will contribute to its better understanding, somewhat as Job's wildest outbursts even were constructive, because prompted by honesty and love.'[4] Unfortunately, the preoccupations of the professionals have not on the whole, since then, been propitious to the kind of thoughts which interested and troubled Jung, though they trouble many ordinary people. Indeed it would seem that few, at any time, are the theologians and exegetes who have cared seriously to struggle with the awkward questions the Book of Job poses, though its central issue, as Richard Kehoe's review says, is by no means a dead one today. His assertion that Jung's book is 'offered as a version, an expanded version, of the biblical drama of redemption, with the Book of Job as its starting-point' is certainly the briefest and most just way of describing what *that* book is about. It would be neither a wise nor a profitable distraction to try to grapple with the enormous complexities involved in Jung's vast personal synthesis. But it will certainly be admirably relevant and useful at the point we have reached to attempt to return to his starting-point. Even if we do so with the help of rather different aids than his, we shall not be able wholly to forget Jung's reading of a book of which most people will at least know the name as a byword for patience. For, whatever it may be necessary to say, there is certainly enough raging in the very text itself to satisfy almost the angriest and most impatient reader, and no interpreter doing his job can fail to face what all this anger amounts to.

If we are to do the Book of Job even a little of the justice its unquestioned greatness demands, we must begin by recognizing that it invites us to step into a world which is very different from that in which even many believers have been taught to move. But, at the same time, it is as well to note that it is not stranger nor intrinsically less plausible than the world of the pioneer psychologists of modern times at first appeared to be. It simply opens up perspectives at least as challenging and as difficult to dismiss as any new dimension of experience can. For as we shall see, although an old book, the Book of Job looks as though it was trying to open up a new dimension of thought. And it lives because it is still doing that. While acknowledging this, we need not feel excused in delivering ourselves over to any theories that happen to come into our heads. It will, however, be reasonable to avoid those exegetes whose primary interest is in textual problems and who wish to labour over the kind of details which they suppose may enable them to place the Book of Job in an exact historical context. We shall need the help of those who are not ignorant of these matters, but who also feel the need to go further. For it is the book in its broad outlines, in the form in which it now stands, that is of compelling and universal interest. This is the book which was regarded as canonical by the beginning of the Christian era, not only in normative Judaism but also in sectarian circles, as the Hebrew text found among the Dead Sea scrolls witnesses. It is not necessary to be a scholar to see that the book itself consists of a prose narrative enclosing a poetic dialogue with one or two linking sentences and, perhaps, as a highly competent modern Jewish scholar suggests, *implying* a few more interjections which, in the heat of semitic argument, would be understood by the speakers. Professor Gordis, who repeatedly argues for the Hebrew origin of the text has, in his study of the whole book, also provided at the end an often singularly happy and convincing English version, which demonstrates the possibility of making something sensible of even difficult readings.[5] We may postpone, for the moment, considering how far it is possible to combine *in life* the two 'radically different Jobs' who stand at least *physically* combined in the biblical masterpiece as we have it now. But the fact of the *apparent* difference cannot be overlooked.

Reviewing the later fortunes of Job, Robert Gordis makes a good case for saying that 'we cannot understand the influence of this powerful and disturbing book on the western world unless we remember that most of the twenty-five centuries that have elapsed since its composition have been ages of faith. During this long expanse of time it was, by and large, the long-suffering Job of the prologue, and not the passionate and pain-racked Job of the dialogue, who occupied men's thoughts.' He argues with skill and discretion that this explains why, although the sceptical sentiments of Ecclesiastes came under repeated rabbinic attack, no one ever attacked the orthodoxy of the Book of Job, a fact which is further attested by versions of it in Greek and Aramaic. Although the translators into Greek clearly felt the need to soften or modify certain expressions throughout the book – where they did not omit many as incomprehensible – it was the folk-tale element about the Book of Job that lived on in both rabbinic and Christian commentators. It is a relief to find a scholar of this kind noting that 'the exegesis that is employed may be ingenious or far-fetched but in any case it frequently has its own independent value and attractiveness'. This is, of course, something that can be said in an eminent degree of the vast commentary of Gregory the Great, which may often be remote from the original meaning of the text, but is not always so remote from the main preoccupations of the book. However, as Robert Gordis concludes, 'not until the modern period does Job the rebel, the hero of the dialogue, become the prime focus of attention'.[6]

Scholars have long been satisfied that the Book of Job should be classified among the 'wisdom' books of ancient Israel. For the general reader this use of the term 'wisdom' could easily be misleading. Even someone who uses the single Hebrew equivalent *Hokmah* for 'wisdom' is compelled at once to say how much more inclusive and concrete are the insights to which this term can refer than those which our commoner uses of the word 'wisdom' call up. Robert Gordis writes that 'Hokmah may be defined as a realistic approach to the problems of life, including all the practical skills and technical arts of civilization.' He then goes on to name activities ranging from those of craftsmen and soldiers to the skills of the midwife. Gerhard von Rad, who has perhaps gone further than any other in an attempt to discuss the range and articulation of this type of didactic literature among the old teachers, finds it necessary to insist that, in any case, for them, the word Hokmah is 'only one amongst others'. Von Rad's [7] rewarding though difficult study, *Wisdom in Israel*, is impressive for the seriousness of its effort to live up to the ideal of its preface. There he says that our understanding of Israel's didactic literature 'is definitely dependent on how successful we are in making contemporary the specific questions it formulates and in subsequently completing its lines of thought; for Israel had to undergo the adventure of liberating her reason in a quite unique way.' This is both a warning and a promise which deserves not to be ignored.

Knowledge about matters of common experience is, as von Rad says, [8] at once one of the most elementary activities of the human mind and nevertheless a highly complex phenomenon to describe. In the case of Israel, what often surprises us is that many of the most elementary experiences appeared quite differently to her, especially because she set them in a quite specific spiritual and religious context of understanding. Within this tradition the Job dialogue must, judged on the basis of its language, be late. But some knowledge of what has preceded it is not thereby made irrelevant if we are to understand what is going on in the book. Even the way, towards the end, in which the younger man Elihu presents what he has to say is clearly rooted in a teaching tradition which goes back to pre-exilic times. Activities representative of those living within this tradition are celebrated in the fairly late Book of Sirach or Ecclesiasticus. Such men will 'seek out the hidden meanings of proverbs, and be at home with the obscurities of parables'. In this connection it is useful to recall a Jewish tradition reported by Gordis that 'Job never existed and was never created, but was a parable'. [9] There is no pressing need to take up a position about this view, but that it should be regarded as a challenge in Jewish tradition is also a reminder that we may need to give this book a kind of attention to which a modern reader is no longer very accustomed. Further, as von Rad observes, 'in the speeches of the friends alone there are four didactic poems about the end of the wicked. Each of these is a self-contained, artistic whole which presupposes discriminating listeners'. We shall note that 'in these poems there is nothing specifically theological in the foreground. Their *subject-matter* is not so much divine punishment as the occurrence of disaster as such.'[10] Again, the dialogue form is repeatedly used as the best medium for the development of a problem. But it would be a mistake to forget that it is a Jewish type of dialogue, and not at all like a Greek or modern dialogue. This does not mean that the dialogue implies movement within a circle. A progress in thought can be discerned, though not only one question but several are tackled and these are passed back and forth at will in the course of the speeches. This movement of thought may be strange to us, rather than defective. It is the intuition that is important above all – 'more important than a perception that can be formulated conceptually and then expressed in a sentence'. The poet always aims at an effect of totality.

The teacher's insight which these didactic forms embody, whether in proverbs, dialogues or fables, slowly comes to be seen as a special gift of God, a view which comes to the fore only at a fairly late stage. By then, the statement that wisdom and understanding come from God has the weight of a considered theological pronouncement. Wisdom and understanding have ceased to be something which is given to every man 'by nature'. As the young Elihu says, when he first comes on the scene:

> It is the spirit in man,
> the divine breath which makes him understand.
> It is not always the old who are wise,
> nor the aged who understand what is right.

This young man feels constrained, like a wine-skin ready to burst.[11] The phenomenon has already been described in other terms by Eliphaz, the first and senior speaker in the dialogue. It is an experience which fills the speaker with awe of the kind which receives its simplest expression at the close of the wisdom hymn found in the isolated chapter 28 of the Book of Job: 'The fear of God – that is wisdom.' The word translated as 'fear' in this sentence, lacks the emotional character we associate with such a term. Von Rad sees it as something much more like commitment to, or knowledge about, Yahweh.

Summarizing the trend of his argument he says:

> There is no knowledge which does not before long throw the one who seeks the knowledge back upon the question of his self-knowledge or his self-understanding. The thesis that all human knowledge comes back to the question about commitment

to God is a statement of penetrating perspicacity ... It contains in a nutshell the whole Israelite theory of knowledge. There lies behind the statement an awareness of the fact that the search for knowledge can go wrong, not as a result of individual, erroneous judgements or mistakes creeping in at different points, but because of one single mistake at the beginning. One becomes competent and expert as far as the orders of life are concerned only if one begins from knowledge about God. Israel was in all seriousness of the opinion that effective knowledge about God is the only thing that puts a man into a right relationship with the objects of his perception, that enables him to ask questions more pertinently, and generally to have a better awareness of circumstances.

Thus, having shown how, according to this way of thinking, faith does not hinder knowledge but liberates it, von Rad throws a stone into the calming waters by saying that this does not mean that everything has now become clear. It is, rather, necessary to say that 'starting from this basis, Israel is led into areas of knowledge of a particular type and exposed to experiences of a particular type. In a word, her thinking has to operate within spheres of tension indicated by the prior gift of the knowledge of God. All that can be said either for or against Israelite wisdom is expressed in this statement.'[12]

It will, perhaps, be consistent with this view to say that here we have a very much more dynamic conception of knowledge than that which presupposes knowledge to be the gradual accumulation of pieces in a vast uniform puzzle. We must bear this consciously in mind when we are trying to follow what is going on in the Book of Job. To this way of thinking there is no concept of 'nature' or of the world as a totality, such as we find in Greek nature philosophers or most typical modern ways of thinking. Although this lack of an overall view could be written off as a grave limitation, von Rad thinks that it can 'perhaps more correctly be interpreted as a significant achievement'. For,

> With no possibility of anticipating what was not known or experienced, Israel was forced to hold fast only to what could be discerned from time to time on the basis of individual questions, at the same time always fixing the boundary which was drawn to prevent her from gaining a total picture. This means that Israel was obliged to remain open, in a much more intensive

way, to the category of the mysterious. When she spoke of mystery . . . she did not mean something vague and inexpressible which defied being put into words. In wisdom and didactic contexts it refers rather to something perceived by the *understanding* rather than by the feelings. The term is precise in so far as it refers to God's activity in the world, in which very special domain the wise men dared to look for rules . . .[13]

These rules must not be thought of as general ethical norms. The wise men see human behaviour as governed rather by the experience of inherent laws, which one can come to understand. But this understanding must operate in a context of faith. Behind the very serious exhortation not to requite evil done to one, not to take matters into one's own hands when faced with evil men, there does not lie – at least not in the way we would understand it – a lofty ethical principle, but something else: namely, faith in the order controlled by Yahweh, in goodness as a life-promoting force. If one is to *live* with this conviction, which is of course the only way to *know* it, one comes to experience the limits of wisdom, but not as a sceptic experiences them. 'To man belong the arrangements of the mind, the framing of plans, the constant planning in advance. That is his field, the one in which he is the master. But it is in the putting of these plans into operation that man meets the incalculable, and God is there precisely in this incalculable element.' The wise men, it may be thought, did not experience this as a sinister notion. For it also means that God could protect man even from his own plans. The aim of this teaching, in fact, is 'to put a stop to the erroneous concept that a guarantee of success is to be found simply in practising human wisdom and in making preparations. Man must always keep himself open to the activity of God, an activity which completely escapes calculation. For between the putting into practice of the most reliable wisdom and that which actually takes place, there always lies the great unknown.'[14]

If one takes time to reflect on it, one sees the enormous advantages of this way of looking at things over an apparently more philosophically strenuous one. By means of their teachings, derived from experience, the wise men set the pupil in the midst of the constant oscillation between grasp of meaning and loss of meaning, and in this way they induced him to make his own contribution in this exciting area of knowledge of life. Thus they probably achieved more than if they had helped their pupils to find

a better solution for theological problems. Reduced to their bare
essentials these regulations for a fruitful life seem determined by a
remarkable dialectic. It is one which involves no underestimation
of the importance of learning. Quite the contrary. 'But you must
always remain open for a completely new experience. You will
never become really wise for, in the last resort, this life of yours is
determined not by rules but by God.' This, it would seem, is the
context in which, especially, the speech of God in the Book of Job
must be seen. In mentioning this, von Rad instinctively recalls the
wonderful psalm 139, *Domine probasti me*: 'Lord, you have searched
me and known me.' The sentences of this psalm are a paradigm
of the intermingling of faith and knowledge, as the psalmist considers his own conception in the womb. The desire for knowledge
is so pressing that, at the limits which are imposed upon it, it
becomes itself a witness to God's inscrutability. The 'fear' of God
not only enables man to acquire knowledge, but also has a pre-
dominantly critical function. It keeps awake in the person who
acquires the knowledge the awareness that his intellect is directed
towards a world in which mystery predominates.

The mysteries of the world have no independent existence. In
them man directly confronts the mystery of God, for:

> Lo, these are but the outskirts of his ways;
> And how small a whisper do we hear of him!
> But the thunder of his power, who can understand? [15]

As in the psalm just mentioned, striking psychological and natural
phenomena have a special interest for these writers, and we find
studies of both in advanced forms in the course of the Book of Job.
It illustrates a very genuine absorption in concrete matters of
detail, which is one of the poles of this school of teaching. The
splendid description of Behemoth, the hippopotamus, with his tail
'rigid as a cedar',[16] or Leviathan, the crocodile, with his back
'made of layers of shields',[17] could stand alone quite outside the
theological context in which they have been placed. Thus we see
that authentic wonder at and interest in the observable is in no way
diminished by the sense of surrounding mystery. This sharpness of
view extends to what is unanimously regarded as an insertion into
the Job dialogue.[18] It is a hymn in praise of wisdom, which
contrasts the skill of mining in the heart of a mountain, of which
men are capable, and the impossible task of putting one's hand on
wisdom itself, though it is certainly *there*, somewhere in the world.

This 'wisdom' must signify something like the 'meaning' implanted by God in creation. It is this which is always out of man's reach. He never gets it into his power as he does other precious things. The world never reveals the mystery of its order. But it does, at the same time, call to man with an unmistakable voice. And it is to creation that God gives, at the end of the Book of Job, the task of opening Job's eyes.

It is now time to turn to the structure of the Book of Job itself. It is possible, but not necessary, to assume that the poet of the dialogue found a traditional folk-tale about a righteous man, enhanced by his survival of difficult suffering, to be an appropriate setting for the discussion he wished to launch. He either took this story over, more or less as it stood, or retold it in his own words. Whether Satan played any role in the original story is not certain. In the text as we have it he appears still only half personalized as 'the' Satan, that is 'the accuser', among the court of heaven. It is, of course, among these beings that he is very firmly kept, even in the more developed later Jewish and Christian theologies, which were always opposed to any form of dualism about the ordering of the world. In any case, the sufferings and agonies of the dialogue make no mention of the accuser's hidden presence, though the story does terminate in the vindication of Job and of God's view about him, as the original tale evidently had. When Job's friends arrive on the scene, after the beginning of his disasters, the stage is set for the debate.[19]

However, before Job's lament that 'what has come is agony', they at first keep a long, respectful silence. Then Eliphaz, 'the most urbane of the friends', begins to suggest that what Job has in the past said to other people in like case, he must now say to himself. Further, it is in the free acceptance of the correction that adversity always implies, that it will be possible for all to turn out well:

> For, with the stones of the field you will be leagued,
> And the beasts of the field will be at peace with you.[20]

Job is so deeply distressed that he seems not to hear this nobly characteristic expression of sound wisdom advice. 'Is my strength the strength of stones, or is my flesh made of bronze? Why should God thus visit man every morning and test him at every moment?'[21] How can it make sense for God to behave as though Job's condition mattered to him? Job is unmistakably parodying the thought of the familiar psalm 8: 'What is man that you are mindful of him?' The question was, of course, in its original context part of a celebration of man's dignity as made in the image of God, of which Job's woeful condition seems such a travesty. The second friend, Bildad, is made so angry that he comes in with an open declaration of the conviction that there is always a direct connection between suffering and sin. This is exactly the implication that Job bitterly rejects. It is only too clear that Eliphaz has been right in insisting that no one can argue with God. But Job cannot possibly see that there is any reasonable connection between what he is enduring and anything of which he may have been guilty. If only there might be a third party between him and God:

> For God is not a man like me, whom I could answer
>     when we come to trial together.
> If only there were an arbiter between us
>     who would lay his hand upon us both . . .[22]

Or that, alternatively, Job might be granted the peace of extinction.

The third friend, Zophar, finds Job's declaration of innocence to be mere arrogance. There is no proportion between what man can understand and what is clear to God, 'for there are mysteries in understanding'.[23] Job is then stung into answering the friends at some length in a tone of disgusted irony. He is sick and tired of these 'proverbs of ashes, replies that are dusty answers'.[24] But Job flees from God to God. 'It is, as he says, no flatterer coming before Him.'[25] He longs for the respite that will enable him to see the truth of his situation before he dies.

In a second cycle of speeches the three friends return to their cause. Eliphaz, shocked at Job's vehemence in the face of the wisdom tradition, concedes that perhaps the ungodly do appear to prosper, seem able 'to play the hero against the almighty'.[26] But they are never without their fears of destruction lurking at some unexpected moment. Job only answers: 'I have heard all this before; wearisome comforters are you all.'[27] He reiterates his contention that for some reason God has 'gnashed his teeth' at him and 'set him up as his target'. Yet still to this God his eye pours out its tears and begs 'that he judge between a man and God, as between a man and his fellow'.[28] He is thus sure that God would vindicate him, and not even Bildad's short and cruel retort shakes this conviction. 'Why do you persecute me like God?', he asks his

friends. 'You will learn that there is a judgement.'[29] This is a
certainty that he feels in his very bones, as the difficult verses 25–7
of chapter 19 would seem to be saying. Zophar replies in conscious
defence of the great antiquity behind what the friends have been
trying to say to Job. This only leads Job to go further in his attack
on their position by contrasting what they *say* happens to the
wicked and what in fact anyone can see constantly occurs. His
words are heavy with irony. 'Their houses are safe from fear and no
rod of God comes upon them. Why not ask the passers-by – you
cannot deny their evidence!'[30] When all the facts are totted up 'in
your answers there remains only fraud'.[31]

The third cycle of speeches has obviously suffered some dislo-
cation. As we have already noticed, a hymn in praise of wisdom,
which could be appropriate to the author of the book, has been
inserted among these chapters, though it probably is an independent unit. If we follow the suggestion of Professor Gordis that
chapters 26 and 27 contain at least *part* of the replies of Bildad and
Zophar in their turn, we then find ourselves with a result that
involves the minimal disturbance of the text as we now have it.
Thus, Job replies to Eliphaz in chapters 23 and 24, is allocated a
few sentences at the opening of chapters 26 and 27, and makes his
final speech in chapters 29–31. Eliphaz has returned to the theme
of repentance which would give Job back his role of both counsellor
and intercessor, if only he makes his peace with God. Job's indirect
reply is simply an expression of his longing that he knew where to
find God, for 'he would surely pay heed to me'.[32] Job's words close
with descriptions of how the world is full of injustices, a fact which
he defies the friends to refute. And the essence of what he has to say
to the other two friends is contained in the single sentence: 'Heaven
forbid that I declare you are in the right; until I die I will not be
stripped of my integrity.'[33]

Now the talking is done and Job gives himself over to memories
of his former well-being and to further descriptions of his present
frustrations. 'When I looked for good, then evil came; and when I
waited for light, there came darkness.'[34] Yet he is still sure that
there could be a satisfactory accounting for it all. 'Oh, that I had
someone to hear me – that the Almighty answer me, and my
opponent write out his indictment.'[35] It is at this point that the
young Elihu begins to speak. He disagrees *both* with the older
friends, who maintain that there is always a connection between
suffering and personal sin, *and* with Job in his repeated assertion of

guiltlessness. He sees suffering, rather, as part of the process of being matured. 'For God speaks through one means and through another, though man takes no notice. Who can prescribe the way for Him; who can say, "You have done wrong"? Be it for chastisement – if they do not obey – or for love, He brings it all to pass.'[36] The concluding words of this long discourse, which Gordis thinks could be 'the product of the poet's experience during a lifetime',[37] already prepare for the coming of God in the whirlwind.

God, when he comes, does not answer Job's questions directly, but puts, instead, two new ones, which suggest much that is implicit in two speeches that are full of implications:

> Who is this that darkens my plan
>     by words without knowledge?[38]

and again:

> Will you even put me in the wrong?
> Will you condemn me that you may be justified?[39]

The speeches themselves expatiate on the mystery of the world, its remoteness from much about which it is possible for man to make a judgement, unless he puts himself in the centre of the picture, where clearly he is not, and cannot be. The world includes creatures like the ostrich whom God 'forgot, when he allocated wisdom',[40] the hippopotamus who can swallow a river, and the powerful crocodile, who is 'king over all proud creatures'.[41] These great animals are not there for their charm or appeal, though they would seem to form part of the natural rhythm of things. Professor Gordis may well be right to suggest that the implication of this section is that, just as the natural order involves things that escape man's ken, so there is a moral order with a pattern and meaning which it is beyond man's power fully to comprehend.[42] The tale closes with an epilogue in which God reveals his anger about the attempted defence of Eliphaz and his friends, and declares that they will only be forgiven for not speaking the truth if they ask Job to pray for them. Job himself is then restored to his former condition and more is added to him, in fact twice the normal life span.

It is certainly a matter of importance that the end of the Book of Job is a conclusion which is no conclusion. Nor does it seem wholly relevant to decide to make a choice between the prose tale and the dialogue, on the ground that to take them together involves one in inexplicable inconsistencies. Is it not the inconsistencies of this book, and above all its silences – both of them so near to those of life itself – that have made it live on? For all the problems of various kinds it poses, there is no other Book of Job than the one we have. Nor can we try to make a better one.[43] In any case, even if we should try to concentrate on the dialogue alone, it is probable that, in the end, we should reach much the same position as we would had we taken the book as a whole. For, in either case, there is an element in the argument which is straining out of every conceivable frame, and leading to an explanation which could never be embodied in even the most faultless text. Even the scholar on whose help we have been leaning in our attempt to get a view of the wisdom tradition in Israel, goes a long way towards admitting this. Within this wisdom tradition which, as we have seen, finds its place in several passages in the Book of Job, there is also a concern to argue for the purpose of divine training or correction in the face of all that threatens life, and thus always to preserve an element of human hope.[44] But why should we refuse to look at Job's twice-repeated assertion that God has taken even this from him, like a torrent that washes away the soil and so, of course, leads to the uprooting of a tree?[45] 'This is a really terrifying perception' – and a still more terrifying experience, one may add. Yet is it not the intention of the Book of Job to go just as far as this? As von Rad writes: 'In the Book of Job – in the prose narrative as well as the dialogue – we are completely incapable of naming any teaching traditions with which these tremendous thoughts could be connected.'[46] Taking the dialogue separately, it is possible to say that 'Job and his friends are equally convinced that the suffering which has overwhelmed Job comes from Yahweh, and that it is saying something. On the basis of this statement, which is not subjected to discussion, the whole dialogue starts.' Yet when we begin to read the dialogue it is wise to add that 'the poet does not raise a finger to guide the reader through this confusion of theological opinions'. However, one thing becomes incontrovertibly clear that, for all Job's willingness to admit *aspects* of what the friends say to him, gathered from a tradition to which he himself shows signs of belonging, he never-theless feels himself to be personally the object of divine visi-tation. 'One cannot but affirm that Job stands face to face with a completely new experience of the reality of God . . . And what was really new was that Job involved God in a quite different way, much more deeply and more terribly, in the suffering.'[47] Thus it

becomes necessary to go on to say: 'While Job's involvement in
"wisdom" questions is unmistakable, it nevertheless recedes in
view of the fact that Job introduces into the debate theological
points of view of a quite different type. The picture of God which
destroys that involvement does not arise from the experience of
orders, nor does the image of God for which he struggles with
himself . . . It is not suffering, as has so often been said, which has
become so utterly problematical, but God.'[48]

This is exactly the question. Indeed one can go on to ask how
many books would have been written on the so-called 'problem of
evil', had it been possible from the depths of a Job-like experience
to say something about that evidently self-renewing idolatry which
strives to identify God with any 'picture', however edifying, and
however appropriate to some circumstances other than those in
which one finds oneself. Only God can answer this desperate cry
for meaning. And just as the longing for this seems to be the true
heart of Job's anguish, so it seems to be clear, on any reading of the
Book of Job, that he does not get an answer appropriate to a man
who is looking for an 'explanation', or for yet one more 'picture' of
God and his activities. *God himself becomes the answer*. We cannot
be told what it is Job's own eyes have seen. Christian commentators, however, will not doubt that it is something that leads to the
one who, hanging on the cross, says: 'My God, my God, why have
you forsaken me?' For as Rupert of Deutz says in the course of
reflecting on the prefiguring of Christ in Job, 'God alone is
humble',[49] and Jung sees this coming together too in one of the
finest pages of his *Answer to Job*.[50] But it is curious that Jung with
his lively interest in oriental scriptures should have missed the
extraordinary similarity between some of what God *says* in the Book
of Job about his presence in the world and what we are told in the
great vision of chapter 11 of the *Bhagavad-Gita*. It is almost equally
striking how the virtual conspiracy of silence that Jung noticed
hanging about the Book of Job should also appear to hang about the
climax of this impressive Indian scripture. It will be recalled that
the soldier Arjuna has been held in conversation about his human
dilemma by Krishna, an 'incarnation' of the ultimate, hidden
principle of the world. At the beginning of chapter 11 he has asked
to be allowed to have a glimpse of the Ultimate itself. Within a
moment or two Arjuna asks to be released from confronting the
vision for which he has begged as 'with hair on end' he sees the
Ultimate.

Beginning, middle or end You do not know – your mouth a
flaming fire, burning up this whole universe with your blazing
glory . . . Gazing upon your mighty form with its myriad mouths,
eyes, arms, thighs, feet, bellies, and sharp gruesome tusks, the
worlds shudder – how much more I![51]

Here surely is both a similarity and a difference between the Jewish
and the Indian poet. The Jewish writer does not reject the experience of God as seeming to be both the creator and in some
ultimate sense the destroyer. In fact his tradition as a whole has
other ways of explicitly acknowledging this. But in choosing
Leviathan, 'round about whose teeth is terror and on whose face
terror dances',[52] to speak for him, the author of Job avoids the
identification of God himself with anything that can be known or
pictured. God takes responsibility for something whose final re-
solution in himself remains hidden.

Outside the Book of Job the fact of God's ultimate responsibility
for everything that happens, pleasant or otherwise, is firmly and
explicitly asserted by Old Testament writers. Amos, the first of the
canonical prophets does this when he writes:

Does evil befall a city, unless the Lord has done it?[53]

Similarly, in Deutero-Isaiah, God says:
I form light and create darkness,
I make weal and create woe,
I am the Lord who do all these things.[54]

What exactly sayings like this can mean may present very real
problems, about which three of the psalms explicitly reflect. Psalm
73 does this in the most personal way of all and in a manner very
near to the mood and experience of the Book of Job. The writer
hears the taunts of those who ask: How can God know? 'But when I
thought how to understand this, it seemed to me a wearisome task,
until I went into the sanctuary of God; then I perceived their
"end".' This last word 'end,' 'that which comes after',[55] for which
the one who prays has to wait, is inevitably also hidden even deeper
in God.

If we can feel some sympathy for the ferocious antipathy Jung
felt for the classical theological definition of evil as 'the privation of
a good that should be present', it will be because, like the psalmist
and like Job, we shall recognize that no 'explanations', however

correct, can ever be a satisfactory answer to life. There are some agonies to which only God can give the answer. And if there are some temptations along the road of the one who must *wait* for the answer, *some* of these may have their origin in the Devil. Certainly by New Testament times he has become identifiable as a distinct person though still, willy nilly, among the servants of God.[56] 'To refuse to go through good and evil is the essential suggestion in all his temptations. He pretends that evil can always be avoided,' writes Richard Kehoe in an excellent passage on the biblical conception of the Devil in his review of Jung's *Answer to Job*.

> Job is for the moment goaded by the devilish doctrine that God ought to answer to man's conception of good, into maintaining that he answers to man's conception of evil; and it is as though Dr Jung should intervene, saying, He answers to both; whereas the Bible would say, He answers in himself to neither. And yet to have communion with the absolute transcendent goodness that he is, man must be ready to accept, to be plunged in, to be himself composed of the two. *None is good but God alone.*

Richard Kehoe continues by saying:

> It is not the argument of Yahweh's speech that is meant to be decisive here, as Dr Jung seems to assume. It is rather the fact of the theophany, or of the Revelation, as we would say. Job is caught up out of the welter of theological debate into the world of divine mystery . . . Job is not left, therefore, pretending out of fear that, in the old sense of the terms over which they have wrangled, Yahweh is not evil but good; he is now left believing that Yahweh transcends these opposites, yet is to be found through the acceptance of them both – along the Way of the Cross.[57]

How far it is really possible to believe that this insight and this experience are already obscurely and implicitly present within the wisdom writers' tradition of life is a matter about which each reader will form his own view. There can be no serious doubt that apostolic and continuous Christian tradition would have believed this to be the case. Many early Eastertide sermons make convictions of this kind clear enough. But the ground for these convictions can never be convincingly demonstrated by argument and documentation alone. They presuppose a respect for at least two profoundly modifying factors which von Rad brings to the fore in the concluding section of his study, *Wisdom in Israel*. In the first place, he points out how the wise men had no term for what we would call *logos* or 'reason'. What King Solomon, the paradigm of the wise man, had asked for in his royal prayer was 'a listening heart'. 'What he wished for himself was not the authoritative reason which reigns supreme over dead natural matter, the reason of modern consciousness, but an understanding reason, a feeling for the truth which emanates from the world and addresses man.' What he was seeking was not 'passivity but an intense activity, the object of which was response, prudent articulation'.[58] This, of course, can only be contrasted with the experience of power which the uses of reason we tend to foster are apt to give us. Even further from our common thoughts is the wise men's conviction that creation so decidedly has something to say to us that it is not foolish to think of it as 'wooing' us. 'To the man who entrusts himself to this order, it is not only that the movements of his environment appear different to him (this we could understand), but *it is actually different things that happen to him.*'[59] Although von Rad does not himself underline the final phrase of this sentence, it is of the utmost importance not to glide over it, as many people's experience will tell them. Whatever the outward appearances, different things really *do* happen to those who make the longing for, and attention to, a listening heart the centre of their desires. Not only the saints of the Old and New Testaments who can be named experience this. It is a truth accessible in ways not all of whose secrets are known to us. It is simply a fact that those who come to these secrets, by whatever paths, can look as ruinous and feel as torn apart as Job, and yet hold together. And this is the sense in which 'different things happen to them'. For *what* it is that happens to them is not to be named or measured by the tale of their anguish, physical or spiritual. Theirs is the state of those who in the end receive a white counter and on it a new name 'which no one knows except him who receives it'.[60] God answers them and answers *for them*, in a mystery.

Living with the scandal of God's ways may involve interior upheavals as shattering as those which racked Job. For the one who looks on from outside they can also be as difficult to reconcile with conventional patience as the two Jobs we find clamped together in the book under that name. It is probably therefore that St John Chrysostom sees crowns, not just of patience but of courage or hardihood as appropriate to Job's case. He was to learn his fill of all this before his own days were done. But John mentions this quality of not being afraid of anything except sin, virtually in passing in a series of sermons preached at Antioch within the first few months of his ordination as a priest. They are concerned with another kind of scandal about God than that which is often hidden in the lives of his saints. The direct purpose of these sermons, which are remarkably restrained and concentrated, need not detain us here, though the question of what it is right to say about the persons of the Trinity can never be wholly dormant. It is rather as a forthright statement of the incomprehensible nature of God, demonstrating the basis of this view in the text of Scripture, that they deserve a place at the close of this chapter.[61] The choice is a deliberate one. For although, as we shall see, these five sermons are not wholly innocent of philosophical influences, they are genuinely representative of the views of the undivided Church on the question of what it is suitable to expect to be able to say about God.

No one will be surprised that Chrysostom will begin his discussion of what we can say about God by referring to the assertion of St Paul that, in the fullness of love which fills the soul in the final vision of God, 'as for knowledge, it will pass away'. 'If knowledge is going to disappear, our state far from getting any better will get worse, for without that we shall lose what is proper to man.' What, then, is it Paul's intention to say? 'He is saying this, not about complete, but about partial knowledge ... Thus it is the incompleteness of knowledge that will disappear.' In any case, human knowledge is a very limited thing, as Paul insists when he compares the present state of our knowledge to that of a child, and our future knowledge to that of a grown man. This is why it is folly to claim total knowledge now, above all on the question of God. It is rather God's knowledge of *us* that ought to fill us with wonder. This thought leads John spontaneously to the reflections of psalm 139, of which it has already been necessary to speak in connection with the wisdom tradition of Israel. John singles out for special mention verses 5 and 6: 'The knowledge that you have of me is wonderful; it is high, I cannot attain it.' 'I give you thanks', he says, 'for this reason, that I have an incomprehensible master.' John begs his audience to note that the psalmist does not speak of God's essence, of what he is, but rather of his omnipresence. He does this 'to show that he does not even know how God is everywhere'. John confirms his interpretation with the help of later verses in the psalm which tells how, wherever the psalmist goes, he never escapes God.

It is this experience which dazes him. As another psalm says:
'Great is our Lord and abundant his power; his understanding is
beyond measure.' These thoughts are, of course, all connected with
the experience of God's providence rather than with what he in
himself *is*. It is his reflection upon this general experience of divine
providence that leads St Paul to write elsewhere: 'What wealth of
wisdom and knowledge is in God! How inscrutable are his judgements!' 'Notice,' says Chrysostom, 'he does not say incomprehensible, but inscrutable.' If they cannot be examined, it is even more
impossible to understand them. This gives John a second limit to
our knowledge of God. He adds yet another, quoting a phrase from
the letter to the Philippians, which says that 'the peace of God
passes all understanding'. Proceeding in this way, John piles up a
collection of texts from the letters of Paul and summarizes them in
a great rhetorical question. 'What will you say? His judgements are
inscrutable, his ways cannot be found out, his peace passes all
understanding, his gifts are inexpressible. What God has prepared
for those who love him, the heart of man has not conceived, his
greatness is without limit, his understanding without measure.'
Thus all in him is incomprehensible. Can he be comprehensible *in
himself*?

Thinking of the cherubim and seraphim, who are said to worship in profound awe, John adds the question: 'Have you noticed
what reverence reigns above, and what contempt here below?
There they worship, here they get lost in vicious circles.' If this –
some of it so near the spirit of an unusual modern writer like Jung
in his reflective moods – may seem so far a cry from a world in
which awe has become a rare experience, it is good to know that
Chrysostom, too, is aware how foolish such talk may sound. It is
with this thought that his second sermon begins. Foolish it may
indeed sound, but this, as Paul says, is part of the folly in which
faith involves one. Like the wisdom writers, John will not seek to
separate these reflections from a way of living. Indeed, it is first to
the contemplation, not of the angels, but of the visible creation that
he turns. It is not only the antiquity and yet the youth of the world
that impresses him, but its vast variety. So many people inhabit it,
from Syria near at hand to the British Isles in the north, and out
across India to races even whose names are not known. And yet he
remembers the word of the prophet that 'the nations are like a drop
from a bucket' compared with God himself, and recalls Paul asking: 'Who are you, man, to answer back to God?' He finds these

thoughts a just reminder of man's littleness before the mystery of God. It is indeed with the aid of another text of Paul that John develops this sense of limitation and inadequacy further in the third sermon. This text speaks of God as dwelling 'in unapproachable light'. Note the precision of the language, says John. He did not say that God *is* an unapproachable light, but that he dwells in unapproachable light. 'This is so that you may know that if his dwelling is inaccessible, the God who inhabits this dwelling is even more so . . . Nor did he say – he who dwells in incomprehensible light, but inaccessible, which is even stronger.' Chrysostom picks up this thought again in the fourth sermon, where he says that it is not the intention of this kind of language to confine God to a place, but rather to bring out more clearly how much he is 'inconceivable and inaccessible'. Even the prophets in their most exalted visions never really claim to see God. Finally, as St Paul observes, there is the light that our own self-knowledge throws on the matter of our knowledge of God. 'Just as in the case of human beings no one can really understand what is peculiar to an individual except his own inner spirit, so no one understands what is peculiar to God except the spirit of God.'[62] This is a lucid translation which admirably conforms to Chrysostom's explanation of the apostle's argument. John goes on to insist that we often do not know ourselves, so that the claim to know what God is seems even more fatuous. 'When on the question of the divine being one is ignorant, not of the fact that it exists, but of what it is, it would be the height of folly to give it a name.'

Thus it should be clear that it would scarcely be possible to go further than Chrysostom does here in his insistence on the absolute mystery of God. It is, moreover, a reminder of how living, classical Christian theology continues to maintain a position very like that of the old wisdom teachers in its approach to the question of God. Nor would it be correct to try to represent, as is sometimes done, the doctrine of the incarnation of the Son of God as some kind of radical mitigation of this ultimate mystery. Individual passages from the Fathers can sometimes seem to say things which amount to this. But Maximus the Great who, writing in the seventh century, had a very sure sense of his predecessors in the tradition of the undivided Church, writes on this subject: 'The great mystery of the divine incarnation always remains a mystery . . . How he who is wholly God by nature became wholly man by nature, with nothing lacking to either nature – these are things whose mystery only faith can discern.' [63] This is why, as the saints discover, Job's encounter with God is typical of a vocation that cannot always be satisfactorily described or explained. None of God's lesser sons can know, in advance, what being a son may in the long run mean.

# 7

## REMEMBERING THE SAINTS

Even so, the preparation which God granted to Job in order
that he might speak with him consisted not in those delights and
glories which Job himself reports that he was wont to have in his
God, but in leaving him naked upon a dunghill, abandoned and
even persecuted by his friends, filled with anguish and bitterness, and the earth covered with worms. And then the Most
High God, he that lifts up the poor man from the dunghill, was
pleased to come and speak with him there face to face, revealing
to him the depths and heights of his wisdom, in a way that he had
never done in the time of his prosperity.[1]

The author of these lines is one of those rare writers of incon-
testably first rank, whose handful of incomparable poems and
many pages of lucid, incandescent prose establish him in the
mind of anyone who frequents him as a unique personality. This is
not because St John of the Cross is ever readily autobiographical.
Struggling to express this aspect of the uniqueness of St John's
works, their most well-known English translator felt he ought to
say that next to their unity, range, and method is 'the intense and
evident subjectivity underlying their marked objectivity of form'.[2]
No one of experience will be likely to contest this view. But it
becomes more convincing when the primary evidence of the writings is supplemented by some knowledge of the life of St John of
the Cross and of what people who knew him thought of him. In-
complete though this kind of evidence must always be, it is in the
case of St John of the Cross quite striking enough to suggest him as
an outstanding example of the paradox of which we have a few
pages ago seen the exegete von Rad speaking. He is a man to whom
not only the movements of his environment appear different, but to
whom different things *actually happen* from those merely external
facts of which it is easy to tell. If it made any sense to do so, two
quite different lives of St John of the Cross could be written. No
such task will be attempted here. There is one reality which seems
to bind events, life, and writing together in one unified whole, and

the force which holds them together is an unmistakable struggle for integrity which already marked St John as a very young man and captivated a woman of shrewd judgement like Teresa of Avila from the moment she met him. 'Although he is small in stature, I believe he is great in God's eyes,' she wrote in a letter he unwittingly carried. 'He has courage. But as he is alone he needs all our Lord gives him so that he may work with all his heart.' [3] It is with characters of this kind, in different times and places, that it seems to be good to dwell a little at this point in our reflections. They have much, at least indirectly, to teach us and it ought not to be neglected.

In the case of John de Yepes the soundest university education in Salamanca of the mid-sixteenth century had done nothing to diminish his sense of a quite special, personal call, about whose outward setting he was still hesitating when he first met the very determined nun who had set out to reform the Order to which he already belonged. Teresa persuaded him to renounce his project of becoming a Carthusian by offering something which he, with perhaps a sounder historical sense than hers, came to see was very like the ideal which the simple, solitary Carthusian life might have given him. [4] There was a short idyllic interlude, beginning in the autumn of 1568, when John and a lay brother went out to put some kind of order into the little, tumbledown farmhouse at Duruelo which Teresa had been given for the use of her newly-approved friars. There three of them, of whom John was one, made their profession to the primitive Carmelite rule at the end of November. It was from this date that John signed himself John of the Cross. The conditions under which they lived through the cold Castilian winter are graphically described by Teresa of Avila in what, other considerations apart, remains one of the most genial travel-books ever written. 'They would pray so earnestly that sometimes when the hour of prime came, their habits would be covered with snow without their having noticed it,' [5] she writes. But there is no criticism like silent action to arouse the bitterest hostility, especially if it can be interpreted as divisive of a group. After some years of mounting background tension, John was kidnapped in Avila on the night of 2 December 1577 and, having been given a taste of the lash, was eventually transferred to Toledo. Through a bitter winter and a stifling summer he was imprisoned in a tiny cell, with no window save a hole high in a wall which received some light from an adjoining room. Here, with the help of regular beatings and various kinds of psychological torments, the friars of his former observance tried to break his spirit as his body was already beginning to be broken.

Only after six months of this did a change of warder afford John some mitigation of a kind which eventually led to his being able to escape one mid-August night, down a rope made of strips of his bedding which left him only a jump to the ground. A scarcely less important feature of the mitigation, from our present point of view, was the fact that John of the Cross had been allowed some paper and ink with which, at least at noonday, he was able to record lines he had been mentally composing. They show him, as they grow in force and accomplishment, not wasting his energies in recriminations or self-pity, but living intensely the doctrine he consistently taught, 'though it be night', as the regular refrain of one of the poems has it.

> Where can your hiding be,
> Beloved, that you left me thus to moan
> While like the stag you flee
> Leaving the wound with me?

asks another.[6] And finally, almost certainly belonging to this group, and best known of all:

On a dark night, kindled in love with yearnings – oh happy chance! –
I went forth without being observed, my house being now at rest.[7]

It is from part of John's commentary on these lines, and written subsequently, that the opening words of this chapter were taken. Life and writings, taken together, make a luminous whole, like that ball of light a lay brother thought he saw enveloping the bed where, after many more troubles at the hands of his own reformed brethren John lay, a few months short of fifty, mortally sick. It is moreover a wholeness which is uncontrived, like his gentle remark when he saw the brethren fumbling for the prayers for the dying: 'Leave it, for the love of God, and be quiet.' He died without agony on 14 December 1591.

As an author he had worked with the same serene simplicity, and of this we are more unanimously informed. He was a man of wide reading, but it is all deeply absorbed. We should not neglect to note the significance of the witness of the friar who lived with him throughout the time of his most intense literary activity. Books from the community library came and went to John's cell, but only two books stayed there permanently, a Bible and a *Flos Sanctorum*.[8] This latter was evidently one of those collections of the lives and sayings of the saints which have their ultimate source in the tales told about the Fathers of the desert, and which had received a classical medieval expression in what came to be called the *Golden Legend* of James of Voragine. From the sixteenth century onwards, even within the Church, there has been a kind of scholarship which has so exclusively fastened on the unhistorical and legendary aspects both of sections of the Bible and of the lives of the saints as to miss the nature and the importance of the role that legendary truths always played and will continue to play in history after the changing fashions of merely critical scholarship have long since been forgotten. If legends spring up and memorable tales return it must be because part of the development of any serious life rooted in reality is to catch and give expression to valid dreams. It would be easily possible to show, from both his writings and his counsels, how for a man like John of the Cross even the most apparently spiritual 'fancies' were profoundly suspect. But this does not mean that it is a matter of indifference to know that vital lives, of the kind which are apt to give rise to legend, have been lived by others in circumstances as bewildering and difficult as our own appear to us to be. To this must be added, if it is to be of practical value, the conviction that holiness and heroism have plenty of room for variety and that both can be achieved within the limits of the realistically possible. The very first of the immensely influential fifth-century Macarian homilies notes this when it says:

> It is given to all men to contemplate and admire the stars in heaven, though it be in no one's power to know their number. Likewise it is given to all those who are willing to take up the struggle to enter into the heavenly Church of the saints. But to God alone is reserved the understanding and grasp of their number . . .[9]

To each, then, his personal secret. That remarkable nineteenth-century priest, Henri de Tourville, expresses the implications of this in another way: 'We are the brothers and sisters of the saints; they were saints in their way. We must become so in ours, and not in theirs . . . The good souls who lived before us cannot be blamed if we think we should absolve ourselves from the responsibility of thinking and deciding for ourselves what is most appropriate to our case.'[10] The history of authentic holiness vindicates intuitions of this kind.

It is, of course, the Bible itself which sets the precedent for this particular way of looking at things. Thus, to name one sentence of considerable liturgical and historical influence from a splendid speech in the Book of Judith, we should 'remember how our father Abraham was tried and, being tested under many difficulties, became the friend of God'.[11] Or, for those who prefer a more respectable source, though not without its own hedge of critical difficulties, there is the entire ample section of the New Testament letter to the Hebrews on the theme of being surrounded by a great cloud of witnesses, most, if not all of them, explicitly heroes of Old Testament stories.[12] And paramount among all New Testament texts are the closing sentences of chapters 2 and 4 of the Acts of the Apostles, about whose later history a small book could be written:

> And all who believed were together and had all things in common;
> And they sold their possessions and goods and distributed them to all as they had need.
> And day by day, attending the temple together and breaking bread in their homes, they partook of food with glad and generous hearts.[13]

Even a conservative modern reader could scarcely fail to see an element of idealism in the picture of the tranquil communism and devout liturgical order in the earliest Church which these verses describe. But it is the task of each subsequent period to guess what kind of idealism that might be. Like the word 'gospel', these words have at different times, even within orthodox Christianity, evoked such widely differing responses. It was at any rate about this ideal description that the young Copt Anthony, afterwards called 'the Great', was reflecting when he entered a church and heard words from the gospel which led to his selling his property and going out to the desert, there to find his integrity by being, as his biographer Athanasius tells us, 'a daily martyr to his conscience'.[14]

That Anthony should have come to be regarded as 'the father of monks' is hardly surprising. Yet he wrote no rule, gave a good deal of advice to laymen, and many of the best authenticated stories about him are calculated to make anyone, in any walk of life, pause. Holiness tends to have this unclassifiable tang of reality about it. Anthony himself would have been the first to suggest that it was not everyone's call to do what it came to him to do. Athanasius, writing as he does with concentrated insight, is careful to tell us that it was the combination of 'remembering the saints' and hearing the words of Scripture that first gave Anthony what was, at least for him, the obvious starting-point in an unplanned career whose 'rightness', as everyone saw, was vindicated, as time went on, by an unusual balance and maturity. That Anthony starts out with the courage to do what he believes to be an old thing in a new way is the mark of all those for whom the 'study' of the Scriptures implies a way of life, 'a daily martyrdom to conscience', rather than the addition to their curriculum of just one more academic subject. The sense of the Latin word *studium* among the Latin Fathers and early Christian writers is defined by a sense of this contrast, and 'study' has not lost this overtone in a seventeenth-century writer like Izaak Walton whose closing admonition to his *Compleat Angler* is that he should 'study to be quiet'. A more profound attention to this older implication of the word 'study' underlies some simple sentences of Isidore of Seville on the relationship between the reading of Scripture, prayer, and life: 'For then the word of God poured into the ear reaches the depths of the heart when, by the grace of God, it touches the very innermost being with understanding.'[15]

The life of John Chrysostom, for whom Anthony's desert tradition was still lively and attractive half a century later, is itself a typical illustration of this absence of plan and openness to the indications of the present. As a young man, with a penchant for exaggeration which he never wholly lost, he had almost killed himself in an attempt to live as a hermit in a cave. But he had to recognize that it was back in the city that he must dream his dreams of total dedication to the things of God. This is not the place to speak of his vast output as a preacher, first at Antioch and then in imperial Constantinople with their congregations of nominal Christians, against which the desert movement had been a silent protest. But it is relevant to note that even in the sermons quoted in the previous chapter Chrysostom is outspoken about those with a taste for a fascinating sermon, but none for the prayers and Eucharist which followed, the true centre of his own life.[16] Nor need the details of his stormy career as a reluctant patriarch of Constantinople detain us. At odds with both the clergy who resented him and the formidable empress Eudoxia, whose hatred he had perhaps intensified by his unnecessary indiscretion, his fate was virtually sealed long before his first banishment. In the end, in an attempt to get him as far away as possible, he was sent to a remote place on the very edge of the empire at the far end of the Black Sea. But he never reached it. There is no reason to doubt the facts as described by our most important biographical source for his later years. Hurried along in all kinds of weather, through rain and heat, John collapsed with a fever and was taken back a few kilometres to the shrine of a martyr at Comona. There he asked for the clothes in which he knew he would be buried, received his last communion, and finished his thanksgiving, 'using his customary formula', says Palladius: 'Glory to God for all things.'[17] There are many grounds for believing that these words were a genuinely personal 'Eucharist' or thanksgiving, and reveal the inner and the other side of a very troubled life. But it is a life perhaps too complex to allow any other message to emerge than that of the extreme difficulty of combining an integral Christianity for a man in high office with being permanently politically acceptable.

In the case of Maximus the Confessor in the seventh century, however, the issues which led to martyrdom and head-on conflict with an attempt at a theocratic state are clearly and *only* theological. The beliefs for which Maximus died are absolutely central to any form of orthodox Christianity, and have nothing to do with any social theories. Thus it is a measure of the changed *political* position of the Christian faith that it should be inconceivable that any politician anywhere today would have seriously to mind how these beliefs ought to be formulated. This is not to say that the issues *in themselves* are either incomprehensible or dead, at least among professing Christians. Indeed there are plenty of signs that a new wave of very old temptations is passing over professional theologians who are concerned to present a statement of their belief which they think may be acceptable to their contemporaries.[18] The sentences quoted at the close of the foregoing discussion of the doctrine of God should be sufficient to show that Maximus was not a theologian of this kind. He was a monk, and a man of considerable learning. On both counts the right use of words seemed to him to be a matter of importance. The calm, essentially undisputatious clarity of his thought made it difficult to overlook him, even in his old age. Where others would bend to imperial intrigues to unite Christians on the basis of a way of talking about the person of Christ which Maximus believed to be a betrayal of the truth and of the intentions of the Council of Chalcedon, he too must if possible be bent. The most recent studies of the pithy and unsystematic writings of Maximus have conspired to show that he was from his earliest years possessed of a unitary vision of his faith and its bearing upon life which gave his thought a seamless strength.[19] Maximus firmly believes that there can be no opposition *in principle* between that which is the fitting fulfilment of created things and that which God intends for them, or to which he calls them. This is particularly important in the case of man, and there can be no explanation of man's call to communion with God, *or* of the incarnation of the Son of God, which does violence to the true nature of man as such.[20] It is not necessary to understand the details of how Maximus defends these positions to appreciate that the two are intimately interconnected. It is, further, important to notice that however we, or Maximus, attempt to explain what he has to say on these matters, he is not trying to make them seem *experimentally* plausible.[21] When he says, as we have seen him saying, that the incarnation is and remains a mystery, he is saying that while as theologians we must say that Jesus, the Son of God, is fully human and fully divine, we cannot see *how* this can be the case. And, although he does not put it in this way, he means that since we ourselves are not fully human and fully divine, we *cannot know* by even the brightest intuition what it could be like to *be* Jesus Christ. This is the strength of the orthodox way of looking at the mystery of the incarnation. For while it leads Maximus in his life, and the undivided Church after his death, to insist that Christ, as fully human, had a human will, this does not tempt him an inch of the way – as many modern theologians appear to be tempted – to go on to say that therefore we ought to be able to talk about the *experience* of this full humanity in life. It is not irrelevant to notice that Maximus's doctrine of the purification and deification of *man*, like that of any orthodox Christian mystic, cannot even make the experience of human purification perspicuous for someone who does not go through it. Just as Maximus cannot believe, with the taste of some Christians of his time, that Jesus Christ was some kind of a man swamped, as it were, by the divine, neither can he believe that the union with God which the saints reach is a pro-

gressive dehumanization. On the contrary, he believes that holiness
is the ever-growing experience of human liberty and fulfilment.
This, naturally, implies a growth in mature responsibility which is
an aspect of liberty, though it may lead to what sometimes looks
like its antithesis.

There are a number of obscurities about the early career of
Maximus.[22] It can, however, be inferred from the questions that
were put to him under examination that he was born about the year
580 and had, as a young man, moved in the circle of the imperial
court, perhaps even as secretary to the emperor Heraclius. Under
what circumstances he became a monk at Chrysopolis we do not
know, but Persian advances on Constantinople were doubtless
connected with his departure for Carthage in North Africa. Here
he remained well-informed on theological developments back in
Constantinople and these led to his moving to a Greek-speaking
monastery in Rome. Once there, he actively assisted Pope Martin 1
in the preparation of a synod in 649, the firm theological opposition
of which to prevailing tendencies in imperial circles was to lead to
the arrest and ultimately the death of both. One night in June 653
Pope Martin was seized, to be carried off by imperial orders to
Constantinople. Already a sick man and abominably treated, he
was eventually condemned to exile in the Crimea where, starved
and wasted, he died in 655. His quiet acceptance of his fate is
impressive. Of the case of Maximus the court was determined to
make more of a show and was prepared to go to great lengths to win
him over. But before alternations between offers of honour and
scenes of violence Maximus stood firm. In 662, being eighty-two
years old, he was condemned to be flogged, have his tongue torn
out and his right hand cut off, and was sent to a lonely fortress in
the Caucasus, where he died on 13 August of that same year. Years
before in his reflections he had seen that those who were planted in
the resurrection of Christ would have to be so by their sufferings in
the likeness of his death, whatever form these might take.
Maximus's own death seals the life and writings of a man who
listens and remembers. If he himself is now remembered as 'the
Confessor' this is particularly appropriate for one whose convictions rest on the clearest foundations of early undivided
Christianity. He is sure that God does not reject his creation and
that he shows this pre-eminently by the incarnation which is, as it
were, the supreme model of his ways and intentions. For as
Maximus says elsewhere, 'the Word who is God wishes always and

in everything to bring about the mystery of his infleshing'.[23]

More than a hundred years before the death of Maximus, political
and social conditions in the West were so threatening the survival
of human values and of any adequate knowledge of the Christian
faith at all as to demand a living confession of another kind. It
would have to take the form of learning to cope with the lifelong
claims of working in, and even creating, a library for the love of
God. It is the library and the ideals of the aged Cassiodorus that
understandably attract most frequent mention today. But it was in
Spain that the combination of a library and a man who would work
in it at this vital time first fruitfully occurred. One living sentence
from the writings of Isidore of Seville has just been quoted above.
Whatever most modern readers may think of this devout and
industrious Spanish compiler, we know that in the last days of his
life, a century later, another writer, whom modern scholars have
not hesitated to call a 'scholar', was preparing for his students
extracts from St Isidore. It was, in fact, in this connection that a
student of Bede tells his friend of the ideals of work which his dying
master had expressed: 'I do not wish my sons to read anything
untrue, or to labour unprofitably after my death.'[24] Only those
who have never seriously tried to live and work like this will think
Bede's an unexacting programme, even today when printed edi-
tions of most of what one needs are, at least theoretically, available.
In the second half of the seventh century a single copy often had to
be sought across Europe by anyone who saw the point of acquiring
it.

Bede was probably born about a year before the founding of
Monkwearmouth in 674, on lands which had been given to the
abbey. At the age of seven, as he himself tells us, he was sent for his
education and upbringing to the extraordinary abbot-founder
Benedict Biscop, the first great collector of books among the bar-
barian peoples of Europe. Not only did Benedict's collection,
discerningly picked up in the course of six journeys to Rome,
ultimately contain the very Bible about which Cassiodorus had
taken such pains, but also a widely representative collection of
ancient Christian learning. Between the fifth and sixth of these
great forages, Benedict founded the house of Jarrow, and Bede was
transferred to its new abbot Ceolfrid. It is difficult not to believe
that the boy who helped his abbot to keep the singing of the
liturgical antiphons going when the choir-monks had been deci-

mated by plague was Bede. At least, having told us briefly of the
role of these two men in his early formation, Bede continues:
'While I have observed the regular discipline and sung the choir
offices daily in church, my chief delight has always been in study,
teaching and writing.' Even to his last hours these ideals, within the
framework of the liturgy, were Bede's. His student Cuthbert, to
whom he was in his sickness dictating English translations, tells of
his singing antiphons with them, such as the lovely *O Rex gloriae*
for the feast of the Ascension, on the eve of which Bede died in May
735.[25] Sir Richard Southern has often returned with affection and
admiration to the topic of Bede in his writing and lectures, but
nowhere more movingly or more appositely for the purposes of this
present book than in the talk he gave in 1970 for the opening of the
new library of the monastery of Mount Angel, Oregon. 'Above all,
the library of Jarrow produced a scholar of the kind that
Cassiodorus had dreamt of in vain: Bede,' he says.

> How shall I speak adequately of Bede? All that I could say of him
> would fall short of his deserts ... Writing in a monastery remote
> from the main centres of power, he was able to put together
> works of learning which show that – alone in Europe in his day –
> he had a thorough mastery of the learning of the Christian past
> ... Quietly, without hurry and without intermission, with the
> calm and unclamorous insight of a scholar, he worked for forty
> years to draw together threads that had long been broken, and he
> produced books that were among the text-books of scholars and
> evangelists alike for four hundred years.

It is Richard Southern's main purpose in this talk to stress that
libraries, though planned to be permanent, tend to be fragile and
that, above all, they must not be 'tombs of learning, but places
where systematic, well-directed work is done'. Of Benedict Biscop
he says that 'he understood that books are made to be used and that
they must be used as a whole if they are to have their full effect'.
Speaking of the many 'great and lowly men' within this tradition,
Sir Richard also memorably specifies the kind of virtues they need.

> It must be recognized that many of the tasks that a library
> inspires and makes possible are humble and laborious, though
> they require skills and talents that are more uncommon than
> people suppose. I mean they require orderliness, system,
> perseverance and an ability to keep the end in view while dealing

with a multiplicity of minute facts. In scholarly work these are not virtues that can be left to subordinates while the great men float off into an empyrean of large ideas and exciting controversies. They are needed at every level of the enterprise.[26]

These observations recall a remark of the great Maurist Jean Mabillon of the life of study that it is indeed 'the most arduous of all lives'.[27] This, as the evidence amply shows, was Bede's daily 'martyrdom to his conscience' and it produced, as his student Cuthbert affirms, nothing but gratitude, a Eucharist over his life which began when he awoke. 'I can truthfully affirm that I have never seen or heard of anyone who gave thanks so unceasingly to the living God as him.' In fact Bede finished his life with a *gloria*, 'and all who saw and heard of the death of our father Bede declared that they had never known anyone end his days in such deep devotion and peace'.

It was not, as we have seen, the peace of a man who had ever been idle since he was a child. The Church Fathers of the fourth century had not been mistaken in their estimate of the role that books would have to play in the battle to maintain any sound sense of Christian orthodoxy. Bede, 'the servant of Christ' as he called himself, had played his humble, ministerial role in this struggle. He had known of the work of Willibrord, who carried with him the memory of the saints of Northumbria and inscribed their names in his calendar at his missionary refuge of Echternach.[28] But Bede could hardly have guessed how much the traffic in books between England and the Continent in the wake of devoted men would determine the future of Christianity in Europe. Willibrord's letters are lost. But those we have of Boniface often return thanks for gifts of books and make requests for others, among them explicitly the works of Bede, of whom Boniface had not known when he first left for Germany.[29] Boniface's own death is like a symbol of that combination between learning and risk which has always been the mark of a faith robust enough to survive. Surprised at his morning reading in his tent in the marshes of Friesland, Boniface put up his book to protect his head against his attackers[30] who, when they had killed him and his companions, found nothing of value but a travelling library which they trampled in the mud.

The confrontation between informed faith and violence which occurs in the life and death of Thomas More is both more shocking and more real for most readers today for several reasons. In the first place, a great painter enables us to envisage More physically, a dimension always subtly informing and often endearing. Erasmus, who had been his friend for twenty years when he described him in some detail, had looked into More's eyes and noticed the 'scattering of tiny flecks in their grey-blue, the normal sign of a very happy disposition'. This observation sorts well with the sensitivity and poise of the face in the Frick Collection portrait.[31] Again, it is somehow easy to forget that the man born in February 1478 was more thoroughly late medieval in his formation than most people can imagine, when they see him as husband and father sitting with his family in a drawing made by Holbein for a picture now lost. Kenneth Clark finds that they look 'alert, sensible people of any epoch'.[32] This is the kind of nearness that makes the waste of More's life seem only the greater perversity. Finally, even those who do not share his faith, can recognize in More one of the first of the victims of a view of the rights of a state over its subjects whose more terrible insanities it has been reserved to our own times to witness. It is not likely that even the last of these considerations has often been explicitly in the minds of the many audiences who have clearly been gripped by Robert Bolt's fine play, *A Man for All Seasons.* It ran successfully on the stage in 1960 and shows no signs of being forgotten since, either in live performance or on film. Bolt's own preface to this play probably comes near to touching the secret of its fascination. 'More, as I wrote about him, became for me a man with an adamantine sense of his own self . . . What first attracted me was a person who could not be accused of any incapacity for life, who indeed seized life in great variety and almost greedy quantities, who nevertheless found something in himself without which life was valueless and when that was denied him was able to grasp his death.'[33] It is, of course, the evidence that qualities of this sort are among the normal marks of outstanding holiness, as of any other kind of heroism, that suggested among other things the value of the present little gallery of portraits. More himself, in his happier days at home, had given another reason for remembering such things which reveals his simplicity and absence of strain at the thought of such demands should they ever come. His son-in-law Roper reports his saying that 'there are some circumstances when you are carried up to heaven even by the chins. But if you live the time that no man will give you good counsel, nor no man give you good example, when you shall see virtue punished and vice rewarded, if you will then stand fast and firmly stick to God, upon pain of my life, though you be but half good, God will allow you for whole good.'[34]

As we look back over his life we see that these are not the words of a man who had ever been either notably self-indulgent or uncritically accepting of what even men of authority and learning said. Briefly at Oxford from the age of fourteen, the vital stage of his early formation occurred at Lincoln's Inn in London and in the circle of people coming and going in the city at that time. It was in London in 1499 that Erasmus first met More, and More had taken him out to meet the royal children, among them the bright boy later to be King Henry VIII. From London Erasmus visited Colet at Oxford and got a clearer view of the ideals he was later to make his own. Louis Bouyer has written that it was Colet who 'helped more than anyone else to restore and fortify Erasmus' faith, strengthening it by his own familiar example of what humanism could bring to a spiritual search freed from the narrow bounds of a decadent religious tradition.'[35] The final phrase is not irrelevant to More's own openness to new possibilities. As More's greatest modern biographer convincingly suggests of this triumvirate: 'Till he met More and Colet, the letters of Erasmus are those of an amiable but aimless scholar not too well befriended . . . In Colet [he] made a friend who was to help him discover his life's work; and with More he made the longest of all his friendships.' More shared to the end of his days the desire of his two elder friends to see the restoration of a living theology, and Professor Chambers is certainly right to see that there was no necessary conflict between his enthusiasm for a literary humanism and his still unresolved conflict about whether he should choose to live the life of a monk. His Greek studies were in fact deepened while he weighed up this problem at the London house of the Carthusians, later to produce its own impressive crop of martyrs. Although More decided firmly for marriage and accepted its responsibilities, joys, and troubles to the full, he never gave up some of the traditional monastic ascetic practices in private or lost the sense of that call to solitude and personal integrity which is of the very essence of the monastic calling, wherever and however it be lived out.

The details of More's life as lawyer and servant of the young Henry who became king in 1509 need not detain us, engaging though they are. The years see the growing frustration of all that the young More had most valued and hoped for. As Chambers saw,

'More, Erasmus and the young Vives working together might have
repeated in the sixteenth century some of the features of the eighth
century, of the age of Bede and Boniface and Alcuin, when England
became the centre of European scholarship, the city of its refuge
... It is difficult for us to realize now, how fair was the promise of
the opening years of Henry's reign, so complete was the frustration
brought about in the second half.' It was in that second half of his
reign that Henry slew Richard Reynolds, Thomas More, and John
Fisher, 'the most learned monk, the most learned layman, and the
most saintly patron of learning in England'. In brief, Henry
'destroyed more things of beauty and more things of promise, than
any other man in European history'.[36]

In explaining why, in his play, he has depicted More as a 'hero of
selfhood' Robert Bolt says that 'it may be that a clear sense of the
self can *only* crystallize round something transcendental.'[37] Since
he is often able to put into More's mouth phrases that the man
himself certainly said or wrote, Bolt must have got close enough to
More to know that More himself would never have been able to
accept, any more than anyone else need, the notion of a necessary
antithesis between the 'rational' and the transcendental. It is in fact
possible that those who wish to assume that reason and 'something
transcendental' are necessarily incompatibles suffer from imaginative difficulties nourished by a one-sided diet of reading. More's
feeling for 'humanity' is not the less universal because it includes a
place for his prayer. There is, indeed, no reason to doubt that his
very 'rational' second wife Alice found exactly the right temptation
to put before him when, visiting him in the Tower, she reminded
him of 'your library, your books, your gallery, your garden'.[38]
More never willingly placed these things lightly in jeopardy, as
every step of the way shows. He had doubtless from his youth, like
the people of Utopia, believed 'that the dead be presently
conversant among the quick as beholders and witnesses of their
words and deeds. Therefore they go more courageously to their
business as having a trust and affiance in such overseers.'[39] It
would perhaps be dangerous to deduce this from a book about
whose interpretation there can be large areas of doubt, were this
not a theme which explicitly came up in one of More's last
conversations with his beloved daughter Meg. For all their
profound differences of character, More, like the Erasmus of the
portrait by Quentin Mastys, looked over and beyond his books to
things of which the books were only reminders.[40] 'I am also,

Margaret, of this thing sure enough, that of those holy doctors and saints who are with God in heaven long ago ... whose books still today remain here in men's hands, there were some who thought some such things as I think now.' This was not, of course, a way of saying that his position was that of a man who hides behind someone else's authority. The remembrance of the saints seemed rather to be a challenge to him here and now, as he said very clearly in the same prolonged discussion designed to persuade him to say and do what would get him released. 'Truly, daughter, I never intend to pin my soul to another man's back, not even the best man that I know this day living, for I know not whither he may happen to carry it.' When it came to what this conviction would cost him he knew, as he told Meg, 'few so faint-hearted as myself'.[41] At the time when he was still being allowed paper and books he had prepared himself for these deliberations at some length in his moving *Dialogue of Comfort against Tribulation*, 'not desiring to be brought unto the peril of persecution – for it seemeth a proud, high mind to desire martyrdom – but desiring help and strength of God if he suffer us to come to the stress, either being sought, founden and brought out against our wills, or else by his commandment for the comfort of our cure, bounden to abide.'[42] In the end More found himself trying to comfort the weeping friend who came to fetch him to the block, convinced as he was that 'we shall, once in heaven, see each other full merrily'. To the scandal of some who heard of it, he climbed the scaffold with a quip and died cheerfully, having declared that he was 'the King's good servant, but God's first'. It was 6 July 1535.

Joy, peace, and a balance which costs the courage to take the next step indicated are to be found among the saints in circumstances which to many would seem at first unlikely. The young Prokhor Mochnin, born into a Russian merchant family in 1759, was a pious boy from the time he could read. At nineteen, with her consent and blessing, he left his widowed mother to enter a monastery in the forest of Sarov, and took the name of Seraphim.[43] From this moment he began to live, externally, a life that goes deeper and deeper into the Christian past. By 1794 he had received permission from his superior to become a hermit and went to live in a cabin on the bank of the river Sarovka. Chopping wood in winter and running his vegetable garden in summer, singing psalms as he worked, he was as solitary as any desert Father of the fourth century and silent when anyone passed. In September 1804 he was so brutally attacked by robbers, against whom he made no attempt to defend himself with the axe they seized from him, that he could scarcely crawl back to the monastery. But after five months he was, though physically broken, back in his beloved solitude. In 1810 a new superior, supported by members of the community who were hostile to Seraphim, insisted on his return to the monastery. Here he chose a cell where he lived as a complete recluse for five years. Slowly, after 1815, he began to communicate a little with those who came to him, and after 1825 he became accessible to an increasing number of people of all kinds who visited him.

What attracted them, and what sort of man did they meet? Dressed like a peasant in birch-bark shoes, he came towards them with a radiant face, full of personal interest for each one. The notes and anecdotes that survive, still inadequately sorted and assessed, reveal the classical frame of his life and formation. 'One must give the soul the word of God for, according to Gregory Nazianzen, it is the food of angels,' he said. 'One must exercise oneself in it so that one's thought swims, so to speak, in the law of God. It is very useful to give oneself to the reading of the word of God in solitude and to read the whole Bible in a sensible way.' But, as he goes on to say, this is the Bible read within the context of the living tradition of the Church. 'For it is necessary also to furnish the soul with knowledge about the Church, how it has survived from the beginning until today, what it has gone through in this period and that. One must know this, not out of a desire to rule men, but in the eventuality of trials that may come.' It is impossible to read the most well-known of all the conversations of Seraphim with a visitor, that with the young landlord Motovilov, without being aware of these two factors in Seraphim's interior formation. He has a ready access to the Scriptures, but it is one which is thoroughly formed by an assimilated reading of patristic and monastic texts, lived and not merely studied academically. Like Anthony the Great, so long before, he gives counsels which are penetrated by the common sense of experience.

One must not undertake activities which exceed one's measure, but must keep an eye on our friend – the flesh – to see that it is faithful and fit to practise the virtues. One ought to be considerate about the weaknesses and imperfections of one's own soul. One should endure one's own defects like those of others and, without becoming lazy, urge oneself to do better. If you have eaten a lot or done something like that out of ordinary human weakness, do not worry about it. Do not add a second evil to the first, but courageously take measures to improve, while compelling yourself to keep your inner peace. Voluntarily to exhaust the body to the point of wearing the spirit is to practise a silly mortification, even if one does it to acquire virtue.

Seraphim has a good deal to say about the importance of peace of soul. 'When a man has attained this state of peace, he is able to turn upon others the light of an informed understanding. Before that time, he ought to repeat the words: Hypocrite, first take the log out of your own eye.' This is, of course, an interior state which has to be acquired by controlling one's tongue, by patience, and by genuine humility 'without which there is nothing but darkness in a man'.[44] Perhaps the most deservedly renowned of all his words on this subject is the sentence: 'Oh my joy, get yourself the spirit of peace and thousands around you will be saved.'

'My joy!' was in fact Seraphim's most common greeting and mode of address and it occurs in the stories of his relations with both men and women. He would also sometimes use the salutation: 'Christ is risen'. He was also credited, as many saints have been, with being able to read people's thoughts, and is sometimes spoken of as a prophet. Although he may sometimes have foretold the future, Seraphim perhaps most justly deserves to be called a 'prophet' in that special New Testament sense of this title to which, as we have seen earlier, the Russian theologian Afanassieff draws attention in his study of the Church.[45] Seraphim is primarily a prophet in the sense that his way of living and teaching renews the living sense of some aspect of the faith too often forgotten. The frequently-translated conversation with the layman Motovilov is very explicitly prophetic in this sense. As one reads it, it is not possible to miss the influence of the fourth-century Macarian homilies on Seraphim's teaching, especially, perhaps, homily 5. We know he read them, but they have been transformed in the experience of a man who lives his theology and Seraphim instinctively places the origin of his doctrine within the tradition of the Church and the sacraments.

The conversation in question occurred with a man whom Seraphim doubtless recognized as, in some ways, a kindred spirit. It is a grey winter day, and the snow is falling, when Seraphim opens the conversation by saying that he is aware that Nicholas has longed from his boyhood to know what the ultimate thing in the Christian life is. Although he has questioned a number of clergy about this he has never received a satisfactory answer. He has simply been told to do the usual pious things and not to meddle with matters too high for him. 'God-loving one,' says Seraphim, 'it is in the acquisition of the Spirit of God that the true goal of our Christian life consists; whereas prayer, watching, fasting, alms and other virtuous practices engaged in for Christ's sake are only the means of acquiring the Spirit of God.' Explaining that by 'acquiring' he means devoting one's energies to fitting oneself to receive the action of God in the same way that a merchant is absorbed in what promotes the good of his business, Seraphim suggests that prayer is the primary preparation and more readily available than any other means. 'Always the opportunity for prayer is open to all men; to the rich and the poor, to gentle and common folk, to the strong and the weak, to the healthy and the sick, to the just man and the sinner. Great is the power of prayer; more than anything else it brings the Spirit of God.' But Seraphim goes on to add that everyone must find what, *for them*, best disposes them to receive this life-giving and enlightening action. If people no longer so readily receive this gift it is because faith has grown cold 'and because of our inattentiveness with regard to the acts of Divine Providence concerning us'. The idea of communion with God seems fantastic, and yet Scripture constantly speaks of this, and it is also common doctrine that the Holy Spirit is given in baptism.

> Indeed this baptismal Grace is so great and so necessary, as well as so life-giving to man, that it is not taken away from the heretic until his very death – that is, until the term placed by Divine Providence upon the ordeal of human life on earth: this will be the testing of what he can do during the time granted him by God, and with the help of that power of Grace given him from above . . . In spite of our sinfulness, in spite of the darkness surrounding our souls, the grace of the Holy Spirit, conferred by baptism in the name of the Father, the Son and the Holy Spirit, still shines in our heart with the inextinguishable light of Christ's priceless merits.

But how, asks Nicholas, can one know that the Holy Spirit is present? 'This, God-loving one, is very simple, wherefore our Lord says: All things are simple to those who have understanding.' As they talk, Seraphim becomes radiant with a brightness which makes it difficult to look at him. It is like full sunshine on the dark winter day, though it is not sunshine, as Seraphim points out, since it does not melt the snow. He points out also that this is a shared experience, otherwise Nicholas would not see him in this way. Seraphim mentions in this connection the lovely words which occur in St John's Last Supper sermon about the woman in labour who forgets her sorrow when the child is born. He says that whatever they may be experiencing at the moment, it is nothing to what they can hope for. 'And now, good father, it is our task, adding effort to effort, to rise from strength to strength and reach the measure of the fullness of Christ.' It is a matter of indifference who one is, monk or layman, Seraphim says. This is a common Christian call. 'It is enough that we ourselves love him, our heavenly Father, with the love of true sons . . . the Lord is merciful to all.'[46]

To the doctrinal aspects of the teaching embodied in this interview it will be necessary to return later in this book. But it is for the moment right to remind ourselves how at the very time when the armies of Napoleon, born ten years later than Seraphim, were devastating Europe and had even invaded Russian territory, at least one monk, only *apparently* 'away from it all', had been learning lessons of universal compassion. And when he explicitly turned to his fellows in his old age, it was with a message that was healing and life-promoting. One January morning in 1833 they found him dead, still peacefully kneeling at his prayers before the icon of Our Lady of Tenderness, who had been his human model of all that is really important in life.

There are, as we have seen, cases where one could feel justified in writing two lives of the same man or woman, so great is the contrast between what everyone knew and what the subject appears to have experienced. Social history is slowly doing something to remedy the perspective of histories that were once lists of kings, wars, rebellions, and other public figures and events. More rarely, however, do we get a glimpse of those in a more humble station who appear to have risen to the challenge of their life in a way that puts them among the princes of the heart. A striking example of this is a pioneer study of Franz Jägerstätter, a peasant from a village in upper Austria who was beheaded in August 1943 for refusing, on grounds of conscience, to serve in Hitler's armies.[47]

Franz Jägerstätter was born in 1907 in the tiny village of St Radegund in the heart of an old Catholic world. He appears to have grown up as a very normal lad and, in his day, rode his motor cycle with the rest. He does, however, seem to have undergone some kind of notable experience of conversion to a more devout practice of his religion, which the nearest of his friends thought ought to be placed somewhere about the end of 1934 or 1935. At any rate, in 1940 he seemed the obvious man to ask to take over the duties of preparing the altar and answering Mass in his village church, on the sudden death of his predecessor in that post. In 1936 Franz had married a girl from a neighbouring village and they had gone to Rome for their honeymoon. When the German army invaded Austria in 1938 he was the only man in the village to speak openly against it. Although he did not belong to any kind of political organization, and even did a brief period of military service, he firmly declared that he would never fight in Hitler's war. He was called up for active service in February 1943, by which time he had three daughters, the eldest already six. Partly on account of his duties to his family, he was advised on principles too familiar to need discussion that he could safely leave the responsibility for the war to those whose business it was to govern. This he remained firmly convinced he could not, in conscience, do. The lawyer charged with his case when he ultimately came up for trial took every conceivable step to avoid the inevitable. He did this partly because Franz deeply impressed him as a human being, a view which appears to have been common to all those who had anything to do with Franz in this last period of his life. Years afterwards, when questioned, they one and all denied any sign of his being unbalanced or fanatical. He received the sacraments and went to his execution in great peace of soul on 9 August 1943.

Although *some* of the issues were much the same for Franz as they had been for Thomas More – Franz always included the Nazi attitude to the Church among his reasons for refusing to fight – we shall not expect his reflections to be so wide-ranging as those of More. Yet there is a striking similarity between their explicit priorities. The letters of Franz express a very real concern for his wife and children and for what his decision is going to cost them – to begin with, even in worry for him. They must, he says, not have a heavy heart: 'For you know well enough under whose protection I stand . . . It will not go worse for me that I had to come here. For God does not wish that we are lost, but that we shall live happily with him forever.' Franz tells them how, in his prison cell, he is saying the same kind of prayers in the months of May and June as they will be saying at home in the parish church. 'And at least I can pray for you. It is also God's grace to have to suffer something for one's faith.' He thinks how the children will be picking strawberries and bilberries and looking for cherries.

In the prison context he was always wise enough never to enter into theoretical discussion with those who pointed out (as More also had been told) that men as pious as he had decided to act otherwise. He simply said that God had evidently not given them the grace to do differently. There is never a word of judgement about them. 'Dearest wife, as long as I am not unhappy, you have no reason to have a heavy heart for me. Do not forget me in your prayers, as I do not forget you. Remember me specially at Mass . . . Oh that we might only remain in the love of God, for even tougher trials of faith may yet befall us. We do not know whether we are living in a time when, as it is said, even the just will scarcely be saved.' In this last letter he begs his mother, who had broken with him over the whole issue, not to go on being bitter about it, or to worry about his bodily survival, 'for the good God will not send me more than I can bear'. Sadly, he tells the children not to despair if he should not return to tell them stories. 'For today there are many children whose father either cannot come to them, or will *never* come again.' Another, probably later, note says: 'I want just to write a few words, exactly as they come into my own thoughts and heart. If I am writing to you with bound hands, I much prefer this to having a bound will. No prison, no bonds, no sentence of death can take from anyone his faith and his free will. God gives strength enough to bear all suffering. This strength is greater than any power in the world. God's power is unconquerable.' Moreover, says Franz, the kingdom for which a Christian fights 'does not need arms, but spiritual weapons, and among these, in the first place, prayer . . . A true Christian is easier to recognize by his deeds and actions than by his words . . . Let us love our enemies, bless those who curse us and pray for those who persecute us. For love will conquer and love will abide for all eternity. Happy is he who lives and dies in the love of God.'

Then, at some point before his execution, Franz covered two sides of a piece of card with some final thoughts:

All my love. The time is getting steadily nearer when I must give my soul back to God. How gladly would I have spared you the pain and sorrow you have to bear for my sake. But you know well enough that we must love God more than our family and forsake everything that is dear and precious to us on earth rather than offend God in the least thing . . . Had I not trusted in God's mercy to forgive me all my sins, I could hardly have lived so peaceful a life in my lonely prison cell . . . One must not think ill of others who act otherwise than I. It is much better to pray for everyone than despise others. For God wishes all men to be saved . . . That one is bound, under pain of sin, to put oneself under oath to our earthly authorities and obey them in all they command is not to be found either in the commandments of God or the Church. Bring up the children as good Catholics, as far as you can. For it is normal that they do not yet understand it much. I can say from my own experience how difficult life can be if one goes on living as half a Christian. It is often not very different from vegetating rather than living . . . Now, my dear children, if your mother reads you this letter, your father will already be dead . . . Pray for your father that we may soon see each other again in heaven.

The last priest to see Franz found him entirely peaceful and, like St John of the Cross, he even turned down an offer to have something read for him from the New Testament. He said: 'I am inwardly entirely united with God, and any reading would only hinder my contact with my God.' Franz then gave him a look the priest was never able to forget, so that he afterwards said: 'This simple human being is the only saint I have ever met in my life.' And the Sister who eventually took the ashes of Franz to his widow told her that all who really knew the circumstances thought that he was 'a special friend of God'.

It is thus that, when the mystery of God is allowed to work freely in the unfolding mystery of a human life, the combination leads to yet one more paradox. On the feast days of martyrs the Church in the West often sings as the opening words of the Mass the strangely appropriate words:

> Many are the afflictions of the righteous;
> but the Lord delivers him out of them all.
> He keeps all his bones;
> not one of them is broken.[48]

# 8
## SOUL-KEEPERS

'And some there are who have no memorial, who have perished as though they had not lived. But these were men of mercy, whose righteous deeds have not been forgotten; their prosperity will remain with their descendants.'[1] It is an essential part of Sirach's familiar 'praise of famous men' that those without a name are not forgotten. In that change of perspective in the Jewish tradition whereby it is *men* that come to the fore and reflect in their lives and on their faces the immense variety of the ways of the hidden God,[2] the *unknown* bearers of the tradition are an essential part of its human continuity. It was on something akin to this that Saint-Exupéry found himself reflecting as he saw the three sons of an old peasant-woman in Provence watching their mother die. What had been passing on through her was life, but it was also awareness and now, separated from their mother anew, as once long ago at birth, they must go on alone, and *hand on* in their turn. In this, his *Terre des hommes*[3] – perhaps the most permanently haunting of all his books – Saint-Exupéry is explicitly preoccupied with the liberation of the human possibilities glimpsed in the comradeship of intense difficulty or on the face of a sleeping child. It is a sense of values so easily lost in the dull, organized anonymity of modern life. The whole book was part of an honourable attempt, which Saint-Exupéry never wholly gave up, to articulate the conditions for a post-Christian humanism. This particular book of his ends abruptly with the desperate sentence, ambivalent in French as in English: 'Only the Spirit, if it breathes on the clay, can create Man.' Many who know only the somewhat later *Little Prince* have understandably felt that they could divine through the mask of its fairytale charm, the deep trouble of a disappointed man. Essentially a man of action rather than a philosopher, Saint-Exupéry died a singularly appropriate death by flying out into the blue and never being heard of again.[4] But as someone struggling with the sense of a task of reflection to be achieved in the face of the human situation created by, among others, the technology of flight, he still commands the respect his surest intuitions deserve. In the last of his writings he says that 'civilization is an invisible good because it rests not upon things, but upon the unseen links which bind them one to another, thus and not otherwise'.[5] This is a variant on his conviction that the fullness of being human, even in one's solitude, consists in one's sense of one's debt to and link with others. A typical expression of this is what he says about his pilot-friend Henri Guillaumet, to whom *Terre des hommes* is dedicated. His courage, says Saint-Exupéry, was first and foremost a result of his 'uprightness'. This is a word Saint-Exupéry does not leave unexplained. Guillaumet's greatness, he says, was to feel himself responsible – to himself and to others. 'To be a man is precisely to be responsible.' These phrases, of which it would be possible to collect many similar ones throughout his works, illustrate how for Saint-Exupéry the theme of friendship – for nothing less rich and complex is meant – returns to its natural place in modern life, not just as the polarization of ideals, but as a forming discipline. With or without worked-out theories attached to it, we find this theme spontaneously returning whenever the removal of the paralysing constraints of mass living exposes people with any spark of vitality to the true urgency of their human situation. It can be found, it would seem, in the camps of governments which would at least wish to insist on their differences of political colour.[6] There will perhaps increasingly be reasons even in ordinary daily life why friendship must be cultivated as an ultimate defence of human dignity. So many links even with the fairly immediate past have been broken over the last thirty or forty years. But not this one. All over the world places like the exposed Blaskets off the Atlantic coast of Ireland are steadily being deserted save for brief, romantic jaunts. Yet it is not just the gentle, civilized tone of the reflections of an old woman who had lived there in all weathers that makes what she says on friendship hard to forget. There are many new and different reasons why men and women under stresses of other kinds will need to weigh up quietly what she has to say: 'We helped each other and lived in the shelter of each other. Everything that was coming dark upon us, we would disclose to each other, and that would give us consolation of mind. Friendship was the fastest root in our hearts.'[7]

It has seemed wise to introduce the subject of friendship at this point in our discussion by reference primarily to a man and a woman who, for all their total differences of background and

formation, clearly responded to the resonances of feeling this experience evokes. Yet neither could lightly be dismissed as mere
dreamers by those who have never flown a pioneer aircraft or
survived in poverty on a windswept island. There will, however, be
some who find this hardly sufficient reassurance to take the matter
seriously. To them it will simply recall a passing phase of adolescence out of which they, unlike some of their 'friends', have satisfactorily grown. For their sakes, as much as for those who dream of
learning to become saints and heroes in the morning along a path of
pure delight, it may be as well to begin by taking a careful look at
some aspects of the element of romance in friendship. Neither
Cicero, the chief transmitter of the Graeco-Latin tradition, nor
his twelfth-century disciple, Aelred of Rievaulx, will do more than
hint at the interplay of hidden psychological factors in friendship,
about which it would seem to us natural and necessary to be
reasonably explicit today. Fortunately we know just enough about
the life and thoughts of the author of a unique novel built around
an imaginary friendship to help us to see what is often involved,
without destroying the integrity of the portrayal itself.

The first chapter of Robert Gibson's second and long-matured
study of Henri Alain-Fournier is entitled 'An atlas of nostalgia'.[8] It
is a frank enough discussion of the problems of writing satisfactorily about childhood and adolescence, and of the possibility of
having an unfavourable reaction to Alain-Fournier's only novel *Le
Grand Meaulnes*,[9] published in 1913, less than a year before his
death in the First World War. The rest of Professor Gibson's book
is, in the relaxed variety of the ground it covers, a quiet defence of
the thesis that 'to write effectively of one's past is, in a very real
sense, to exorcize it.' But it is also an attempt to show that *Le Grand
Meaulnes* is something more than 'the most delicate rendering so
far achieved in literature of the romantic adolescent consciousness',[10] though it would, of course, be great for that reason alone.
This is not the place to defend a novel to whose merits one suspects
its denigrators often pay tribute by the force of the negative
emotions it arouses. It is, however, valuable to notice the evidence
in the novel itself and in Alain-Fournier's correspondence, for the
role the young Meaulnes plays in the imaginative life of his author.
We shall hardly get our perspective right if we do not appreciate a
point which Robert Gibson seems to have been the first to analyse.
Even before the hero, Meaulnes, arrives on the scene, and right to
the end of the story, our impressions are being mediated through

SUMMER IN THE SEED

the eyes of a narrator, François Seurel, who is by no means the empty name he has sometimes been taken to be. Seurel is 'timorous and over-protected', and this is why 'he readily casts Meaulnes in the role of a vigorous and free-ranging hero; indeed, he never ceases, thereafter, to see him through a highly-coloured romantic haze.' Although Professor Gibson does not express the matter in this way, one could say that Seurel's dramatic function is to create a feeling of tension within the novel which also existed, in fact, in Alain-Fournier's own life. There is a holding-back, combined with a longing to break out, which it is sometimes part of the function of our friends to help us to resolve. As Robert Gibson says, 'In the course of the action Seurel has lost everything he holds most dear – and in the fifteen years which have elapsed since all these momentous events occurred, he seems to have found no adequate consolation.' He thinks that, of all the characters in *Le Grand Meaulnes*, Seurel has 'by far the most in common with Fournier himself'. This is seen as being most importantly revealed in the fact that Seurel and Fournier 'are both artists. Each has to learn the artist's bitter lesson that before he can re-create his Paradise, he must first lose it utterly.'[11] Not perhaps artists alone . . . Yet, of course, there is really a lot of Fournier in Meaulnes too. To the closest of his many friends, Jacques Rivière, Fournier wrote: 'Meaulnes, the hero of my book, is a man whose childhood was too beautiful. Throughout his entire adolescence it trails after him.' This he explains, is why after an adventure 'he comes back into class like an insolent and mysterious young god'. The phrase is not fortuitous. Fournier goes further in this characterization when he says to Jacques: 'I'm beginning to believe that we have an obligation to be happy, that while Meaulnes may be a great cruel angel, he's not a man. And, whatever you might think, I believe I have within me a great ability for being happy, and I have also the capacity hitherto unused, for giving happiness. All that's required of me now is the courage to put this to the test.'[12] Here we surely have clearly enough Fournier's sense of being haunted by dreams which are not quite serious because they have never been brought down to earth. Meaulnes is 'an insolent, young god', in so far as he is the mirror in which Fournier sees some of his ideals beckoning him on. But he is also 'a cruel angel', in so far as he represents demands that take too little account of human existence in the round. Fournier both loves and hates his dreams because they keep him alive to intriguing possibilities which would necessarily have to take on a rather different form were they ever to be realized in life. Interestingly enough, there are a couple of letters to a friend from his *lycée* days, René Bichet, in which Fournier admits his impossible expectations of a real friendship. On one occasion he writes: 'What's the point of having a friend, if he is too riddled with doubts and is overwhelmed by the impossibility of everything?' It is the kind of remark that both friends and husbands and wives tend to make to each other sooner or later. But not everyone gets as far as recognizing what Fournier comes round to in a second letter four years later:

> The only serious criticism I have to make of you is the same as it has always been . . . you are not sufficiently like *le grand Meaulnes* of the first part of my novel, a chap in whose company anything is possible, who's got faith in himself . . . All the same I have to level this same charge against myself, and I must admit that if I were still a chap like that, I wouldn't be needing another to be him for me. I'm also to blame and the reproaches I'm addressing to you ought really to be directed against that awkward couple we used to make in years gone by.[13]

It is because of the need to make explicit the kind of thing Fournier is saying here that studies of the theory of friendship sometimes need to be written, if it is to bear its finest fruits. We inevitably show ourselves to each other by reflecting, or failing to reflect, real possibilities which no one but we ourselves can realize. It can become a common task, valuable to both parties where friendship is real and intimate, to ground our dreams and canalize our energies into authentic, healthy growth. The best of many human lives runs to waste for want of a discipline informed by the insight of love.

Whether friendship arises as a common and natural response to the demands of difficult and special situations, or as a factor in personal and psychological development, it is not generally felt as a challenge or a threat to those who are not immediately involved in it. But once one begins to talk about it as an ideal, to be consciously favoured and fostered, misunderstandings and suspicions can arise, of two of which it will be as well to dispose, at least in general terms, before we go further. Classical discussions of friendship are, as we shall see, not likely to deal directly with either, though they take very specific account of them by implication. In the first place, it has not been common until comparatively recent times to think of the lives of those who are not kings, rulers, or politicians by profession, as necessarily leading lives with a political dimension. It is scarcely possible for even the most politically indifferent in the modern world to remain unaware of the fact that the views and actions of the population at large have an enormous political influence. This is the case even where this influence is chiefly marked by passive acceptance, whether voluntary or enforced. Now this knowledge must be seen as creating a variable, but ultimately inescapable, degree of political responsibility. Deliberately to renounce the degree of responsibility one has is, in practice, to accept – and not just for oneself, but for others – that human beings may excusably be herded like cattle. Thus it comes about that friendship may not rightly be thought of as alternative to soiling one's hands with the activity which may be necessary to prevent such things happening, where that is clearly a duty. For that each human being has a dignity which ought not to be publicly alienated is a presupposition for friendship, as we shall speak of it here, to exist at all. No political system can prevent people from choosing to fall below their human dignity in one way or another. And in a society in which the quality of life is not enriched by the practice of the virtues which friendship encourages, it is quite likely that human dignity *will* tend to fall low. But a relationship of warmth between a few, bought at the price of acquiescing in gross human injustice to the many, cannot be and does not deserve to be called friendship at all. It is hoped that this will presently emerge clearly enough. When it was suggested above that situations *could* arise in which friendship might become the ultimate defence of human dignity, this was a remark based on the unhappy observation of political fact that situations already exist in many places in the world in which the right of friends to live and die for each other's good is the only political right which has not been, and cannot finally be, denied them. No one in their senses would wish to suggest that this is a commendable state of affairs, or one which ought not to be remedied.

The second reserve which sometimes arises in connection with the discussion of friendship is almost the opposite of the first. Those who do not fear that friendship may be thought of as an alternative to politics and political action are often, consciously or unconsciously, so exclusively politically-minded as to feel certain that friendship always implies a sinister form of hidden political power. They are apt to reach this conclusion by seeing that friendship is an enormous source of strength, not only for private life but also, if need be, for public action. Where they go on to suppose that the source of this strength is *invariably* sinister, they reveal not only a misunderstanding of the true nature of friendship, which it will be our purpose shortly to discuss, they also reveal a common feature of the more sinister psychology of groups. When friendship between people of the same or opposite sexes becomes more than a passing romantic dream, it is apt of its very nature to further independence of mind and personality in those who benefit from it. What this costs the people involved is the most hidden thing about it. It is the *results* that cannot be concealed, and it is these that are often experienced as sinister by larger groups. This phenomenon can, alas, be seen as frequently in cloisters as in other social, political, and religious groupings. And sometimes the more ideal-istic the group, the greater will be their temptation to identify with their ideals and to exact of their members a kind of conformity stultifying to all the human forces that alone could enable them regularly to renew their life. In so far as conformism produces conformists, these groups generally ensure their own death the more certainly they are chiefly preoccupied with fighting for their life. Eventually they breathe an atmosphere heavy with fear and none appear to them to be more sinister than those in the group who, however silent, are clearly neither cowed nor afraid. There are, unfortunately, in every century a good many legitimized exe-cutions, in one form or another, of those with whose challenge the group found it too uncomfortable to live. Given the appropriate circumstances, the argument of Caiaphas that 'it is expedient that one man die for the people'[14] never fails to find its ready sup-porters. In his alternative ending to *A Man for All Seasons* Robert Bolt makes his Common Man address the audience as 'friends' in what is truly that word's conspiratorial sense: 'It isn't difficult to keep alive, friends . . . just don't make trouble – or if you must make trouble, make the sort of trouble that's expected.'[15]

Thus to allude again to the haunting figure of Thomas More, of whom Erasmus wrote that 'one might say he was born for friend-ship',[16] is to be reminded of the invariable connection between humanism and friendship. Genuine friendships had, of course, certainly existed in the spontaneous groupings of the early Christian monastic tradition. That the matter was sometimes dis-cussed as a feature of ascetic training is clear from the fact that it forms the subject of one of the *Conferences* of John Cassian,[17] that eminent Latin reporter of the desert teachings. But one of the encouraging features of a hard life was perhaps more frequently accepted with gratitude rather than deliberately discussed. We have noticed how a great deal of the work of Bede and of the English missionary monks who followed in his tradition is penetrated with the sense of reliable connections to whom one could appeal for help and advice. But doubtless Richard Southern is right to say that it was first in the circle of Anselm of Bec in the late eleventh century that friendship returned as a topic on which to reflect and express oneself in a very specific way.[18] The impulse which generated the Cistercian reforms at the very end of that same century was a conscious and reflective return to the riches of the monastic past of the undivided Church. The fresh and glowing eloquence of Bernard of Clairvaux gave the reform its most influential, but not its only voice. A convergence of social and religious factors ensured the rapid spread of the movement and gave it a stability of purpose to which a number of gifted people felt drawn. Among these Aelred, who at the age of twenty-four had joined the abbey of Rievaulx not far from York, had not only known the founding group, under the leadership of a man who had been a secretary to Bernard; he had also been prepared by an unusual boyhood and upbringing at the court of the francophile King David of Scotland to play his role in the formative period of early Cistercian thinking. A cloister open to new impulses would make this possible for him, and even require it of him. First as master of novices in his early thirties and then as abbot of Rievaulx before he was forty, it was his duty to discuss with his fellow monks individually, and explain to them publicly, the ideals of their way of life. It is clear from many things he wrote that nothing appealed to him more about these ideals than the notion that the cloister was a school of Christian loving. No one knew better than he that it could be a very exacting school. But, as he understood it, it was not the purpose of this school to maim its pupils. It should create, rather, the conditions under which, by prayer and reflection, each could reach the wholeness appropriate to his gifts and bent. Aelred often returns to the image of the different kinds of trees in a fruitful orchard, or the variety of flowers in a border. As far as we know anything about his government of what, by the time of his death at the age of fifty-seven, had become a very large house, it was generous to the wayward and difficult to a degree that must have cost him many troubles and certainly brought down on his head a good deal of hostile criticism. No empty theoretician, he worked as and where he could at his own integration and that of others. The list of his surviving writings witnesses to his having made something of almost all the very varied influences on his life. Yet there is no reason to suppose it to be a mere literary convention that makes him refer to most of his works as instigated, at least in their final form, by others. In referring to himself as 'the handmaid of the Lord',[19] as he lay on his deathbed, he confirms the impression made by the more personal aspects of his writings as having been an unusually disponible person.

It must have been not many years before his death in 1167 that Aelred at last put together what is stylistically the most polished of his writings, *On Spiritual Friendship*.[20] As he tells us in his preface, Cicero's dialogue *On Friendship*[21] had been known to him long before he became a monk. What had struck him initially about this little book, produced in an intense period of literary activity at the end of a full life, was the contrast between the mature ideals of a pagan with philosophical training and his own youthful instability 'tossed hither and thither between changing loves and friendships'. Aelred's problems about a book whose ideals he had at first thought too demanding seemed rather different when he became a monk. Now he had made his choice, and began to see about him walking pictures of an ideal that was lived. One monk whom he specially admired is described in his first book, *A Mirror of Charity*, a kind of vast map of the theology of Christian love: 'The rule of our Order forbade us to speak, but his face spoke to me, his bearing spoke to me, his silence talked.'[22] This was an attraction which, as we know, was never put to the prolonged test of true friendship, for Simon died young. Perhaps a closer acquaintance would have anchored the romantic side of Aelred's nature sooner. This was left to others of whom we know, on the whole, even less. But Simon's evident and undivided devotion to the person of Christ must have emphasized that sense of the living presence of Christ as the centre of the monastic life which so discreetly yet definitely informs the rule of St Benedict. Attention to this point was one of the features of the Cistercian reading of the sixth-century rule, and brings out a contrast with the philosophical idealism of Cicero, or even the monastic pursuit of a rather abstract 'good', which we find in Cassian. It was this contrast which Aelred first experienced as a monk, as he was afterwards to say. This probably also explains why his very first essay on the role of friendship in the Christian life, which comes at the end of his *Mirror of Charity*, consciously avoids the direct use of Cicero. Aelred could not have known how deeply Ambrose, on whom he there chiefly depends as a source, had assimilated Cicero's thought, as he himself was later to feel free to do. He doubtless needed not just to think, but to *live* the matter through. When finally, at the request of a number of monks some of whom are featured in it by name, *On Spiritual Friendship* was written, Christ's presence was alluded to at the beginning and the end as naturally and as quietly as it is in the Holy Rule itself. That is to say, Christ is neither dragged in nor tacked on to a cleverly edited version of Cicero's dialogue. His is rather a presence which has transformed the model without betraying it. The dialogue form is retained, but Cicero's main points have been thoroughly and respectfully rethought in the light of Christian tradition, and enter the discussion as and when they are needed. The dimension which is really new is an explicitly Christian sense of the mystery of the human person which, at every turn, explains Aelred's moderation, forbearance with the inexplicable, and courageous conviction that 'it is already a great thing to attempt great things', especially since this is not done alone, but with others whose needs are like one's own. If one had to venture to name a contrast between this book and Aelred's first sketch of the ideal of friendship in the last chapter of his *Mirror of Charity*, one might say that the old enthusiasm and warmth are still authentically there. What has gone is a vaguely erotic haze, whose ultimately impersonal character is often mistaken by the unexperienced for love and leads to many a bitter disappointment. It is the object of books like *On Spiritual Friendship* to help one avoid these often mutually wounding catastrophes.

It seems honest and useful to offer here what may be called a 'reading' of Aelred's little book, rather than a detailed summary of its contents. Not only do summaries of this book tend to be inordinately dull and muddling since the dialogue form extended over three overlapping sections is unhelpful and unfamiliar to a modern reader; the difference of tempo and total remoteness of its setting also make it difficult for anyone without direct experience of monastic life in any form to envisage the importance and weight of what is not explicitly said. Later in this chapter we must at least name some of the problems created by the want of a 'setting' for the practice of Aelred's doctrine of friendship, other than that which friends can create for themselves. But, even on historical grounds, it would be entirely misleading to underestimate the importance of the fact that the three discussions of which this little treatise is composed are presumed to occur in a house in which people have a common way of life, rising at fixed times, praying and singing together, sharing meals together, and also being silent together both for reading and for sleep, at regular hours of the day and night. Thus one can say that the pattern of life which most people have to discover for themselves by mutual agreement is, in a general way, presupposed to the monastic life, and accepted in advance by those who choose to enter it. The fact of free choice at entry does not, of course, eliminate the difficulties which any life involves, arising out of temperament, fatigue, and other transitory factors. All these are explicitly allowed for in St Benedict's rule, as in most monastic rules. And when these rules are implemented, as they evidently were at Rievaulx in Aelred's day, there is sufficient room for very real spontaneity. But it remains the case that while the rhythm of monastic life can, at least theoretically, be used as a kind of pillow on which to abdicate from a large number of personal decisions, it has in-built 'awakeners' which even the most listless and indifferent can hardly hope indefinitely and invariably to avoid. It is St Benedict's view that it must be discovered of a novice 'whether he truly seeks God'. This, as we have tried to see perhaps most explicitly in chapter six of this book, can be for anyone a sufficiently mysterious business. But the purpose of the pattern of life Benedict lays down is to keep his monks aware of their sense of vocation by offering them the training of a very considerate school, which makes explicit allowances for variety in the capacities of its pupils.

If we bear all this in mind, we see that what Aelred explicitly intends to offer in his dialogue, *On Spiritual Friendship*, is an entirely optional extra help in the way of personal development and training. It goes without saying that anyone, in any way of life, if they are to mature must slowly find ways of enlisting all their capacities. There is also certainly no one who can achieve this on the basis of purely formal relationships alone, though even those with the greatest gifts for intimacy will probably be grateful for not needing to make new decisions about absolutely everything all the time. It has perhaps become a real problem for many in the modern world that this is exactly what is required of them in circles where total spontaneity is overvalued or improvisation is the rule. In circles like that, friendship in Aelred's sense can only rarely and against great obstacles survive since, as he sees it, however friendship may begin, it involves in the long run a considered and responsible choice. Why this is the case, we see if we ask his and Cicero's initial question, namely What *is* friendship? It is, says Cicero, 'an accord on things human and divine, accompanied by good will and love'.[23] The part of this definition which may well require most reflection on the part of a modern reader is hardly a serious problem for Aelred, given his monastic setting. He feels that Cicero's 'accord on things human and divine' could hardly be more completely fulfilled than it is said to have been in those sentences on the life of the early Church which appear in the Acts of the Apostles and were regularly cited later as the basis of the ideal of the common monastic life.[24] As we shall see presently, it is this deeply traditional sense of the monastic life as a form of the *Christian* life that makes Aelred's thought on the subject of friendship applicable in a wider context than that of which he is explicitly thinking.

In any case it is his comments on the words *good will* and *love* that introduce us to his more personal contribution to this subject. By 'love' Aelred understands 'personal affection' and by 'good will' the expression of that love in action. This commentary immediately becomes more enlightening when Aelred expresses his interest in the connection between the Latin words for friend and for love. Later in the discussion he will say in one sentence something that is already implicit in the beginning. The source and origin of friendship is love, that is to say, that love is presupposed to friendship, though they are not the same thing. 'For love can exist without friendship, though friendship can never exist without love.' It is also at this later point that Aelred makes it clear how extensively we must understand the concept of love. It can begin either as a spontaneous 'liking' or as an intuitive sense of human worth or, naturally, a combination of both. This helps us to feel more secure in our interpretation of what Aelred has earlier said about his understanding of the implication of the word 'love'. He speaks of it as that sort of 'directive desire that drives a rational being'.[25] It is his explicit use of the word 'rational' in this context, like his notion that love can be inspired by a judgement of worth, that reminds us that it is of a *human* Eros of which he is here speaking. Thus, although working with the minimal use of technical language, Aelred succeeds in keeping Eros in the picture from the start. As we shall see, he thinks that Eros *could* become debased under the name of friendship, but that of its original nature love is a good and innocent thing of which something can, and often should, be made.

But the first sign that there are going to have to be conditions for this happening occurs at this very early point where he is first noticing the connection between friendship and love. For he adds something on which he is going to feel the need to say a little more at the very end of the discussion. If love, in one or other of its forms, is the presupposition of friendship,[26] this must mean that a friend is the keeper of one's love or of one's very soul. This last is really probably the key to Aelred's view of the role and value of friendship, and it appears to have been too little emphasized. All that he has to say later about the rules which ought to govern friendship flow out of this sense of mutual responsibility which the notion of being a keeper of someone else's love or of their very soul implies. To share the responsibility for what drives someone else, what constellates their ideals, is a very considerable responsibility indeed. For it is, as we shall come to see, to take a real if limited responsibility for what is the most mysterious about things that are human. And not everyone is capable of this.

The reason why not everyone is capable of taking responsibility for the defence of the leading forces of someone else's life is that not everyone is capable of keeping a confidence. Let it be said at once, for Aelred's every return to this point confirms it, that the chief concern here is not secrecy for secrecy's sake. There are, about everyone, aspects of character which require time to develop as they should or, in some cases, to become integrating forces in a personality where they might otherwise lead to its destruction. We are, I believe, going to see that at the summit of the ideals Aelred is expounding there is the conviction that a personality can become so transparently authentic that it has nothing to hide. A few great saints seem to have struck those who knew them as being like this. It is not an argument for hypocrisy to say that there are few who at the beginning of their life can fail to be damaged by full exposure to public view. We need those who can bear to know us in our worst moments to be few enough and reliable enough for us to be able to avoid the strain of being put on our mettle all the time, especially on those points about which we are weakest. We need these people also to help us to see how we have to handle ourselves in a way that will not *for us* be warping, and to say a word of encouragement when we have got through what *for us* was a difficult matter. I was once able to turn cartwheels in a gymnasium in the presence of the only man who was ever able to make me feel capable of it. A physical example is deliberately chosen. There *are* matters of greater importance for our well-being and maturity which may need long spells of understanding and support from those who never give up looking beyond our failures and hesitations to our real possibilities. This is why, to return to Aelred, and to Cicero, both think that friendship has a touch of the everlasting about it. For in a certain sense it includes the end in the beginning.

Nothing about the honest demands of such an ideal ought to make us hesitate to pursue it, even if it should lead to our having to lay down our life for our friends – which, according to a word of Christ, is the greatest possible sign of love. It is a natural step for a Christian writer like Aelred, who thinks of this phrase, to remark that although the law of love requires us to love everyone, friend and enemy alike, only those can be called our friends to whom we are not afraid to commit what is in our heart. To do this with *everyone* would involve us in the kind of risks to which relationships which often go under the name of friendship are exposed. It is therefore necessary to take a look at those too. Cicero sounds a good deal the sterner of the two on the subject of what Aelred calls 'carnal friendship'. For Cicero says dismissively that there are some men who 'after the manner of cattle' [27] judge everything by the standard of pleasure. Aelred is nearer a modern view when he describes those sorts of relationships which are entered into 'without reflection, never submitted to sound judgement or ruled by reason, swept on through everything by the impulse of feeling'. [28] Such people are driven on by attractions which quickly burn themselves out. Whatever it is they feel for each other it cannot be love for, as the psalmist says, he who loves evil hates his own soul, and anyone who hates himself certainly cannot love anyone else. Then there are the 'mundane friendships, whose basis is less titillation, curiosity, and intrigue than a concern with straightforward gain'. They 'follow the bank-book'. [29] This too is generally 'friendship for a season', though it can happen that through the pursuit of common commercial interest a sort of permanent camaraderie is established. It does not, however, deserve to be compared with true friendship which is, of its nature, 'spiritual'.

When a modern reader looks at how Aelred describes this 'spiritual friendship' he will be aware that what is being depicted reaches the level of what is properly personal in the way that neither of the other kinds of friendship does. It is not sought with a view to advantage or for some ulterior motive, but for its value in itself as the fulfilment of a human need. Thus it is, in itself, its own fruit and profit. This last is a very Cistercian conviction about love, namely that true love is its own reward. And in that conviction, of course, lies hidden the factor which makes it really searching and demanding. For a love which is its own reward gives the other person the intrinsic value one gives oneself. It cannot be childishly egoistic, but pays the price of maturity, whether one's own or that of one's friend. To say this by way of comment is not to leap further than Aelred suddenly, but not inconsistently, seems to do when he says that his argument illustrates the meaning of a saying of Christ in St John's Gospel: 'I have appointed you that you should go and bear fruit' – that is to say, that you should love one another.[30] For this is indeed the overall context of these words in the Last Supper discourse on the 'new commandment' of love. There love and its expression in life and action are inseparably related. When Aelred goes on to point out how this doctrine illuminates the pure gift of creation – that God makes things which are good for their own sakes and not because he needs them – he returns to what is the governing thought in his early *Mirror of Charity*. But here, as earlier, Aelred points out that, although created things are given their own intrinsic value, everything from the stones in the brook to the trees in the wood is related in the cycle of life. Thus, although it is the mark of the things that are not God that they have their own value within the whole, it is part of their situation that they also have their needs. Aelred sees it as 'a very special incitement to love and friendship'[31] that God creates man *and* woman. For it is 'not good for man to be alone'. Even more interesting for some points to which we must return at the end of this chapter is Aelred's express conviction that the creation of the woman out of the side of the man is a sign of *equality* between the two. They are to be collateral. Nor, at least in the ideal world of human things, should there be superior and inferior, for equality is the *proper mark* of friendship. Thus, as Aelred sees it, to find one's way through the aberrations of un-regulated Eros back to this original sense of the truly personal value of each one, in love, is to reach the heights of wisdom itself.

This is perhaps all very well and good as a vision. But what the young monks want to know is this: Since friendship has become necessary as a *special* virtue, because not everyone wants what ought to be normal for everyone, would it not be better to leave aside something that sounds so demanding? Aelred cannot agree. Not only does friendship help life along, so that by joining shoulders we bear each other's burdens; it is, in fact, only one step short of the knowledge and love of God. With its help, 'from being the friend of man one becomes the friend of God, according to that word of the Lord in the gospel: No longer do I call you servants but friends'.[32] Pulled firmly back from any mystical flights, Aelred can be quite brief on what is simple and fundamental. True friendship can only arise between the good, grow between those who are growing, and reach its fullness between those who are spiritually mature. He agrees with, and for a moment, returns to Cicero in saying that 'it is no excuse for a sin, if you do it for the sake of a friend'.[33] For it is not difficult to show from experience that friendship cannot survive between people who cannot depend on each other's uprightness. At the sight of downcast faces in the group, Aelred hastens to add that it is not his intention to say that friendship can only exist between people who have no faults, but simply that one must have come far enough not to be indifferent to one's own integrity, for that is the basis on which friendship rests. Aelred would, in fact, gladly make his own Cicero's dictum that 'those who would take friendship out of life would seem to take the sun out of the world'. He later continues, in a characteristically personal passage: 'I would say that they are not so much men as beasts who say that one should live without being a comfort to anyone, taking no delight in another's good, causing no trouble to others by one's faults, loving no one, and caring to be loved by no one.'[34] Here again he dismisses what he calls mercenary as much as merely puerile friendships, all unregulated feeling, since both are contrary to that valuing of the person which true friendship fosters and expresses. As Aelred says: 'That man has not yet learned what friendship is, who wants of it any other reward than itself.'

This gradual emergence of the value of the developing person as the test of friendship makes it necessary to recapitulate certain points before the close of the dialogue. To be stable, friendship presupposes careful choice and a sensible period of probation before the door can be opened to its fullest development. Aelred names four things one needs to know about a friend. First comes his capacity for fidelity. This ability to stand the strains of friendship is, of course, intimately linked with what Aelred calls 'intention' – namely, what the friend expects from the relationship. This he regards as decisively necessary.[35] There can be no nonsense about this. The command to love one's neighbour as oneself implies that one must love oneself. Without this ultimate integrity, especially in relation to divine things, one will never be able to address one's friend as another self. Then there is the question of discretion which implies knowing when to say what. And finally there is the question of patience. As Cicero had already noted, there are some people who expect their friends to possess all the qualities they themselves still lack. Friendship, to endure, implies mutual help in growing. Because this function of furthering each other's human and spiritual maturity requires the intuitive discretion appropriate to something alive, Aelred returns near the end to the idea of the friend as one's soul-keeper. We have seen that, of the four qualities of a possible friend about which one needs to know, his intention is singled out by Aelred as decisively important. For someone who seeks something other than the friend's total good is bound, in the long run, to strike at the root of the relationship. Similarly, once the friendship is really growing, Aelred would think that it consists *chiefly*[36] in the open sharing of all one's secrets and plans. Although he does not expressly use the word 'soul-keeper' when he says this, Aelred clearly refers to this particular function, named at the beginning, for in the fulfilling of this lie both the value and the risk of the relationship. It is that one can be known by another as one knows oneself, for the advantage of seeing who one is and where one is going. Since Aelred with his complex Northumbrian background was not out of contact with the old Celtic world, it would be interesting to know whether he unconsciously remembered a very ancient tradition by which the man – not invariably a priest – who heard one's confession was known as a 'soul-friend'.[37] In any case it is impossible not to notice how very closely Aelred's description of the functioning of friendship corresponds to the function of a true spiritual director. He will not, of course, be that kind of bossy man whom St John of the Cross, in a word of unusual sharpness, once said was rather like a blacksmith.[38] But he will rather be the kind of person to whom one can reveal one's projects and weigh up their suitability in realistic relation to one's weaknesses and strengths. The deeper this intimacy goes, the more it requires an unselfish love, and the more it is likely to have to be sustained by prayer. It is this thought that enables Aelred to bring his treatise the full natural circle back to

Christ. At the beginning, although Christ is, as it were, *in principle* present with the two who are talking, he is there perhaps most because they desire not to exclude him. Later, through the caring for each other throughout the mysteries of life and development, Christ becomes almost palpably present.

> And so, praying to Christ for his friend, and longing to be heard by Christ for his friend's sake, he reaches out with devotion and desire to Christ himself . . . As though touched by the gentleness of Christ close at hand, he begins to taste how sweet he is and to feel how lovely he is. Thus, from that holy love by which he embraces his friend, he rises to that by which he embraces Christ.[39]

Because of this utter openness created by true caring, the two can look forward to that condition of things where no one any longer needs to hide his secrets, and where that which one can share with only a few on earth can be shared by everyone and God be 'all in all'.

Even some Christians in the modern world would probably feel disappointed if one closed this subject at this point without linking the notions Aelred has been discussing with problems about which we are used to being rather more articulate today. Only a few fundamental matters can be noted, for their detailed treatment would require whole books, some of which no one is yet ready to write. In the first place, it is necessary to note how Aelred's experience leads him instinctively to choose fidelity to the oldest convictions of Christian theology about the life of love. He cannot believe in a kind of tenuous 'supernatural' love which has no connection with the mysterious forces of Eros. But his own efforts lead him more and more in the direction of seeing that Eros is itself a blind force, even though it may be specific people who evoke it in us. Friendship consists in the transformation of Eros by love which is directed to the well-being and life of others as valuable in and for themselves, and not merely in their relationship to us. Aelred certainly did not know, but would not have been surprised to learn that St John Climacus, a Syrian monk of the late sixth century, had written: 'Those who have been humbled by their passions may take courage. For even if they fall into every pit and are trapped in all the snares and suffer all maladies, yet after their restoration to health they become physicians, beacons, lamps, and pilots for all.'⁴⁰

It is sad that so many of these lamps have been so long hidden under bushels. For there are few who do not need to be faced with the fact that many of their first impulses of love are profoundly indifferent to the real person, whose name they may be whispering under their breath. These things need to be explicitly recognized, not only by those who propose to themselves abiding friendship, but by those who seek stable marriages. Neither the one nor the other can endure if untransformed Eros is their necessarily precarious link. For it is a link that is bound to break at the first serious test. If Aelred can say that *some* kind of love is presupposed to friendship, though they are not the same thing, so one can say that friendship is necessarily presupposed to happy marriage, though these may not always be the same thing.

At this point it is as well to say that just as marriage sometimes goes to pieces for want of the dimension of friendship, so it is an illusion to suppose that the fact of physical intimacy in marriage will or should lead to the abolition of personal integrity. Not even the most loving wife or friend can relieve us of the burden of being ourselves and indeed to promise or expect this is the beginning of a betrayal. There is a very consistent tradition among the Fathers of the Church that each human being is, in its depths, so valuable that there is something about it which cannot be given away. It is that aspect of our being which links us to that ultimate mystery which God is. St John Chrysostom, whose teaching about marriage is so consistently positive,⁴¹ makes a point of saying in one of his commentaries that St Paul is quite certainly speaking to the married and unmarried alike, when he says: 'I have espoused you to one husband that I may present you a chaste virgin to Christ.' This is certainly sound exegesis and, as St John says, the reason why this is so is that 'the incorrupt soul is a virgin, though she have a husband'.⁴² In other words, that integrity which is implied in the secret name of the Book of Revelation is not renounced, but protected by marriage, as it ought to be by any friendship worthy of the name.

But this is, of course, still not the complete story, even in its broadest outlines. That story is better understood by reflecting as the Fathers do on the universal significance of the image of the *Theotokos*, the one who is the God-bearer because she is both virgin and mother. The integrity which she keeps in relation to God is meaningful, even in relation to men, because it is the source of a fruitfulness which nothing can destroy or diminish. And it is, further, a kind of fruitfulness which is as appropriate to a man as it is to a woman. Indeed the great teachers are never afraid of insisting, as St Paul does, that 'in Christ there is neither male nor female'.[43] This is not because either is abolished, but because both, in that equality on which we have seen Aelred insisting, are experienced by being transcended in love. Guerric of Igny, another Cistercian abbot of this same early period, says to his brethren in one of his sermons:

> O my brethren, this name of mother . . . is common to all of you who do the will of the Lord. For all of you are indeed mothers of the son who is born to you and in you, in so far as you conceive in the fear of the Lord and bring forth the spirit of salvation. Take care, then, holy mother, take care of the newborn child, until Christ be formed in you, who is born of you.[44]

The fact that virtually no one would dream of saying any such thing to a group of people of either sex today is a matter that deserves pondering. The result of doing so will not invariably give us cause for unmixed satisfaction.

While the points being made here are explicitly connected with and arise out of profound and central Christian theological convictions, the need for something rather like them will often be discovered by non-Christians. This does not, of course, argue for the truth of the oldest Christian ascetics of love, though it is a suasion in favour of their harmonious compatibility with mature human needs. Indeed it may be asked whether any truly humanistic view of life can ever be satisfactorily sustained without a deep and certain conviction of the value of each human life in its dynamic development. Of all the studies of Turgenev, some aspects of whose work we were considering in chapter three of this book, there is probably none more informed and impressive than a longish essay by Isaiah Berlin, recently reprinted.[45] This essay has as its sub-title 'Turgenev and the liberal predicament', and it explains probably as well as anyone ever could why Turgenev was so tormented by a genuine sympathy with radical views and quite unable to give any political expression of them his unreserved support. But the essay is curiously silent on the one subject which may surely explain why Turgenev, as he knew only too well, was never able to be accepted by thinkers of either the left or the right.

It is a reserve in him which has nothing whatever directly to do with politics, but a great deal to do with that painful distrust in *any* ultimate value in human life, which does not have to be clearly expressed to be felt. It would be quite contrary to the intentions of this book to insist that the two writers chosen to represent the post-Christian sense of life as an illusion, with 'nature' as the heartless enemy, were the best or fairest choice. Both, as is well known, were men with different and never wholly resolved emotional problems in their personal life, which may in part be responsible for their tendency to feelings of hopelessness and frustration. But it certainly looks as though what both men – and certainly not the only ones in modern times – lacked was any view of human beings which would enable them to feel that all they found most moving about them was in any serious way ultimately valuable. It is, again, not the intention of this book to decide whether any satisfactory view *can* be found apart from a Christian one, but merely to expose the acute need for such a view if the possibility of meaningful action and meaningful love is not to be withered at its root. As a story told with consummate art by St Luke at the end of his Gospel reminds us, there were even those in the circle of Christ whose doubts went so far, after the crucifixion, that they felt the whole story might have to end with the words: 'We had hoped . . .'

# 9

## 'AND WAS MADE MAN'

Since the beginning of chapter six of this book we have been consciously moving on the frontiers of mystery. For these frontiers defend themselves and cannot be crossed either by will or ingenuity. It is frequently possible to turn one's back on them, or to steer a course which keeps one just clear of them most of the time. But this can only be done at the cost of a very considerable human deprivation. Naturally, no one can hope in the course of a lifetime to meet many people of the imposing stature of some of those whose lives we were considering in chapter seven. But everyone can hope, and most of us have an urgent need, to go far enough in the development of our capacity for love to encounter at least one other person sufficiently intimately to know the wonder and joy and awe of sharing the responsibility for their very soul. This encounter is more likely than any argument to lead us to an indelible awareness of the essential aloneness and uniqueness of each human being, which cannot ultimately be invaded, but only supported and reverenced at the point where it stands on the brink of a hiddenness which is not altogether its own.

It is these values and these experiences which are, as it were, seen in terrible reverse in one scene at the beginning of the tradition about the arrest and suffering of Christ, of which all the evangelists have *something* to say. Not untypically St Luke, reflective artist that he is, actually has *two* mockings: one before the prisoner is delivered to Pilate for judgement, and another in an interlude before Herod, where the reversal of values is heavily underlined by the use of a gorgeous robe.[1] That something of the kind actually occurred there is no reason to doubt – and not only because it seems so often to occur to those whose very existence appears to challenge their fellows deeper than they can bear. In this case it is not only the art of the gospel writers, but the existence of the Christian faith at all that must convince us that sooner or later the particular person round whom they revolve posed and poses in a disquieting way the question: Who *is* this?

There is on the wall of a cell he decorated in the convent of St

Mark in Florence a painting of Fra Angelico so unexpected in its power to suggest the significance of the mocking of Christ that it seems surprising that it has not been more frequently mentioned.[2] The seated figure of St Dominic in the right foreground is often reproduced as a harmonious independent unit. But his absorption is not that of a man reading the book that lies open on his lap. He, like the feminine figure opposite him, is profoundly withdrawn. This is natural enough if what is occupying them is connected with the bewildering scene in the background, at which they are not looking. This scene depicts spiritual violence reduced to its simplest terms. There is, as we must say in a moment, a dimension of this unusual picture which we should hardly expect easily to find later than the death of Angelico in 1455, and which we should more readily associate with a time fifty years or even a century earlier. But should we not also expect to have to look more than 500 years *later* to find these hands flying in the air that strike the face, pluck the beard, or doff a hat, or the trunkless man who launches a shaft of spittle at the haloed head? Picasso or Chagall might have done it; but who else in the long interval of progressively conventionalized, humanized, and often sentimentalized representations of this particular scene? Even the psychological fantasies of Hieronymus Bosch belong to another world. For this synthesis of the evangelical details, and possibly an element of popular tradition, is primarily a monumental human and theological statement.

It is doubtless legitimate, and even inevitable, to read it at these two levels. The blindfolded figure of the seated Christ corresponds to the gospel accounts of the horseplay which included the requiring of a blindfolded man to say who had hit him. But the veiled face is also an unconscious reduction of even the human dignity of the victim. The mockers need to do something like this, even for their own sakes. It is impossible to mock what one might suddenly find oneself compelled to take seriously, and thus be forced to rein in one's outraged passions. Mockers and mocked can, of course, have agreed to be merely playing a game. But true mockery – which this is evidently meant to be – requires the mockers not only to forget that they themselves are human, but to be able to forget this about the one whom they desire to humiliate. The unanswerable argument of sheer meaningless violence must be allowed free play.

To achieve this total abolition even of human dignity was obviously difficult in the case of Christ, as a number of details in the gospels are concerned to stress. Angelico tells us the same by the

authoritative calm of the seated figure in its robe of almost transparent white. Even the Christ of the transfiguration and resurrection in adjacent rooms [3] are not more, and perhaps really not so,
imposing. And herein lies the theological statement, and the element in the picture which separates it so firmly from the products
of a piety of a quite different kind, which has gradually come to
affect not only the way people tend to read the gospels, but even the
way some professional theologians tend to think. The picture
conveys a profound sense of shock, read at either level, but there is
not a hint of anything simply pathetic about it.

To an Englishman who knows her a little it may seem natural to go
back about fifty years [4] to that day in May 1373 when Julian of
Norwich had her revelations, or 'showings', of divine love. For in
the little book which records these and their meaning we can, with
hindsight, glimpse how two kinds of piety about the passion of
Christ could come to a serious divide. [5] Mother Julian tells us, by
way of introduction, how before the grave illness during which the
visions occurred, she had long cherished three spiritual desires.
The first of these was to have 'truer recollection of Christ's passion'. The phrase is a careful one, and its deepest meaning the
book as a whole makes clear. But at its first mention we are led to
suppose, and rightly, that she means the 'recollection' to include
that 'going down' in true compassion which must have been that of
the friends of Jesus who watched him die, and even means some
intuition of the sufferings of Christ himself. [6] There will, as we
know to our cost – for their sentiments are reflected in some of the
more lubricious hymns sung by Catholics and Protestants alike in
the last hundred years – be later writers and artists who will not
hesitate to depict the sufferings of Christ as an object designed
primarily to evoke our pity. This intention can sometimes be
exploited with such a degree of emotional self-indulgence as unwittingly to reverse the most fundamental New Testament values.
A Christ who needs our pity a great deal more than we need his
would hardly have been the object of the mocking described in the
gospels, and certainly not challenging enough to need crucifying.
From any temptation to create this, among many possible Christs
of our imagination, Mother Julian was preserved in advance by a
deeply traditional sense of values. Not only does she tell us at the
point where she introduces this subject that she had never been
able to pray about this desire for deeper insight into the passion

without reserve, but that she had actually forgotten about it at the time when the 'showings' occurred. It was really only the third desire about which she had been able to pray as a later saint, Philip Neri, would have said *assolutamente*, undividedly. This was also the only desire she had always had with her. In its composite of three aspects it embraces everything an ordinary Christian of the faith of the undivided Church could desire, whether he ever has visions or not – 'the wound of true contrition, the wound of loving compassion and the wound of longing with my will for God'. It was really this third desire which seems to have regulated and swallowed up the other two on the day on which Julian was believed to be dying, as she had once felt she wanted, and the ministering priest held up before her a crucifix. She found herself wanting the 'compassion which would lead to longing for God'. 'I never', she adds, 'wanted any bodily vision or any kind of revelation from God, but the compassion which I thought a loving soul could have for our Lord Jesus, who for love was willing to become mortal man.' Almost at once she was caught up in two apparently contradictory experiences, about which, as the two drafts of her 'showings' reveal, it took her many years to decide how to write. On the one hand she saw the blood running down from under the crown of thorns, and on the other was simultaneously overwhelmed by the joy of God in three Persons. Throughout the 'showings' the thought of Jesus was, she insists, inseparable from that of God in Trinity. This ultimate mystery, to which, as Mother Julian says at various points, the incarnation and passion give us access, is very profound. Words are difficult to use about it, and always will be as long as we live. The experience gave Julian the simple conviction 'that God is the Creator and the protector and the lover'.[7] This business of not being able to talk adequately about it all is, in fact, going to go on until God shows the reconciliation of the apparently irreconcilable in the opening of a secret of another kind than that special secret of which Christ himself is the embodiment. It seems right to use the phrase 'special secret' about the person of Christ. For Mother Julian herself makes a clear distinction between the great ultimate reconciling secret about which it is not right even to speculate now, and those secrets which God wishes us to know *now*, which are the ordinary Christian teachings.[8] These teachings are, to use Mother Julian's own word, 'open' secrets, because *something* correct can be said about them. Their essential nature remains lost in the mystery of God. And the chief of these is undoubtedly the person of Christ. Probably many discussions of the incarnation, that is to say of the doctrine of Jesus as truly God and truly man, would take a different form if it were from the beginning more explicitly borne in mind that the primitive, undivided Christian tradition, whether 'mystical' or not, has from the first prayed to Christ as to God, while strongly insisting upon the reality of his birth of a human mother. Perhaps in the latter point lies the problem of what can be correctly 'said' about this secret. It has been so from the early days of Christianity, and still is in our own day, though usually for reasons that look rather different from the old ones. It would be as well to remind ourselves at once of a point to which we shall return later in this chapter, that the notion of speaking of Christ as an 'open secret' of God is not a novel fancy either of the writer of this chapter or of Mother Julian. It would not be a misleading way of paraphrasing the phrase in the letter to the Christians of Colossae, which says that Christ is *the* mystery of God. 'God's secret, which is nothing less than Christ,' as Bishop Wand writes.[9] It is noteworthy that in her account of the opening of her experiences Mother Julian, although not designedly thinking about her, is led straight from the strange antithesis of suffering and joy, to the thought of Mary. She sees her 'marvelling with great reverence that God was willing to be born of her who was a simple creature created by him'. In general terms, Mother Julian will say that among all the means God has given to help us to understand and live with that goodness in which we are 'clad and enclosed' . . . 'the chief and principal intermediary is the blessed nature which he took of the virgin, with all the intermediaries which preceded and followed, which are a part of our redemption.'[10] It is doubtless this fundamental conviction that made it so difficult for Mother Julian to sort out what the beginning of the 'showings' seemed to be trying to teach her. Her experience forbids her *either* to let go of the reality of the physical sufferings of Christ *or* of the awareness that this is truly God involving himself in the human situation in a unique way. The way is unique because the name 'Jesus' applies to a person who is truly human and truly divine. Hence, too, it is impossible for Mother Julian to forget the Trinity, a doctrine about the ultimate mystery of God himself which had to find *some* expression as a result of the belief that Jesus Christ should be accepted as God and not simply honoured as man. No one should allow themselves to be fobbed off with the suggestion that the prolonged struggles of early Christianity to find

correct ways of talking about the mystery from which it takes its
name were a lightly dispensable luxury overlaying a primitive
belief of innocent, rustic simplicity. Neither those trying to take a
first serious look at orthodox Christian belief, nor those trying to
look at it afresh, while already claiming to hold it in some form, will
be able reasonably to satisfy themselves that there is no problem to
be faced here, embedded in the very earliest evidence we have. Of
course, belief in Jesus Christ as truly God and truly man as an
experience is in its own way always simple, whether it is a Galilean
fisherman or a trained philosopher who has it. It is simple with the
evidence of all that presents itself in a way that cannot be denied.
Problems only begin if one is asked or feels driven to *talk* about it.
Then, when all the documents of early Christianity have been
examined with rigour, and doubts and queries multiplied, there
would still seem to be no room for doubt that the crucifixion
occurred because of something which is most conveniently sum-
marized in an accusing phrase incorporated in St John's Gospel,
'because you, being a man, make yourself God'.[11] Any of the major
New Testament materials will confirm that this was what Jesus,
though clearly truly human, was believed, directly or indirectly, to
have claimed. That his followers accepted the truth of this claim
about him and gave some kind of liturgical expression to it was
among the very few simple things an interested pagan governor
could discover about Christians, living in Bythinia in the early
second century.[12] To try to circumvent this, one of the most
consistently attested facts about late Roman antiquity, argues a
degree of perversity not likely to be amenable to reason.

It is, of course, a rather different question to ask what role reason
should play in the consideration of these primordial Christian
claims. To this question the greater Church Fathers were acutely
alive, being in most cases men with the finest education available in
their day. They also frequently became gifted and lively writers
and, even in the defence of their faith, left little to be desired as
representatives of all that was best in late antique culture. It is
therefore an important and noteworthy fact that by far the greater
number of views about the person of Christ which the undivided
theological tradition of the whole Church felt it had to reject are
marked by an attempt at an imaginative philosophical consistency
and plausibility ultimately inconsistent with the irreducible mystery of faith. To embark upon a full discussion of this subject for

the patristic period would require a whole book, if not several
books. But those who have been accustomed to read a great medieval theologian like St Thomas Aquinas in the light of his predecessors, unrefracted through the often curious lenses of later
times, will probably find it just as useful to notice a few of the
things he has to say on this subject, neglected as they often are
today. It is not necessary to agree with all that St Thomas will find
it possible and desirable to say about the person of Christ to feel
that here, as generally elsewhere, he has an uncanny sense for the
minimal essentials of the claims of the unbroken Christian tradition. In reference to the perspective in which this present book is
being written, it will seem apt to turn to the only one of St
Thomas's works which has at least a superficial accessibility today.
For, although his monumental dialogue with Islamic philosophy,
as he knew it, is marked by the scholastic forms in which he had
been trained and was continuing to work in the second half of the
thirteenth century, it nevertheless has something of the shape and
style of a modern book.

Thomas begins the impressive final section, in which he is
intending to speak of the scandal of the person of Christ and all that
follows from it, with a wisdom quotation from the Book of Job:

> Lo, these things are said in part, of his ways: and seeing we have
> heard scarce a little drop of his word, who shall be able to behold
> the thunder of his greatness? [13]

This sentence produces a marked change of tempo and mood,
which those who read the work slowly without commentary will
savour. In this single phrase of his choice Thomas finds an allusion
to several different, though interrelated, matters. In the first place,
it is connatural to man to derive his knowledge from his senses.
Thus there is no true proportion between the knowledge of created
things, however noble, and God, whose mystery cannot be apprehended by the senses. Nevertheless, since all these things are
wisdom's work, they hint at ultimate wisdom in two general ways.
They suggest an ultimate wisdom in their origin by bearing
wisdom's mark, each according to its kind. They also suggest the
unified nature of that wisdom in their interrelationship of de-
pendence and variety, traceable to causes of a more interiorly
complex and unified kind. Thus it is that these 'ways of God'
could, at least theoretically, be used as a way of ascending to some
sort of dim or partial knowledge of him. It does not matter that this

is implicitly a very neo-platonic view of the world, at least as Thomas describes it. For his comment on it is the same as it would be for any other view, even the modern scientific one. He thinks that *this* road to knowledge of God is full of the doubts and uncertainties that everyone who works with the deliverances of the senses sooner or later discovers, either in their own methods or in the things they study. Thomas never says more clearly than he does earlier in this same big book that, even the kinds of argument which he himself believes conclude *in principle*, are not necessarily *seen* to conclude by more than a mere handful of people.[14]

For these reasons God has been good enough to show us things we could not know if he did not reveal them. There are thus three kinds of human knowledge about divine things. A first, which could be the term of a sound investigation of nature. A second, by which divine truth is spoken of without being made self-evident, thus making the claim of faith upon the mind if it is to be embraced at all. And a third by which the human mind is raised to the immediate sight of divine things. The second kind is like those 'little drops' which come by the hearing of faith and are still, as St Paul insists, far from seeing face to face, the only evidence which could be compared to thunder. Thus the wisdom sentence from the Old Testament makes a suitable link with the matters Thomas will now discuss. Those who have read his book as a whole will also find it appropriate to recall something he said near the beginning. He observes that 'there are some people so confident of their mental powers that they believe they can measure the nature of everything, judging that what is evident to them is unreservedly true and what is not, simply false.'[15] At least he himself has taken three-quarters of his huge project to ventilate matters which he believes will suggest the truth about divine things or will remove obstacles to their acceptance. Now he must talk about those things which are proposed precisely for belief. Thus we must see what those things are and accept the fact that we are entering obscurities of another kind than those we meet in philosophical or scientific studies. Here are mysteries about which no one can claim perfect knowledge in this life, since it is precisely as mysteries that we meet them. 'But', adds Thomas, 'it must be shown that these things are not *opposed* to reason, so as to defend them from the attacks of unbelief.'[16]

Although Thomas explicitly formulates this principle several times in his writings in a way that may justly be thought of as characteristic of his firm theological confidence, it would be a mistake to think of it as a merely personal view. It makes explicit, in a form determined by Thomas's own interests and methods, a profound conviction of the undivided Church, which also commands the discussions on the person of Christ. This conviction of the Church, which is truly universal in its outlook and genuinely 'catholic', is that although the word of creation, with its own proper obscurities, and the word of revelation are not the same *in kind*, they do not proceed from two different gods, and therefore cannot be in ultimate disharmony. If one looks back, for instance, at Athanasius in the fourth century, one will find him expressing a clear preference for using the text of Scripture to discuss a theological matter like the doctrine of the Trinity. But should anyone bring forward a philosophical concept in the discussion, he shows himself by no means backward in the analysis of how far this may be compatible with sound belief.[17] He, in so many ways a key figure in the formulation of the Church's view of the incarnation, was himself to use a philosophical term in defence of orthodoxy, where it seemed helpful.[18] This very initiative is itself, as later in St Thomas, the expression of a fundamental conviction of faith. It also reminds us of the very different way older theologians regarded the appeal to Scripture from that which has been, and still sometimes is, taken for granted since the Reformation.[19]

Returning to Thomas, as he introduces his presentation of the mysteries proposed for our belief, we find him seeing that they fall into three groups. There are those things which concern what God is, the doctrine of the Trinity; those things which God has done which reason cannot penetrate, such as the mystery of the incarnation and what follows from it; and finally those things which man still expects God to do for him, like the resurrection and the glorification of the body. In each case Thomas proceeds by presenting some traditional scriptural texts for these articles of belief, and only then discusses the difficulties which may be thought to arise out of them. When he comes to the real *context* of the incarnation, which will show how it links both the doctrine of God and the doctrine of man, he says:

> If anyone considers earnestly and devoutly the mystery of the incarnation, he will find such a depth of wisdom as exceeds human knowledge. 'For the folly of God is wiser than men,' as the apostle says. Thus it is that to faithful meditation more and more remarkable reasons for this mystery will be shown.[20]

These two sentences are one of the many hints of the contemplative side of St Thomas the thinker, which link him to those writers of whom we must speak later. For the moment, economy suggests going to the last section of his great unfinished survey of theology, which opens with a clear statement of some of the fundamental aspects of the doctrine of the incarnation, and gives us some of his reserves on certain kinds of even devout speculation about it.

Here, the starting-point for discussion is the scandal or the suitability of God's becoming man. Like creation itself, this event is to be seen as the expression of God's goodness, as the great theologians and councils of the past have seen it. Although he does not mention this at once, Thomas will not forget that, like creation itself, the incarnation is dependent on God's choice and so, in an important sense, deeply obscure to us, save in so far as it manifests itself. If it seems to be a shock that the unchangeable should involve himself in the world of change, Thomas answers by saying that the change occurs, not in God himself, but in the world to which God unites himself in a new way, or rather, *it with him*. To begin with Thomas concentrates his interest on what we should nowadays agree, looked at historically, was the determining factor in many of the debates on the person of Christ in the early Church – namely, the relation of the incarnation to its revealed purpose, the salvation or healing of man. Thomas at once agrees with anyone who says that, as far as we can see, this might have been achieved in some other way.[21] All the way through his discussion Thomas will keep firmly before him that the possibilities in this area are vast, but that we can only talk about what is given in the Christian claims, and that involves us in problems enough. Taking the incarnation as given, its suitability is explored and expounded in a vast mass of patristic writing both Latin and Greek. Thomas gives a very representative slice, more representative than he can explicitly have known. No one will be surprised at the large number of quotations from Augustine, which also have a more representative quality than those who do not read Augustine often imagine about him.[22] More interesting in their mediatorial function between East and West are the two quotations from a Christmas sermon of Leo the Great that has long been, and still is, in use in the Latin breviary. Especially significant is the exhortation to Christians to remember that they have become 'sharers in the divine nature', as one New Testament letter has it.[23] With an equally sure instinct Thomas has also chosen a single sentence which exactly expresses a conviction dear to Athanasius and other Greek writers, and sometimes claimed by polemical authors to be an exclusively Greek notion. 'God was made man that man might become god.'[24] Under the cover of some authoritative name or another this notion certainly continued to circulate in the West at least until the time of St Thomas. It is when Thomas confronts the question as to whether the incarnation would have occurred but for the fact of sin that he feels he has to make an important statement of principle, which deserves to be considered seriously in any theological context. He admits that he does not really know the answer. For it must be said that 'those things which occur by God's will alone, beyond all the exigencies of creation, cannot be known to us save in so far as Holy Scripture, by which we know God's will, tells us about them.'[25] As this particular article and this whole section of his work show, Thomas is not blind to the aesthetics of these matters, but very reserved about allowing them to occupy the centre of the picture.

Having, then, kept the fact of the incarnation in the only context about which tradition is undivided, what can be said about the phrase 'God became man'? Thomas will, in a very short summary, suggest that unacceptable views about its meaning can be classified in one of two ways. They will tend, on the other hand, either to make the person of Jesus not really God *or* really man, but some kind of mixture of the two, a sort of semi-divine hero. Or they may tend to think of Jesus as *a* man in some quite ordinary sense, in whom God operates and lives permanently and decisively, he being as it were a passive instrument of God. For what must be one quite rare occasion Thomas resolves the discussion between the alternatives he has been reviewing by quoting the authority of a council, which he introduces by saying that the Catholic Church holds the balance between the contending points of view. The council he quotes is the Second Council of Constantinople, but he also makes general reference to the preceding councils as condemning any other view than that the two natures, the human and the divine, in their integrity, are united in the person of the Son of God.[26] It was this that the Council of Chalcedon had defined, declaring that Christ was true God and true man, in the two natures unconfused. A modern patristic scholar has made a not wholly dissimilar assessment of the theoretical factors at work in creating the need to find 'a middle position'. He says:

On the one hand was the conviction that a saviour must be fully divine; on the other was the conviction that what is not assumed is not healed. Or, to put the matter in other words, the source of salvation must be God; the locus of salvation must be man. It is quite clear that these two principles often pulled in opposite directions. The Council of Chalcedon was the Church's attempt to resolve, or perhaps rather to agree to live with, that tension. Indeed, to accept both principles as strongly as did the early Church is already to accept the Chalcedonian faith.[27]

What is, perhaps, especially striking about this way of describing the issues is the suggestion of a dynamic tension, something or rather *somebody* alive. For, of course, all through its history, then as now, the Church is living with somebody. The question is, who? It is the answer to this question which can never be finally resolved in satisfactory words, though more or less satisfactory words may from time to time be found for answering particular sorts of questions about this person. At the same time as defining the correctness of speaking in the way we have seen about the person of Christ, Chalcedon reaffirmed what had long been the expression of the Church's conviction, namely the use in relation to Mary of the title *Theotokos* or 'Mother of God'. This title was and is understood to mean that Jesus truly had a human mother and that she was, according to his humanity, the mother of the one who was in fact the second person of the Trinity, and so God incarnate.[28]

At this point it will be useful to go back a further twenty years to a sermon preached on this very title by St Proclus in Constantinople, the city of which he was to become patriarch. It looks as though it may have been intended for the feast of the Annunciation, the festival which celebrates that mystery of Mary, whose acceptance of God's condescension had so impressed Mother Julian. Proclus begins by referring to Mary as virgin and mother, and invites all mankind to dance. For

> He who is by nature impassible became in mercy most passible. Christ did not by progress become God – heaven forbid – but in mercy he became man, as we believe. We do not preach a deified man; we confess an incarnate God. His own handmaid he acknowledged as his mother – he who in essence is without mother and in the incarnation is without father ... The self-same person is born without mother, as creator, and without father, as creature ... He became man (he himself knows how –

to explain this miracle is beyond the power of speech) . . . and the transgression of those who killed him he turned into the salvation of the transgressors.

In accordance with the oldest Christian traditions Proclus sees the prophets, 'the physicians who were sent to us', as anticipating this fulfilment. 'When the prophets saw that our wounds were beyond human resource, they cried for the heavenly physician.' The preacher piles up a collection of texts from the Old Testament, and continues in a style full of biblical allusions:

He came to save, but he also had to suffer. How were both possible? Mere man had no power to save. One who was solely God could not suffer. What happened then? He who was God became man. By what he was, he saved; and by what he became, he suffered. When therefore the Church saw the synagogue crowning him with thorns, she bewailed the outrage in the words: Daughters of Jerusalem, go forth and behold the crown with which his mother crowned him. For he both wore the crown of thorns and undid the sentence of thorns. For the self-same was in the Father's bosom and in the virgin's womb, in a mother's arms and on the wings of the wind, adored by angels and dining with tax-collectors.[29]

Although, as anyone can see, this way of talking is not quite like those glimpses of the Church's first sermons we get in the Acts of the Apostles or in passages of the New Testament letters, it is clearly in some genuine kind of continuity with them. It is not denying that Jewish inheritance without which its language and allusions are not fully comprehensible, but it is also working free of it. A still earlier writer, Athanasius, is very explicit on this subject, and the full implications of what he says have still to be weighed as completely as they will probably have to be. In his wonderful little book *On the Incarnation*, echoes of which occur throughout the entire tradition of orthodox theology, Athanasius is explicit on the universal significance which the Jewish Scriptures have acquired in the context of the incarnation of the Son of God. 'Neither was the law for the Jews alone, nor were the prophets sent for them only, but though sent to the Jews and persecuted by the Jews, they were for all the world a holy school of the knowledge of God and the conduct of the soul.'[30] This must seem to a modern reader to be an invitation, if not a challenge, to take a serious general

view of the message of the Jewish Scriptures about the mystery of
God.

We should doubtless be safest to put ourselves into the hands of
a scholar who devoted his life to these studies and seems to have
tried explicitly to grapple with the problem of what the Jewish
Scriptures say, and what they do not say. In the introduction
to each of the two volumes of his *Old Testament Theology*, Gerhard
von Rad states with great modesty how young his enterprise still
is, and what are its limits. In particular, no one with a special
interest in the interpretation of religious texts, whether Jewish or
otherwise, will fail to note his insistence that a view about their
meaning is always implicit in even the most elementary investigation of them. As the second of these prefaces points out, one
can either attempt to treat the Old Testament as a self-contained
entity, or one can see it principally as 'the ceaseless saving movement of promise and fulfilment'. When this is our view, and it
is the one which von Rad finds himself compelled to adopt, 'then
it becomes apparent how the expectations it contains fan out ever
wider. Then it is absolutely open, and the question of its relationship to the New Testament becomes the question *par excellence*.'[31]
As he later says, a survey of Jewish history gives us the impression
of 'a lack of repose – and the constant emergence of new religious
ideas seems to leave her a stranger in time'.[32] Traces of this
mysterious pointing towards the future are to be found in the least
forward-looking of the Hebrew writings. When we consider the
work and teaching of the prophets, we are struck by their absorption in something quite new that God is going to do. There is
in them 'a mysterious combination of close attachment to the old
saving tradition and its radical supersession'. In their handling
of this accretion of the past the prophets are moving with a charis-
matic freedom. It is, von Rad thinks, something we must bear
in mind when we see the way in which the apostles treated their
references to the Old Testament. For there is an element of
continuity here. The apostles no more improvised than the prophets did. Yet although the apostles felt more bound to the texts
of Jewish tradition than some of the prophets, their convictions
led to a completely new interpretation of the Old Testament. 'Every
page of the New Testament rings with the exultant awareness of
standing in a new era of God's activity.' Such a transformation
of the traditional material in the light of a new saving event was
as proper for early Christians as were many other transformations

which had already taken place in the Old Testament itself. 'The Apostles clearly take the view that the texts of the Old Testament only attain their fullest actuality in the light of their fulfilment.' We can and must say that, in the gospels, Jesus speaks as the one who 'fulfils' the Old Testament. As von Rad says, the foundations of Christianity rest on the Old and New Testaments taken together.[33] This is, of course, a conviction to which the oldest liturgical texts have always given a clear expression.

However difficult it may be to define this correctly, one of the chief convictions which runs through the two Testaments is that it is in history that God reveals the secret of his person. That 'lack of repose', referred to above, means that Israel never developed anything like the Greek view of an organic cosmos, and was again prevented from settling down to the seductions of a mythology of the world. Von Rad finds what he calls 'a breakthrough into the secular world' in the historical works ascribed to the humanists of the age of Solomon. Nearly-related to these is the wisdom literature at which we have been looking in connection with the Book of Job. The isolated twenty-eighth chapter of that book von Rad regards as the last attempt to shed light on the world by this method.[34] The prophets evidently made an advance into the realm of the secular of a very much bolder and more far-reaching kind. Their very assertion that God ruled the other nations, and not Israel alone, drew them all, however puzzling this might seem, into the sphere of his mysterious activity. Even the very development of Israel's cult, which underlined the difference between sacred and secular, also contrived to do it without identifying the sacred with a special place. Israel's holy place was specifically movable because, to begin with, the presence of God moves with his people. And once a settled sanctuary is established, its holiness comes from the fact that it is the place where 'Jahweh puts his name'. For it is in the *name* that God is mysteriously present. The whole subject is complex and never systematically worked out, continuing indefinitely to resist crystallization. Von Rad also believes the Jewish view of man – in so far as there is one at all – to be as completely demythologized as its view of the world. It is a view which is not afraid to see man abandoned to the forces of fate.

These views are not dependent on just a few isolated details. But when we have assessed them all, we can and must say that the total effect was that 'Israel's world was exposed in all its parts

to God. Her language is appropriate to such a world. It can therefore be said that when God began to reveal himself to her in history,
he also gave her her language. For the peculiar thing is that in
conversation with her God Israel learned to know and name her
world.' This language of conversation, pre-eminently as we meet
it in the psalms, the Church has felt able to go on using without
any problem. This naturally does not mean that the entire language
remains static. Its terms and concepts belonged to a faith which
was constantly reshaping them, and which was warranted by God's
revelation of himself in Israel. The main burden of von Rad's
argument is to insist how dynamic *in principle* these views are.
'Mankind and the world only had an identity in their relationship
with God.'[35]

This language was 'minted by a faith on which it directly
depended'. That faith, in turn, was constantly driven forward by
specific revelations in history. As von Rad insists, and as even
an untrained reader can observe when reading the Bible, the strands
of interest that *could* be plucked out are interwoven in a complex
thesis under constant transformation. The knowledge of God
which the movement of history reveals is non-speculative, frag-
mentary, and sometimes apparently contradictory. Thus, if we say
that 'history becomes word, and word becomes history', we must
resist the temptation to resolve this formula into something simpler
than it is. Israel has to learn to do a lot of waiting. At the proper
time she will be told what God does. We are, as it were, given
history in the raw, unshaped by reflection. Some stories are told
in a way which contains their interpretation, but not all are.

Thus we note another kind of continuity between the two Testaments. The question of the meaning of history is posed once more
in the light of Jesus Christ. St Paul, writing to the Romans, will
feel that we can now see better what the long past was about
because it was written 'to instruct *us*'.[36] Von Rad will feel that
he can write that 'all presentation of history in the Old Testament
is in one form or another inherently open to the future, a future
to be released by God'. Even the story of the Creation in the Book
of Genesis is told in this way. The *way* of looking forward may
change, but it is always there. It will often be more firmly inserted
by a reinterpretation, and one which is in harmony with something
inherent in the basic point of view. As we have seen, there is no
real point of rest in the Old Testament, no constellating centre
as there is in the New. Moreover, looking back over the Old Testa-

ment from the New, elements can be seen to take a shape which could not have been theirs with any other point of reference. One analogy between the two Testaments is seen by von Rad as their 'divergence from all forms of mythological speculation' by their insistence on the interconnection between revelation in word and revelation in event.

But he feels that 'the supreme analogy between the Old and New Testaments is the way in which men are confronted more and more painfully with a God who continually retreats from them'.[37] Von Rad makes a very prolonged and well-argued protest against the notion that we can cut our way down to a religion of Israel under the accretions of tradition. 'When the Old Testament is allowed to speak for itself, in the end it always confronts us with an event, an act of God either past or future.' Searching for an illustrative analogy between the two Testaments, von Rad decides among others for a story dear to the Fathers and the old liturgies, that of Joseph in Egypt. It is a story in which we find 'the first faint sketches of something far greater which reached its climax in the story of Christ'. This kind of analogy always needs very careful handling, for 'what we extract is not general truths, but we see acts in a context of movement'. The New Testament letter to the Hebrews really believes that the old heroes saw a goal from afar.[38]

'The mark of the New Testament saving event is a deep *hiddenness on God's part*. In Christ, God divested himself of his power and glory, indeed, he did his work among men ... veiled.' But then we remember that 'the man whom the royal psalms envisage as designated by God to be king of the whole world ... is a man who carries little conviction in the world of power politics.' The prophets often had to go so far as to speak of God in a way which outraged pious feeling then, and often does so even now. All this is bound up with the mystery of God's hiding. Isaiah will say: 'I will wait for the Lord who is hiding his face ... and I will hope in him.'[39] But experiences more extreme than this find their place in the Old Testament and several psalms speak of a sense of total abandonment by God. We recall that one of these is quoted on the cross. Von Rad finds the clearest general statement of this theme in Deutero-Isaiah: 'Truly thou art a God who hidest thyself, O God of Israel, the Saviour.'[40]

Relative to this hiddenness is, of course, the summons to what we should call 'faith', for which Hebrew has no consistent or

adequate term. On the other hand faith as a theme is very promi-
nent. Von Rad sees David's words that he came not with weapons,
but in the name of the Lord to meet Goliath as 'a high water
mark' among Old Testament utterances on the subject of faith.
Abraham's faith clearly embraces the idea of delay in fulfilment.
Thus near to the theme of faith is the fact that it is always directed
towards a person in a way which involves the abandonment of
oneself. When for the Christian it is to the person of Christ that
faith is transferred, it still implies the abandonment of oneself to
the future fulfilment of Christ's promises. The similarity here
could obviously be stated in a misleading way. For, on the whole,
it is as if Christ himself were entering into the Old Testament
events, expanding their meaning and extending their reference.
Towards the end of this section of his survey of the theology of
the Old Testament von Rad has found it necessary to say that
the phenomenon of God continuously hiding himself inevitably
also gives rise to the question: Who was this Jahweh? He concludes
the section by expressing his conviction that 'if Christianity is to
be saved from falling into the traps of mythology or speculation
it needs the Old Testament view of history'. He is led to this by
articulating the question which, it may be thought, is the very
question which may truly be said to keep Christian theology alive.
'Is it really true that we know exactly who Jesus Christ was and
is?'[41]

This is, naturally, the question which must lead us back to the
New Testament, to the tradition of the Church and the men of
prayer, particularly as these grapple and live with that tension,
as we have seen Maurice Wiles calling it, of which Chalcedon
speaks in its definition and with which it can only continue to
invite and encourage us to live. In the New Testament we have,
in the opening chapter of the letter to the Colossians, a hymn for
Christ, which must retain its ancient authority whether St Paul
be its author or not.[42] It is in itself a splendid example of continuity
within the tradition of which we have seen von Rad speaking. Of
Christ we are told that 'He is the image of the invisible God, the
first-born of all creation; for in him all things were created ...
all things were created through him and for him; he is the beginning, the first-born from the dead, that in everything he might
be pre-eminent. For in him all the fullness of God was pleased
to dwell.' And in the next chapter this phrase is explicitly extended

to saying that this fullness dwells there *bodily*.[43] Thus the meaning of creation is seen quite differently because of the incarnation and resurrection, and it is encountered dwelling in Christ bodily. Who, then, is this? In the East the continuous struggle on the part of some to insist upon the element of hiddenness which remains implicit in this and other New Testament statements, and to do so in a way that diminishes the element of visibility, rumbles on into the eighth century in the controversy about whether Christ should be represented in images. The defenders of the use of icons do not see themselves as defending simply a pious practice, but as defending the two elements in revelation about Christ, between which it is not possible to choose without ceasing to hold the true Christian faith. For, says Theodore of Studion: 'The incomprehensible is contained in a virginal womb ... And when the unbodily has taken a body, he says to his disciples: Take and eat, this is my body. Thus he is both bounded and boundless.'[44] This business of being bounded or 'depictable', as St Theodore will say later in the same work, applies to Christ *as a person*, although according to his divinity he is not depictable. And it does not, he firmly adds, apply to the natures which come together in him. He will not have anything to do with the kind of talk which implies abstractions.[45]

Anyone who seriously meditates on Theodore's arguments will see that he is working in a direct line that goes back through Irenaeus to the tradition of Paul. The enemies of painting images of Christ are saying that these are really a kind of lying because 'behind the face', so to speak, is really the eternal Son of God who cannot be depicted. No, answers Theodore. Behind any real face there is always a person and Christ, as incarnate, really has a human face because he is truly human. Of course the divinity is not depictable, and neither is either of the two natures which are found together in the incarnate Son of God. Irenaeus had said that the glory of God was 'a living man' or 'a man alive'.[46] Theodore's thought is that if it were ever possible to meet a supreme example of 'man alive', we meet it in Christ. It is probably only if we really appreciate the true force of this conviction that we come to see why it is so difficult to answer the question: Who is this? For while the answer is simple in itself, with a living simplicity, there is no way of elaborating our answer univocally in words. There are no very evidently 'helpful' ways round an explanation of the central conviction of the Christian faith – apart from those the Church continues to use – which do not either deny it or lead us gently away from it.

There is, unfortunately, no convincing way of showing that the intellectual currents within theology in the West, since roughly the end of the twelfth century, have tended to do anything other than banish these matters to what has come to be called 'the devotional life'. This is, of course, not the same as saying that theologians have not often been devout or that people of prayer, both simple and trained, have failed to go on being confronted with these central truths. We have seen someone like Mother Julian, through her prayers and reflections, reaching a contemplative state and finding it impossible to look at a vision of the face of Christ without being simultaneously aware of the mystery of the Trinity. Her 'showings', read as a whole, are a striking testimony to the integration of elements in an undivided theological tradition which mere reflection could never, by itself, produce. It is no denigration of the value of theological studies in the conventional sense to insist on this. For they clearly played *some* part in the final version of what Mother Julian felt she ought to say about her experience.

In the case of St John of the Cross we have an instance even more striking. Not only had he received a normal late medieval scholastic training, as many an analysis of his works has shown. He had actually been rector of the Carmelite college in Alcala. In the beautiful commentary he eventually wrote on his *Spiritual Canticle* we are dimly aware of all this as we follow its development. When he comes to the line, 'He passed through these groves in haste', John writes:

He passed, because the creatures are, as it were, a trace of the passing of God, who made them, as it were, in passing. The greater works, wherein he revealed himself most clearly and which he wrought most lovingly, were those of the incarnation of the Word and the mysteries of the Christian faith, in comparison wherewith all the rest were wrought, as it were, in passing, and in haste.

'And looking upon them as he went, left them, by his glance alone, clothed with beauty.'

To behold them and find them very good was to make them very good in the Word, his Son ... He became man, and thus exalted man in the beauty of God, and consequently exalted all the creatures in him, since in uniting himself with man he united himself with the nature of them all – I, if I be lifted up from the earth will draw all things to myself – And thus, in this lifting up of the incarnation of his Son, and the glory of his resurrection according to the flesh, not only did the Father beautify the creature in part, but we can say that he left them all clothed with beauty and dignity.[47]

Of these things, stanza seven of the poem had said 'something that they are stammering leaves me dying'. What is this 'something'? There are, says John in his commentary, three kinds of pain in this business of loving. There is the wound, which the soul receives from the creatures. There is the sore, which takes a firmer hold. 'And this sore is made in the soul by means of the knowledge of the works of the incarnation of the Word and mysteries of the faith; which, being greater works of God and comprehending within themselves a greater love than those of the creature produce a greater effect of love upon the soul.' And then there is a third kind, pain, which is like dying. 'And this dying of love is effected in the soul by means of a touch of the highest knowledge of the Divinity, which thing is the "something" they are stammering.'[48] When he eventually comes to talking more of this highest knowledge, John tells us that at that high stage, when the soul can be said to have reached 'spiritual marriage', or intimate union with God, God 'describes his works to her, for true and perfect love can keep nothing hidden. And in particular he communicates to her sweet mysteries concerning his incarnation, and the mode and way of human redemption, which is one of the highest works of God, and is thus most delectable to the soul.'[49]

These passages are sufficient to show that, for a mystic like John, as also for Mother Julian, the incarnation is by no means peripheral to the mystery of God. It is a doctrine of faith which he meets again in a different and incommunicably sure way in mystical union. No less clearly does the commentary on the *Spiritual Canticle* explain how integral to growth and development from the beginning, is the pathway indicated by the humanity of the Son of God. In two short paragraphs of comment on the words 'Let us enter farther into the thicket', John gives us what is in fact a tiny concentrated treatise on the ascetic life and its disciplines, whether active or passive. They take their flight from an anguished text from the Book of Job, in which Job begs that if anything kills him, it will be God himself. 'Oh', writes John,

> that it might be perfectly understood how the soul cannot attain to the thicket and wisdom of the riches of God, which are of many kinds, save by entering into the thicket of many kinds of suffering, and by setting thereupon its consolation and desire! And how the soul that of a truth desires Divine wisdom first desires suffering, that it may enter therein − into the thicket of the Cross. For this reason Saint Paul exhorted the Ephesians not to faint in tribulations, but to be very strong, and rooted in charity, that they might be able to comprehend with all the saints what is the breadth and the length and the height and the depth, and likewise to know the super-eminent charity of the knowledge of Christ, so as to be filled with all the fullness of God. For the gate whereby one may enter into these riches of his wisdom is the Cross, which is a strait gate. And the desire to enter therein belongs to few, but the joys to which it leads belong to many.[50]

The link to the next passage on the words 'And then we shall go forth' is again the mystery of the incarnation, known in the deeper joys and wonders of the spiritual marriage. For there 'the soul will know the sublime mysteries of God and man, which are sublimest in wisdom and are hidden in God.'

There is probably no writer in the later western tradition who gives us so profound an impression of the complete integration of faith and experience as John does. But there are sufficient reasons for supposing that many less articulate people have followed, and are even following, a similar path.

But when we have said all this, it must be admitted that the balance which experience has frequently rectified has often been lacking in theoretical studies of the spiritual fulfilment of man. It cannot fail to be a little worrying that St Bernard in the twelfth century is undoubtedly the last spiritual writer of major stature in the West to insist that the saints are not complete without their bodies, that is to say without all that makes them specifically and fully human. Owing to the extreme and increasing intellectualism characteristic of life in the West, not only among professional theologians, these worries though doubtless often a hindrance to sound spiritual maturity, have only in our own day tended to surface with the force of an angry protest. That they have often been released by factors quite alien to faith was only to be expected when much even apparently 'orthodox' Christian teaching had become so tenuously 'spiritual' as to be able to be blown away with a puff of wind. The repercussions of these protests were bound in the end to confront explicitly the doctrine of the incarnation. There had been a protest against these tendencies on behalf of the sanctification of man in his wholeness, by a great Greek theologian in the fourteenth century. But that, integral as it is with an understanding of the doctrine of the incarnation, deserves a chapter to itself. We may not leave Angelico's noble figure of Christ being mocked, without trying to see why it was that to earlier believers all true humanness also seemed to be mocked in that mocking.

# 10
## 'THAT MAN MIGHT BE MADE GOD'[1]

> But God's own descent
> Into flesh was meant
> As a demonstration
> That the supreme merit
> Lay in risking spirit
> In substantiation.

These lines, quoted by Robert Poirier in what may justly be described as an elegant study of that poet, are followed by the comment: 'As Frost phrases it, the incarnation of God was an achievement similar to the writing of a poem, to the "figure a poem makes" . . . For the "figure" of Christ or of poets, "knowing" is through the act of revelation.' It is possible to have one's reserves about some of the language of this comment in its context, just as it would be about some of Robert Frost's own language on various philosophical and religious topics. For, as Poirier says, 'he cannot be called a religious poet in Eliot's sense'.[2] But what can be stoutly defended here is Frost's intuition of the likeness of the incarnation to the unbreakable, unassimilable quality of any work of art that really comes alive. And the defence can begin with Frost's own words on the subject, to which we have seen Robert Poirier alluding. For Robert Frost's main point in the little essay 'The Figure a Poem Makes' is to insist upon the uniqueness of what comes to birth in the poem, which cannot be prepared for by thinking it out in advance, or really alternatively explained once the poem itself exists. 'It should be the pleasure of a poem to tell how it can.'[3]

For an orthodox Christian it is almost impossible not to think at once of that little phrase St Luke puts into the mouth of the shepherds, after the departure of the Christmas angels. Authentic and doubtless conscious Hebraism as it is – although written in Greek – its force designedly disappears in most translations, since it is alien to their idiom. Of the classical versions, only the Douai keeps it, presumably because the Latin Vulgate correctly had. 'Let us go over to Bethlehem and let us see *this word* that is come to pass, which the Lord hath showed to us.'[4] This, and only this, is literally what Luke writes. For more than an idiom of language is involved here. The shepherds go, not to hear a lecture on the incarnation, but to attend to an event by which it is God's pleasure to 'say' something that takes the risk of being misunderstood. To the Old Testament background of all this, as explained and formulated by von Rad, we have already referred at some length in the previous chapter.[5] The issue here is a 'word' that says more than many sentences about it ever can and, as we know, is often only explained by being explained away.

There appear to be two main factors at work to prevent the mystery of the incarnation *itself* remaining the constant point of return in all discussions, many of which are, alas, rather like discussions of poetry by people who never read poems. On the one hand there is the necessarily vacillating impression, in *any* context, of what it means to be 'human'. I say 'vacillating' because the positive sciences, while all of them working with at least an implicit view of what is normal, and certainly conveying this in popular communications of their findings, are also compelled by those very findings to make constant adjustments to their picture of the norm. It may reasonably be supposed that the population at large has a much more static, even dangerously static, view of itself than even the most sceptical specialist can allow himself to have. We have seen earlier in this book how at least one able British biologist, who pours scorn on what he thinks to be Christian belief, is repeating throughout his study a plea for the development in individuals of possibilities which are not biologically determined. We have also seen how doctors alive to their profession are constantly confronted with the importance of a dimension of being human which it is not scientifically easy to measure or describe, but is of vital importance to the survival of men, and consequently of what it is to be human. It is therefore – according to one's point of view – either a piece of good fortune, or an act of divine providence that orthodox Christianity has never been *dogmatically* committed to a specific point of view on this subject. The letter to the Hebrews in the New Testament says the one thing that determines the boundaries of what orthodoxy can say about Christ himself. 'Since the children share in flesh and blood, he himself likewise partook of the same nature ... tempted as we are, yet without sinning.'[6] This appears to be consistent with the other

New Testament documents. Whatever the speculations of theologians at different times about this condition as the experience
of the one who lived it, the undivided Church has never felt able
to commit itself to any of them.[7] It has firmly confined itself to
insisting that Christ has a human soul and a human will. For it
cannot allow that the divine life and the divine will are simply
substitutes for what gives any ordinary man life and some degree of
freedom. Thus orthodox Christianity has remained open to another
view of the significance of the humanity of Christ than that which
supposes it to be so unusual that it necessarily has nothing to teach
us concerning those selves, about whose depths we seem to remain
in a large measure unclear.

The force of this point will probably be better appreciated if we
consider the alternative type of temptation against orthodox belief
in the incarnation. One can either identify the 'human' with com-
pulsions and states of which human beings are quite commonly the
more or less involuntary victims, or one can insist that human life is
characterized rather by a capacity for intellectual or psychological
transcendence. It will thus be 'the spiritual life' conceived as
'wisdom', in whatever form the times find most attractive, that is
the only human life convincingly worthy of the name. Thus we shall
be able, by one means or another, to climb up to the unknown God
without his really needing to come down to us. We shall ensure his
hiddenness, if not his banishment, that way. It must, unfortunately, be admitted that many Christians, both ancient and
modern, have a weakness for avoiding having to live with the
scandal of the incarnation by creating the mental image of a disincarnate Christ, according to prevailing fashion. Augustine, although he knew no Greek, was certainly right to see that either or
both of these temptations can lead to what St Paul meant by
'carnal-mindedness'. 'For the man who makes the soul's nature the
greatest good and rejects the body's as evil, evidently desires the
soul in a carnal way, and flies from the body in a carnal way. This
gives the impression of being human folly rather than divine
truth.'[8]

It is probable that the greater number of the readers of this book
will find it difficult to envisage how far a certain kind of intellectual
theology could go in the direction of the 'folly' of which Augustine
is here speaking. But one very great Greek theologian, St Gregory
Palamas, who had to contend with a theology of this type in its

most aggressive form wisely decided not to use his very obvious intellectual abilities to argue directly with it.[9] For, as he liked to say, 'every argument refutes another argument, and none can hope for anything other than its own defeat'.[10] But once, after a review of the contentions of those 'who have faith in their own reasonings and in the difficulties they present', he adds a remark memorable enough to embody something of the spirit of his entire work.

> It is said that every argument refutes another argument, but what is the argument that can refute a life? We believe that it is impossible to know oneself by the use of syllogisms and analyses unless one makes oneself free of arrogance and baseness by a complete conversion of heart and exacting self-discipline. For he who has not taken his own soul in hand by these means will not know his own deficiency in knowledge, an invaluable foundation for the knowledge of oneself.[11]

Gregory's situation as a theologian can, for our present purposes, be very briefly described. Born in Constantinople in 1296, he had retired as a young man in his twenties to lead a simple monastic life of prayer on Mount Athos. Turkish invasions soon made it necessary for him to live elsewhere for some years. But in his early thirties he was able to return there, and became the spokesman for his less articulate brethren in a controversy with a representative of a type of intellectual theology which has never been wholly without its adherents since late scholastic times. For men of this kind, often of notable intellectual ability, it is inconceivable that 'contemplation' could be anything other than a speculative exercise, even when devoted to theological matters. Often formidably agnostic themselves, they are readily apt to suspect that those whose way of life leads them to undertake a training of another kind are helplessly exposed to every sort of illusion and even heresy – especially if growing experience appears to lead them to an awareness of divine things which cannot be acquired by reading books alone. A glance back at the passage just quoted, in which Gregory is explicitly arguing for the unanswerable quality of a way of life, ought sufficiently to show that Gregory is no naive anti-intellectual. Although, like many great thinkers, including Thomas Aquinas, never the creator of a co-ordinated system, Gregory generally chooses his words with great care if one reads them in their context. Were it not too large a distraction, even a study of Gregory's position on these matters within the bounds of the writings on which this chapter is based, would adequately demonstrate that he acknowledges that natural philosophy has its own value and competence. But profane education needs to be penetrated and complemented by faith and the love of God if it is to lead to that kind of wisdom about divine things which Christianity offers us. As he argues, 'Now the Word of God has come in the flesh' – that very person 'who has become for us the wisdom of God', as Gregory loves to repeat in Paul's phrase [12] – these philosophical theologians seem still to be maintaining that, instead of purifying our hearts and devoting ourselves to prayer, we should go on 'sitting uselessly around a smoking lamp'.[13] This latter is a fairly untypical thrust in a style of writing marked by a deeply meditated use of Scripture and earlier writers, which does not readily reveal its riches at a first reading. Gregory writes as someone solidly grounded in that tradition of theology as integral to the life of prayer which is unquestionably the patristic one. For, as he says in several slightly different ways, 'the mere business of thinking and talking about God and divine things, does not give you the experience of them'.[14] And it is the opening phrase of the long sentence that ends with the ironic twist about the smoking lamp of philosophy that indicates the glowing heart of Gregory's thought and endeavour. It also gives him his modest and sane sense of human equilibrium. This is the conviction that 'the Word of God has come in the flesh that, in Christ, God is truly incarnate, and in this very "showing" of himself saying something to which we ought to attend'.

The inseparable connection between the object of Gregory's contemplation and his doctrine of the spiritual life is explicit enough in a passage in which he has been stressing that the aim of that life is not to be confined to any one of the aspects of being human in particular. The 'rule of the spirit' has to be established in us as a living whole. By this we fix a measure appropriate to every power of the soul and body. In the background is the thought of two very concentrated sentences of a letter of Paul, which are now quoted. 'The God who said "Let light shine out of darkness" has shone in our hearts to give the light of the knowledge of the glory of God in the face of Jesus Christ. But we have this treasure in earthen vessels.'[15] Here is, as it were, the paradox of God's ways which must be lived with to be known. Gregory's comment is this: 'Thus having, as in earthen vessels, that is our bodies, the light of the Father in the face of Jesus Christ to know the glory of the Holy Spirit, shall we fail to receive the great things of the spirit if we hold

our attention within our bodies?'[16] We must return presently to
the clear reference to the memory and prayer of God in the heart,
the centre of one's being, which this sentence implies as the integrating principle of the spiritual life. It is enough for the moment
to note how it also embodies a conviction which Gregory endlessly
repeats in one form or another as one aspect of his grasp of the
significance of the incarnation.[17] It is an intellectual deception to
seek some kind of remote and lofty understanding of the new light
which God, who once called the world out of darkness, throws
upon himself in the person of Jesus Christ, if we try to do it by
pretending not to be the kind of beings we are. Firmly basing
himself on the teaching of St John Climacus, Gregory declares:
'Among men it is not an angelic impassibility we should seek, but a
human one.'[18]

The other side of this disciplined acceptance of the human
condition is a supreme confidence in Christ as really God incarnate, which makes it natural for him to interpret the words of St
Paul just quoted in a trinitarian sense, as Gregory clearly does. The
consequence of this can be expressed in a very simple form in St
Paul's words in his letter to the Romans: 'If you believe in your
heart that Jesus is the Lord, you will be saved.'[19] 'Thus', says
Gregory, 'it is not by acquiring the knowledge of created things
that one possesses God. One possesses God by believing in one's
heart that Jesus is the Lord through the establishment of the
simplicity of faith within oneself.'[20] But this, as Gregory sees, is
still not the whole story of the way of living he feels called to
defend. Does not the incarnation mean that 'Christ himself is our
only master'? God himself is the teacher of the knowledge of divine
things which is accessible to us. For it is not an angel, not a man,
but the Lord himself who instructs us who are saved. No longer do
we know God by approximations, for that is the knowledge which
comes from creatures. But *now* 'that life is made manifest which
was with the Father and was made manifest to us'. According to
this same New Testament tradition, 'God is light', and those who
really believe in him become 'children of light'. 'What we *shall* be
does not yet appear, but when it appears we shall be like him for we
shall see him as he is.'[21]

Passages of this kind could appear to be claiming for the life of
prayer things which Gregory is continuously careful to deny.
Prayer does indeed give us a simple 'knowledge' of God and lead to
some sort of 'seeing', which are different in kind from even the

subtlest conclusions of philosophy or speculative theology. But this is not to claim that God ever ceases to be invisible and incomprehensible as both philosophers and theologians agree. As Gregory once says, 'they agree with us, even if they do not understand what they are saying'.[22] For Gregory thinks that the life of prayer, honestly and faithfully lived, leads one to an even deeper conviction of God's invisibility and incomprehensibility. The problem is that there is only the language of knowledge and sight with which to talk about these things. 'I have spoken', he says, 'of "spiritual eyes", for it is with them that in the power of the spirit these things can be seen; even though this holy vision of the divine ineffable light transcends even the spiritual eyes.'[23] If, on account of their conviction of the primary importance of the life of prayer as also itself 'a way of knowing', some of the Fathers and spiritual teachers appear to suggest that even the reading of Scripture is useless, this is to misunderstand their intention. Every true contemplative is faithful to his 'holy reading'. But, adds Gregory, they know that 'it is the practice and not the knowledge of the Scriptures that saves us'.[24]

This is the constant emphasis of Gregory's teaching – that the protection of the soul from error and its own weakness is the 'memory of God' and ceaseless prayer as the very centre of one's life. It is one of Gregory's strengths, as we read him today, that his teaching is quite explicitly not tied to any specific philosophical or physiological view of how ordinary human knowledge functions. We are, as he sees us, *one* unique reality, to whose centre we may conveniently and rightly refer as 'the heart', which is also the common usage of Scripture.[25] However we speak of it, it is to this very centre of ourselves that we gather ourselves together by that prayer which brings us into living contact with the mystery of God. Not, of course, without a struggle. For in common with all who pray at all times and everywhere, Gregory finds that 'the enemy of God is the enemy of prayer'. Of those who, disciplining their tendency to dispersal and coping with their temptations, reach the conviction that we cannot do anything without God, there are some who are carried away by the longing to unite themselves with the Lord of all. To them prayer comes as a gift, sometimes 'like music to the one who hears the song'. All who seek a prayer like this must try, as far as possible, to live without letting go of the memory of God. 'Such a one strives to fix the thought of God upon their soul like an indelible seal, as Basil the Great says . . . For if you have not

received the glorious gift of prayer, persevere and you will receive
it.'[26]

In saying all these things, and, in not concealing that there will
be difficulties and discouragements along the way, Gregory is also
careful to say that all efforts only dispose us to that gift which God
alone can give. As he says, 'the perfect contemplation of God and
divine things is not just a purification but it is, beyond the purification, a sharing in divine things, a gift and a possession rather than
a purification.'[27] But, as he then goes on to say, in common with all
orthodox Christian mystics of both East and West, this contemplative gift cannot be described in words. It can only be talked
about by using images and analogies. It is a light, as the whole
passage has been saying, which is at the same time dark to our
minds, a kind of vision which is an absence of vision involving, as it
does, *seeing* that one does not see. It is therefore that Gregory
immediately repeats what he has several times had occasion to say,
on account of the controversy in which he is involved, that the gift
of contemplation is *not* the same as what speculative theologians
call apophatic or negative theology. As he says elsewhere, not
everybody comes into this divine darkness though 'since the coming of the Master in the flesh' apophatic theology is accessible to
everyone, and not to just a few gifted specialists.[28] For the incarnation plunges us, at least in principle, into the mystery of God
in a new way. Thus Gregory will even feel able to say that 'this
knowledge above conceptions is common to all those who have
believed in Christ'. What is *not* necessarily common to all is the
experience to which that faith is meant to lead through the faithful
following of Christ in life and prayer. For this leads beyond created
knowledge of every description into 'that uncreated light which is
the glory of God and of Christ as God and of those who are
destined to be conformed to Christ'.[29] Naturally, this cannot be a
permanent experience in this world, though occasionally the man
of prayer is granted a little glimpse of this light as a kind of foretaste
of future vision. It is this light which 'deifies' those on whom and in
whom it shines. Among those whom Gregory believes had an
experience of this kind is St Benedict, whose vision of the whole
world in the light of God is recounted by Gregory the Great in a
life that circulated in the East in a Greek translation.[30] Very like
Pope Gregory, Gregory Palamas speaks of those who attain these
contemplative heights as seeing 'God in God'.[31] It is the kind of
experience which can be said to be, here and now, a pledge of the

age to come. This is indeed the end to which the life of contemplation tends.[32]

These things will perhaps all seem very exalted and not altogether surprising in a work designed in the first place to defend
a very specifically withdrawn form of monastic life favourable to
these developments. Thus the question will inevitably arise: Is this
an invitation open to everyone? And Gregory's answer is an un-
equivocal 'yes'. Just as every Christian is at least in an elementary
way a theologian by profession of faith, so it is a natural consequence that he or she should penetrate *by living* into the meaning
of their faith. The one condition for doing so is a radical change in
the orientation of life. This consists in the abandonment of evil and
the acknowledgement of things as they really are. This must pre-
cede 'the holy work of divinizing and unifying the soul'.[33] The
result, as we have seen, in looking at the lives of the saints of the
past, and shall doubtless continue to see in those of the future, is
different in different souls. 'For the Lord dwells with men in
different ways according to the character and manner of the way in
which they seek him. For it is different for the man of action and
different for the contemplative.'[34] Gregory recalls a lovely phrase
of Basil to describe how natural the result appears to be when it is
appropriate and genuinely God-given. Deification manifests itself,
as Basil the Great says, 'like an art in a man who has mastered it.
For the saints are the instruments of the Holy Spirit.'[35]

This tranquil vision of integration in the love of God is, as we
have already seen, supported by a conception of the transformation
of the life of the passions which is determined by the value which
the incarnation has given to the human condition. 'For the abuse of
the powers of the soul produces diverted passions, just as the abuse
of the knowledge of creatures engenders the wisdom which has
become folly.' The desiring appetite must be transformed by love
and the irascible by perseverance. It is not a question of killing off
the passions but, through the constant memory of God, of training
them to function as they should. Gregory is very insistent that it
should not be something *dead* we offer to God. 'Thus we should
offer the passionate part of the soul to God as something living and
active that it may be a living sacrifice, as the apostle says of our
bodies.'[36] Neither St Paul nor the Fathers are recommending a
kind of spiritual suicide.

What impresses Gregory through all this is that it is not an angel,
not a man, but the Lord himself who has saved us. 'Shall he who

did not refrain from becoming man for us, submitting to the cross and death for us "while we were yet sinners", as the apostle says, fail to come to dwell in man?' – always provided, of course, that we have prepared ourselves in the ways of which we have already given some indication, and laboured responsively in what Gregory once calls the 'school of God', under the guidance of the Holy Spirit.[37]

For anyone who has tried to look at the teaching of Gregory Palamas as the integrated whole it undoubtedly is, it will not be difficult to appreciate how, although many centuries separate them in time, it is to this school that a saint like Seraphim of Sarov also belongs. To say this is not to assert that Seraphim had read much, or even any, of Gregory Palamas explicitly. What they primarily share is common sources of doctrine imbibed within a living tradition of life. It is very ancient tradition which lives with the conviction that the experience of the apostles on the mountain of the Transfiguration is a common Christian and human call. It is a conviction shared by a great Latin pope like Leo in his teaching on both the incarnation and the transfiguration.[38] But, save for a lovely last flowering of the undivided monastic tradition among the early Cistercians, the force of convictions of this type has been seriously diminished in the West under the impact of developments which have often been described. In the East, the monastic tradition goes on being fed, fairly directly, from the primitive sources, many of them very largely Syrian in affiliation. Sometimes these sources are mediated through anthologies, of which the most famous is the *Philochalia*, originating on Mount Athos in the eighteenth century. This big collection of texts is gradually, according to the best traditions, being itself anthologized in translation.[39] At the point we have reached it is perhaps most useful to illustrate one or two of the convictions which it has been the purpose of two chapters on the incarnation to stress from two influential earlier sources, which often appear in the collections.

Of the predecessors of Gregory Palamas, St Simeon the New Theologian in the eleventh century is undoubtedly the greatest. Attributed to Simeon in the *Philochalia* is a short paragraph which summarizes in simple form the way all the great early writers we have been citing see the mystery of the incarnation:

What is the aim of the incarnate dispensation of God's Word, preached in all the Holy Scriptures but which we, who read them, do not know? The only aim is that, having entered into what is our own, we should participate in what is his. The Son of God has become Son of Man in order to make us, men, sons of God, raising our race by grace to what he himself is by nature.[40]

It perhaps needs specially emphasizing that the process begins by 'entering into what is our own'. There is an explicit and conscious revaluation of all that is truly human in this common doctrine. To go back once more to the implications of the Angelico picture with which our previous chapter began, part of the dignity of the Christ being mocked is not the feeling that what is divine is merely shining *through* the human. The human itself has a beauty which it is hardly an exaggeration to call 'terrible', when we see it for what it is – so terrible we prefer to see it veiled.

Of a piece with this conviction that there is a dignity which is proper to man which we can betray in ourselves, but only wilfully abolish, is the conviction of the soundest monastic writers that monasteries are not the only places or, for some, even the right places, to be true to this dignity. Simeon certainly says, as the *Philochalia* also quotes:

Some praise life in a desert, others life in monasteries, still others a place of authority among people, to instruct and teach them and organize churches where many may find food for body and soul. I would not wish to give preference to any of these, nor to say that one is worthy of praise and another of censure. In all ways of life, blessed is the life lived for God and according to God in all actions and works.[41]

And of the descriptions of the result of a life lived *anywhere* 'according to God', one of the most memorable and, in one form or another most frequently remembered, is from a much earlier Syriac source: 'And what is the sum of purity? A heart full of mercy unto the whole created nature ... And therefore even in behalf of the irrational beings and the enemies of truth and even in behalf of those who do harm to it, at all times he offers prayers with tears that they may be guarded and strengthened ...'[42] Whoever wrote these words seems to have had a sense of things, at least on these matters, consonant with what is clearly an evangelical picture of perfection in likeness to the God 'who makes his sun to rise, on the bad and on the good alike, and sends the rain on saint and sinner'.[43]

It would be impossible to close this particular chapter in the world
as it now is – especially perhaps in what honesty already compels us
to call post-Christian societies – without at least a word on a
question which appears spontaneously to arise for anyone who
believes that the mystery of the incarnation and its human consequences are mysteries of divine compassion. It is possibly even a
little sharper in its urgency for those in whom the desire to reflect
the divine compassion is strongest. It should be obvious to anyone
who reads Mother Julian that she was notably bothered about how
the reassurances she was given in her visions that 'every kind of
thing will be well'[44] were reconcilable with the fact that so many
people appear to have no belief in the things her faith told her are
necessary, not only to make life meaningful, but actually to fulfil it.
Already in the fourteenth century Mother Julian knew how it felt
for the Church to seem to be shaken 'as men shake a cloth in the
wind'.[45] To her repeated questions, even in relation to one of her
nearer friends, she never received any definite answer, and was very
explicitly told that this is the kind of thing with which we cannot
meddle. 'For I saw truly in our Lord's intention that the more we
busy ourselves in that or anything else, the further we shall be from
knowing.'[46] The history of orthodox mysticism is at least consistent on this point, for Anthony the Great had been told much the
same in the fourth century.

From the point of view of commonly accepted theological teaching there must also be, even in principle, a large measure of
uncertainty as to how God makes himself available by means other
than those to which orthodox Christians believe he has promised to
be faithful. That he is free to make himself available in any ways he
chooses, and therefore probably does so often, would appear to be
at least implied by New Testament statements which say unequivocally that Christ is the saviour of all men. In that same
section of his great final work which begins with the incarnation, St
Thomas Aquinas quotes two of the more important of these texts in
discussing the question as to whether Christ is the head of all
men.[47] In brief, he finds it necessary to say that humanity at large
may be related to Christ in various possible ways, some of which
have yet to be realized. While the possibility of such a relationship
which, in itself, is always an open one, also remains open from its
human side, it may yet be realized at a time and under circumstances we cannot see. He does not in this article refer to an unusual
circumstance which is bound, in spite of its quaintness, to have

some interest for the modern reader and which does appear in some
questions he discussed while teaching at an earlier period in
Paris.[48] On that occasion the discussion turns upon how explicit
faith has to be in order to be worthy of the name at all. The main
body of what he has to say employs his usual distinction between
the different times and circumstances in human history about
which this particular question may be posed. For neither a medieval theologian nor a modern exegete would think that 'faith'
implied quite the same experience for Abraham as for St Peter. But
Thomas's general perspective here is determined by a text from the
New Testament letter to the Hebrews, which he regards as em-
bodying a statement of principle about what is, we may say, minimal for 'faith' to be a meaningful term to use. 'For whoever would
draw near to God must believe that he exists and that he rewards
those who seek him'[49] – however obscurely they may comprehend
what this involves, we may with probable certainty permissibly
add. And, as though for good measure, Thomas expresses a view on
what *might* happen in the case of a human being brought up by
wolves in the woods with no possible contact with the teachings of
the Christian faith. One can, for the purposes of discussion, obviously choose one's 'wood', and the plausibility of an equivalent
situation arising in a forest of tower-blocks can by no means be
excluded. I remember how, as a small boy many years before the
Second World War, I overheard while standing outside a baker's
shop not far from a large London church, two girls speculating as
to why there should be crosses on Good Friday's 'hot cross buns'.
Thomas at least gives a view which aptly applies to all cases where
lack of contact with the teachings of Christianity occurs for whatever reason, whether physical or psychological. He says that 'it
pertains to divine providence to provide for each person what is
necessary for their salvation, so long as this is not impeded on *their*
side'.[50] Thus he goes on to say that, in an extreme case – and who
can easily say what that might be? – God would reveal what is
necessary for faith 'by internal inspiration', or would send a teacher
of the faith to the person concerned, as we are told in the Acts of the
Apostles Peter was sent to the centurion Cornelius.[51]

Obviously views something like these are the only ones which
may be regarded as being compatible with others which must be
held as having a greater certainty of faith. Mother Julian, at least,
learned a similar attitude to her worries, and expressed it perhaps
more attractively: 'He wants us to know that he takes heed not only

of things which are noble and great, but also of those which are little and small, of humble men and simple, of this man and that man. And this is what he means when he says "Every kind of thing will be well". For he wants us to know that the smallest thing will not be forgotten.' [52]

# 11

## THE LONG RESULT OF TIME

There is more than a suggestion in the words of Mother Julian with which the previous chapter closes that there would be a grave want of modesty in expecting to compete with the God who hides, for the moment, how he keeps things which are 'little and small' in view. In common with all the orthodox masters of prayer she consistently teaches that the experience of life with, and in the service of, God leads to a firmer and more realistic grasp of one's own creatureliness. But neither she, nor any great mystical writer in whom the instincts of the undivided Christian tradition are alive, can rightly be accused of teaching that we can or should be indifferent to the factors in the development of human history and the world immediately around us which thrust themselves upon our attention. They indeed not only form a part of the material about which we have to make decisions; these are the factors which provoke us into making choices, even when we only make them by *failing* to do so when we could and should. A true choice evaded is invariably a choice made. For those who take the trouble to lend themselves to the thought of Gregory Palamas as a whole, or to any of those who through their lives and writings have gone on leading others in the certain, or deeply mysterious, ways of God, it will become impossible to conceive of a mysticism apart from a searching morality. Indeed, we may come to suspect that just as the authenticity of a 'mystical experience' may well be doubted if it has no effect on the rest of our lives, so it may be doubted how far it is possible to find a morality which has, as it were, no living centre. A life can probably only begin to be 'moral', in any sense worthy of the name, when it begins to take steadily into account the consequences of a developing relationship with *somebody*. It may possibly not be necessary to have any obviously supernatural belief to agree with this point of view. And it would be a mistake to suppose, as some believers can appear to come to suppose, that the relationship of prayer to God supersedes and is even in necessary conflict with other kinds of relationships. With the growing sense of creatureliness grows a deepening sense of compassion. Indeed one of the more obvious fundamental Christian beliefs is that the one cannot exist without the other in *some* form. As a letter in the Johannine tradition in the New Testament has it, 'he who does not love his brother whom he has seen, cannot love God whom he has not seen'.[1] This does not, of course, exclude the possibility of considerable differences in the ways this love may be appropriately expressed according to place and person. But these are wider questions to which we must return later in this chapter. For the moment we are confronted with the kind of consideration which would seem to bring us back the full circle to where we began this book.

Even a positive attitude to the theories which remind us with evident honesty how determined our lives are is not incompatible with considerable problems about how to cope with the consequences of taking these theories seriously. In 1837 Tennyson, who all his life was fascinated by scientific theories and the advance of technology,[2] had written a poem which at the personal level is, as Christopher Ricks so effectively says, full of 'blustering timidity'.[3]

> Here about the beach I wandered, nourishing a youth
>    sublime
> With the fairy tales of science, and the long result
>    of Time.[4]

There is, of course, no hint here – as there probably would be in anyone writing these lines today – of anything pejorative in speaking of the theories of science as 'fairy tales'. These two lines, indeed, contain a reminder of one of the few aspects of the bitter view of life of which *Locksley Hall* is an evasive expression about which Tennyson never seems to have had a pessimistic doubt. In an earlier poem, using much the same language, he had expressed the wish to be able to go to sleep for long spells:

> And every hundred years to rise
>    And learn the world, and sleep again;
> To sleep through terms of mighty wars,
>    And wake on science grown to more,
> On secrets of the brain, the stars,
>    As wild as aught of fairy lore.[5]

Many others in Tennyson's own day and since must have felt much the same excited enthusiasm, though they might not have wished to express it in the same way. What Tennyson never learned to cope with was the stratification of social life determined

by wealth, which had made an early love affair impossible, and is
the poem's real subject. As for everything else, a bit of him was
always inclined to think that, given time, things would of themselves get better and better and more and more fascinating. The
candid rebel in him, who seems never to have died even in his old
age, equally seems never to have reflected that it was not simply
lack of consideration for him personally that led to the development of Freshwater Bay and made it necessary for him to buy up
land at £1000 an acre to preserve his view from Farringford of what
his devoted wife Emily called 'our down' and 'our sea'. Tennyson
was, naturally, no more shortsighted than many even in our own
time who fail to grasp the often inseparable connection between
social and technological change and loss of personal amenity. As his
latest biographer writes, 'one cannot help feeling that Tennyson
was lucky to have enough money to buy land at a ruinous rate to
preserve the view of "our sea" '.[6]

Nowadays everyone is gradually having to learn that a phrase
like 'our sea' or 'our down' necessarily has a much more general
and public significance, whether anyone assumes adequate responsibility for this or not. During the course of the writing of this
book thousands of tons of oil have sunk to the sea-bed off the coast
of Brittany, with consequences that no one can predict. No one
counts this as a merely private sorrow. An incident of this kind,
indeed, readily gets ample international coverage. But there is still
a considerable time-lag in taking in the consequences of other kinds
of events affecting the quality and even the possibility of certain
ways of living which have been occurring at a much accelerated
pace roughly since the beginning of the Second World War. One
vital area which has a strong personal interest for the present writer
has recently been described, particularly in its effect on the English
setting, in Ian Niall's tightly written *To Speed the Plough*.[7] This
book is all the more effective for having been written by a man with
direct experience of agricultural change, an immensely accurate
eye for detail, and a capacity to assess a wealth of interrelated facts
in a way that is at once human and quite unsentimental. It is his
final chapters which concern us most here, especially from the
point at which he begins to talk about the introduction of the
combine harvester, the aesthetic and personal effects of whose
work filled those of us who knew and lived with the older ways with
almost inconsolable horror. As Ian Niall says: 'What lay beneath
this relentless change was a matter of pure economics. People who

had been leaving the land for decades prior to the advent of the tractor and the combine had gone to live in towns and urban communities . . . They had become producers of everything but their daily bread.'[8] It was this need that had to be met and it lay, and lies, behind a great deal of virtually irreversible change – 'no tea in the hedgeside'.

> No one seems to have noticed that farming has sub-contracted its main enterprise in so many ways that the business bears little relation to what it was when the yeoman sat at the head of his table with half a dozen hired men, each with a different part to play, eating their dinner . . . The contractor's men are the same countrymen as ever, but mechanically minded. They once changed teams at noon to have fresh horses for the long hard afternoon in the field. Now they rest the combine for five or six hours when it overheats, as it sometimes does . . . New-mown hay is gone in a few days. The meadow-sweet doesn't grow in the ditch. The crab apple and the blackthorn have been grubbed out.[9]

Well, that is, briefly and sharply told, the story. And not all of it on the negative side. Although Ian Niall does not mention this, anyone who has watched with mingled bewilderment and admiration a big suburban London store providing a fairground of customers on a Saturday morning with an assortment of English and foreign cheeses and everything from marshmallows to mangoes will appreciate how important it is that 'the modern strain of bird will lay more eggs in the one year of its life than the free range hens kept by nineteenth-century Giles or Hodge laid in their life-time.'[10] On the way to saying things like this, Ian Niall is constantly reminding us how much of all this has happened without most of those involved in producing the result thinking very much about it. And it has, of course, changed both consumers and producers. 'Neither Giles nor Hodge is the man his father was, but a different man produced by a different environment. He doesn't think the same way.' Further, 'the working horse has been out of date for forty years. The internal combustion engine may not last as long as the horse.'[11]

Both these latter observations were made in a similar, though more general context by the biologist Desmond Morris in the final chapter of his *Human Zoo* ten years ago.[12] How many remember it now, and especially its vital remarks on the truly human

alternatives? As Desmond Morris pointed out, of those who consciously try to react against these developments, 'even if they
somehow contrived to de-train their highly activated brains, such
individuals would still remain extremely vulnerable in their small
rebel communities . . . They would either be exploited as a tourist
attraction . . . or, if they became an irritant, they would be attacked
and disbanded.' Having said this, Morris then made his first crucial
observation: 'If we are condemned to a complex social existence, as
it seems we are, then the trick is to ensure that *we* make use of it,
rather than let it make use of us.' His is the case for the development of real creativity within the context as it exists admitting, as
he does, how few are favourably equipped for this on the basis of a
sufficiently positive childhood experience. On the other hand, a fair
degree of creativity would be possible, granted his second main
contention in this same chapter. 'The secret is to provide a social
environment capable of absorbing as much inventiveness and novelty as it sets out to encourage in the first place. This requires
careful and imaginative planning. Above all, it calls for con-
siderably more insight into the biological demands of the human
species on the part of politicians, administrators and city planners,
than has been evident in the recent past.' Morris predicts that, on
biological grounds alone, when enough people 'feel themselves
trapped in a planners' prison they will stage a prison riot'. The
alternative implied by their continued passivity would be a gigantic
lunatic asylum.[13]

If anyone who has read so far is beginning to think that these
remarks are peripheral to the main interests of this book, then it is
time they thought again. It would do Desmond Morris a grave
injustice to suggest that he is pinning his faith to merely external
solutions, as at least the first of his main points should make clear
enough. The genuine wish to implement either, or both of them,
demands a degree of human maturity which it was, at least originally, the business of the oldest Christian view of the 'moral life' to
foster. The varying campaigns in which freedom banners of one
kind or another are constantly carried can never really liberate
anyone who only wants some imagined 'equality' but is not, in the
long run, prepared to bear the burden of rising above the 'repetitive
mediocrity' which Morris rightly sees the type of society we are
evolving appears to encourage. And to do this we need to find the
bravery to tolerate 'stimulating heterogeneity'.[14]

Was it not the fact that undivided Christianity consciously embraced challenges of this kind that made it so alive at its first beginnings? And was not the monastic protest, when it came, at its most authentic a protest against the planners, not in the form of an alternative plan, but in the form of insisting that life can only be renewed from its centre? And that this, moreover, involves risking one's life as the young copt Anthony, afterwards called 'the Great', risked his? This risk, as it seems he was constantly insisting in his counsel, need not, and often *should* not, necessarily involve doing anything externally similar to what he himself felt called to do. As we must see again in the case of a master like Barsanuphius in the desert of Gaza, never have there been spiritual masters so insistent on stimulating heterogeneity as they were. Opposed as they were to mere eccentricity, the one thing of which they were the declared enemies was repetitive mediocrity. Why did so many people from so many different walks of life travel to consult these people if not to be awakened to possibilities in the lives they were already leading to which they had become blind? Of them might be asked the question which Jesus is reported to have asked of John the Baptist: 'What did you go out into the wilderness to behold? a reed shaken by the wind?' [15]

In the hearts of these men, who so often proved to be not just exacting but singularly merciful liberators, there was a deep sense of personal liberation. We can still find it in the oldest tradition of icon painting and, behind this, perhaps most strikingly in the Gospel of St John, 'the theologian' or 'the divine' as he so understandably came to be called. It is his Gospel that inspires an early, monumental depiction of the raising of Lazarus on a beam from the monastery of St Catherine on Mount Sinai, where it makes a natural complement to the scene of the transfiguration of our Lord, which the Synoptic Gospels all record. [16] The Lazarus story, which is peculiar to St John's Gospel, appears to be an unassailable part of the New Testament tradition. As Maurice Wiles, who has made a useful survey of early interpretations of this Gospel says: 'There are some books of the Bible whose interpretation has been so completely revolutionized by modern critical methods that the exegesis of earlier centuries is unlikely to be of much value to our understanding of them. There is probably no book of which this is less true than the Fourth Gospel. It is of such a nature that it seems to reveal its secrets not so much to the skilful probings of the analyst as to a certain intuitive sympathy of understanding.' [17] At the same time Professor Wiles notes how it was particularly in relation to the details of the story of the raising of Lazarus that earlier writers were impressed by the historicity of this Gospel.[18] This view is equally not without its modern defenders. It is interesting that both Greek and Latin Fathers tend to see Lazarus in his graveclothes as also a symbol of the spirit of man bound by that deviation from the path of life which sin is. The icons, by contrast, show the head of Lazarus as he emerges from the tomb surrounded by a nimbus of the light of a new kind of life as the attendants release him from the constraining bands. Those who remember Epstein's fine Lazarus in New College Chapel in Oxford will recall its unusual evocation of someone in the very act of coming to life.

Professor Dodd in a study, *The Interpretation of the Fourth Gospel*,[19] to which one constantly returns, points out how the story of the raising of Lazarus is the longest compact narrative in this Gospel apart from that of the Passion itself. He succeeds in stressing its powerful compactness in a way we must note. As he says, 'the interweaving of narrative and dialogue is complete'.[20] There is, in fact, no story separable from what the characters say, nor could the conversations be understood without the story. The theme is clearly that of life, and of the special kind of life which Christ himself gives. It is also made very clear in the course of the conversation with Martha and Mary, the sisters of Lazarus, that this life is not just the promise of something in the future. It is something which begins now. Lazarus, who is being raised to life, is going to die *physically* again. But the kind of life to which he is being called out of the tomb is one which already essentially implies victory over death. As Professor Dodd writes, 'Resurrection is the reversal of the order of mortality, in which life always hastens towards death. The Hellenistic society to which this Gospel was addressed was haunted by the spectacle . . . by which all things pass into nothingness.'[21]

In an independent examination of the language associated with 'eternal life' in this same book, C. H. Dodd finds that it is clear that such a phrase was quite unknown to pagan philosophical writers at anything like so early a date as we have it in St John's Gospel. But, while John's use of the phrase has some demonstrable late Jewish background, it is at the same time a development of the Jewish idea of the life of the age to come. 'In the dialogue preceding the raising of Lazarus the evangelist appears to be explicitly contrasting the popular eschatology of Judaism and primitive Christianity with the doctrine he wishes to propound.' Professor Dodd is convincing in saying that the narrative of the raising of Lazarus is so constructed as to correspond to the words of Jesus which imply that eternal life is something not just for the future, but something that can begin now. Especially through partaking of the Eucharist, which we shall find all the Fathers stressing, 'the believer already enjoys eternal life'. 'When the life of the age to come, with its specific quality, is transplanted into the field of present experience (which is never the case in Rabbinic Judaism) then the chief thing about it is its difference in quality from merely physical life.' [22] As we have seen earlier, this is exactly the doctrine of Gregory Palamas who had never read a modern exegete. What the modern exegete has so usefully done for us is to bring out the affiliation with its Hebrew antecedents in the thought of John. 'For the Hebrew conception of life is always one of action, movement, and enjoyment.' At the same time, as the story is presented in the context of the Gospel itself, this is 'not only the story of Lazarus raised to life; it is also the story of Jesus going to face death in order to conquer death'. The meeting which, in principle, condemns him is surely correctly seen by Dodd as 'the pendent to the episode of Lazarus'. Thus, as he says, in summary, 'the theme is Christ himself manifested as resurrection and life by virtue of his self-sacrifice'. [23]

This, of course, by no means tells us all that the icons tell us and the Fathers living in the tradition of the evangelist and St Paul believed. For life now, alive in the light of this miracle, is also seen as a liberation from all about the business of living that is merely death-dealing and confining. Life received as a gift, instead of a series of impossible demands made from without, is a very different experience from that of a prison of moral constraints. Before we look, in this connection, at one very vital aspect of the thought of St Paul – that most maligned of the saints – it will perhaps be useful to see how St Thomas Aquinas felt he thought he ought to discuss the whole question of the gospel of grace. It may well surprise as many professing Christians as it does those who know their Christianity only through caricatures for which Christians share at least some measure of responsibility.

Although he does so for reasons different from those which would be likely to occur to those who approach this subject for the first time, it will doubtless seem appropriate to many modern readers that Aquinas should begin to talk about the gospel of grace in relation to the idea of law. For that is how even some Christians will have tended primarily to think of it. A new law perhaps, but a law all the same. As Father Ernst notes in the introduction to his translation of the relevant section of Thomas's big final theological work, ' "Law" for St Thomas bears a wider range of senses than we ordinarily allow it . . . In its highest sense law for St Thomas is identical with divine providence in one of its aspects.'[24] Father Ernst suggests that, as a source of cosmic order, Thomas's idea of eternal law may be compared to such archaic concepts as that of Tao though, as we have seen, we cannot find any certain reference to divine will and purpose in this or similar concepts of great antiquity. We may, I believe, however, go as far as to say that the notion of Tao is not incompatible with Thomas's notion of eternal law, and this will perhaps be of some importance to those reflecting on certain ideas discussed in this present book. At least it is against some such dynamic overall background, in which men can have a share in virtue of their capacity to understand and choose, that Thomas begins to consider 'the law of the gospel, which is called the New Law'.

He begins by asking the question whether this law is something we find primarily written in books or is an inward one, and he gives a firmly dynamic answer. 'It is the grace of the Holy Spirit, given through faith in Christ, which is predominant in the law of the New Covenant, and that in which its whole power consists. So before all else the New Law is the very grace of the Holy Spirit, given to those who believe in Christ.'[25] As Father Ernst writes in a note, 'St Thomas's answer shows that he considers the Gospel primarily as reality and life, and only secondarily as written text "Scripture".'[26] This point of view is substantiated in the answer which St Thomas gives to the first of three subsidiary difficulties. Here he elaborates the point he has already made that, in so far as there is anything else about the New Law than its own inward dynamism, it is the kind of thing which either disposes us for the action of grace, or helps us to see how we should exercise it. In that which disposes us he includes explicitly all those aspects of the gospels which manifest Christ's divinity or his humanity. He adds, further, that when we speak of the inwardness of the gospel, we mean not only that it suggests what we should do but also helps us to do it.[27] Thus we already see that we are talking about something very alive and very flexible. It is flexible, I believe we may add, in a way which it is not necessarily easy to distinguish outwardly from living flexibility wherever we meet it in human beings. But, not forgetting a matter to which we have referred at the close of chapter ten of this book, Thomas adds as a statement of principle that 'no one has ever had the grace of the Holy Spirit except by faith in Christ, whether this faith be explicit or implicit . . . Hence anyone who received the law of grace inwardly by this very fact belonged to the new Covenant.'[28] This is a wise reticence, and we should obviously not try to go beyond it. It is very wide in the scope it allows for a relationship of life in different times and places to that special work of God in the world which goes beyond creating and sustaining and implies 'health'. This is, of course, basically what the word 'salvation' means, in a sense defined by the context of our discussion.

In going on to examine closer what is involved in the gospel of grace precisely as health, Thomas continues to keep his eye on the dynamism of what he is saying by stating unequivocally something which perhaps needs saying more often. 'Even the gospel letter kills unless the healing grace of faith is present within.' As Father Ernst comments: 'It is difficult to imagine a purer and firmer expression of evangelical truth than this.'[29] Having said these very fundamental things we can then, of course, say as Thomas does that 'the state of men can vary according to the sort of relationship, more or less perfect, they have to the same law . . . This diversity is also to be found in the state of the New Law, in accordance with a diversity of places and times and persons, where the grace of the Holy Spirit is received in a greater or lesser degree.'[30] St Thomas, like every orthodox teacher, cannot admit that there can be a further phase of the work of healing than that which is already present in the faith preached by the apostles – though, naturally, that healing can draw into itself more extensively the various peoples of the world. The undivided Christian faith is, in fact, the only religion which is *explicitly* universal. It will thus be appreciated that the sheer human enrichment of the experience of the gospel as it is allowed to come into contact with different kinds of culture could *potentially* be much increased in our own times. But this naturally also demands a certain degree of mature openness to the possibilities of existing situations, to which we have seen both scientifically-trained men and theologians, in their different ways, are constantly referring us.

To say this is inevitably to say that, although such an enrichment must begin at a level of interiority, it will also find expression in ways which are externally visible and apprehensible. St Thomas is careful to relate these two aspects of the working of grace to the mystery of the incarnation which, as it has been apprehended by generations of believers, may be said to define an important sense of the undivided Church. There is a real value in actions and practices which may not at first appear to be consonant with saying that the New Law is primarily an inner one. The comment of Thomas on this is to repeat that 'what is primary in the New Law is the grace of the Holy Spirit, shown in faith working through love'. He then continues:

> Now men obtain this grace through the Son of God made man; grace first filled his humanity and thence was brought to us . . . Thus it is fitting that the grace which overflows from the incarnate Word should be carried to us by external perceptible realities; and also that certain external perceptible works should be brought forth from this interior grace, by which flesh is made subject to spirit.[31]

These external works can draw us to grace, as the sacraments do, in their use of things like water, bread and wine, and oil. Or they can be, to return to Thomas's own words 'works which are brought forth by the inner stirring of grace'. Among these Thomas notes that it is important to distinguish between those things which are absolutely clearly in accordance with or contrary to the very nature of the gospel, and these can be known and specified in precepts. But there is a still wider area of actions which may or may not be incompatible with the gospel, and are therefore more clearly left to personal initiative. As Thomas writes:

> Works of this kind are not enjoined or forbidden in the New Law in its primitive form, but they are left by the lawgiver Christ, to the individual, according to his responsibility for others. And so each individual is free as regards works of this kind to decide what it is best for him to do or avoid doing; and each man in authority is free to make arrangements for his subjects in such matters as to what they should do or avoid doing.

We should, of course, note that many of the arrangements made by recognized civil authority ought to be obeyed ultimately because love requires it for the good of others, as certain regulations for public health and safety do. St Thomas underlines this by saying that 'if the kingdom of God is interior justice and peace and spiritual joy, it necessarily follows that all external actions which are contrary to justice or peace or spiritual joy are contrary to the kingdom of God.' But whether we eat this kind of food or that is, generally speaking, a matter of indifference 'for the kingdom of God is not there', as St Paul says.[32] Thus we have a picture of a very wide spiritual freedom, which is nevertheless not merely individualistic. It works by its own inner dynamism, and its only constraints are those which are contrary to the very nature of the life that keeps it going. For the lesser constraints which arise from the fact that we are living this life in the midst of others are the constraints of an ever-developing and more widely liberating love.

Before we leave St Thomas on this subject, as it affects the theme of the present book, there is perhaps one point which has earlier been several times mentioned in principle and deserves to be mentioned again. St Thomas alludes to it in an answer to the question as to whether any truth can be known without grace. He replies with a clear and quiet confidence: 'Every truth, by whomsoever it may be said, is from the Holy Spirit in the sense that he imparts the natural light and that he moves the mind to understand and utter the truth. This is not so, however, in the sense that he dwells in the soul by sanctifying grace.'[33] Truths of this latter kind are the things of faith of which St Paul speaks in his letters, to which we must in a moment turn. But the sense here expressed by St Thomas of a hidden harmony between the work which God does in creating and that which he does in redeeming is fundamental to the undivided Christian faith as centred on the mystery of the incarnation. It should also evidently be the basis of its confidence in living and acting in the world as it happens to be at any moment of time.

In assessing the results of his investigation of the early tradition about St Paul, Maurice Wiles recognizes that the waters seem later to have become much muddier than they ever seem to have been in the case of St John.[34] But it would be a mistake to suppose that modern exegesis has been entirely destructive and negative in relation to certain themes alive in Church tradition, even if not always based on the kind of interpretation of individual texts which we should feel it necessary to give them today. Among these themes is one which occurs in the writings of Paul, to which more recent scholarship, both Catholic and Protestant, has been devoting a good deal of attention of the kind that has a special interest for this book. The importance of 'discernment' or 'discretion' in spiritual matters is a familiar enough theme in traditional monastic writing. Perhaps few before our own times will have noticed how important a Pauline theme it also is.

The Greek verb which can loosely be translated 'to discern', and words related to it, are of very frequent occurrence in the writings of Paul, and it is very much to our purpose to look briefly at some of these.[35] It is of this business of discerning and being discerned, as *God* discerns, that Paul is conscious in relation to his own vocation as giving him the right to make any comment at all on the gifts of others. He tells the Thessalonians, to whom he presents his own credentials in the opening verses of his first letter to them not 'to quench the spirit',[36] but to test everything as he feels he has himself been tested. The whole content of St Paul's thought makes it clear that he is thinking of 'prophecy' in the sense several times mentioned in this book, as being the function which draws attention to the will of God in situations arising here and now in the life of the Church. The test of relationship to the good of the community is a real test, but it is one which is not to be invoked as an excuse for reducing the life of the Church to a mere bureaucracy.[37] How is this test to be applied? It is to be applied by a certain moral connaturality. This is very difficult to define, but we can rightly see that it is that protection of the Holy Spirit which saves the Church – at least in the long run – from being deceived about views which are not compatible with the genuineness of faith. Thoughts of this kind – so like the sense of liberty at which we have just been looking in a later theologian – are continuously at work in Paul's letters. In the letter to the Galatians we have a clear statement of the love of the common good as being the criterion and a presupposition of a liberty which is authentic. It is a question of 'bearing one another's burdens and so fulfilling the law of Christ'.[38] This can only be done by those who are aware of themselves as they really are. Any kind of settled self-sufficiency is the enemy of this kind of self-knowledge. And this is why everyone must 'test his own work'. It is evident that this sort of assessment is to be based on the tenor of one's life as a whole, and not of individual acts seen in comparison with what others may do. It is difficult for anyone who has been deeply influenced by it not to think at once of the lovely chapter 72 of the Rule of St Benedict in this connection. It urges on the community that 'good zeal' which leads to God and everlasting life, and which prefers nothing to Christ, who has called us *all alike* to eternal life.[39] Modern exegetes often say these things, but not always so memorably.

In St Paul's letter to the Romans we are confronted with several
more complex matters, but the main sections which concern our
present interest come towards the end of the letter. The Romans
are, St Paul says, to allow their moral sense to be 'renewed' so as to
discern what the will of God is. The Greek word for renewal here
used is the same as that used in connection with the transfiguration
of Christ in the accounts of both Matthew and Mark.[40] Thus it is
clearly a question of opening oneself to the action of the spirit.
Those who find themselves liberated under this action are also to
use this strength to bear with those who have not necessarily
reached the same degree of maturity. Thus we find ourselves once
again confronted with the love of all as the criterion of what each
may permit himself. The letter as a whole clearly celebrates
Christian liberty as that which puts us at the disposition of Christ
for the good of others, even when this leads to tribulations.[41] Again
one remembers the conclusion of the prologue of St Benedict's
Rule, where he speaks of sharing in the sufferings of Christ by
patience that we may have a place in his kingdom.

It is perhaps in the first chapter of the letter to the Philippians
that we find the most deeply penetrating account of Christian
moral discernment in Paul's writings. It is in these verses that the
criterion of love and the sense of eternal life, as something here and
now, come together and break into a song of praise. Paul prays that
those who receive his letter may 'abound in love more and more
with knowledge and discernment'.[42] This is plainly a growth
which comes with living, a certain 'taste' which a way of living
brings with it. It is a continuous rediscovery by 'connaturality' of
what the will of God is, here and now. It is a lived liberty, endlessly
liberating.

In summary, we can say that an investigation of this single
theme within the letters of St Paul, far from leaving us with a list of
laws and rules for the Christian life, leaves us with a call to
continuous growth in that kind of understanding which is only
possible for someone who is wholly committed to whatever form of
life a growing discernment confirms as right for us. It is the
common Christian call, whether lived in a monastery or outside it.
This is why so many of the finest monastic texts are appropriate to
those whose obedience to the will of God leads them and keeps
them elsewhere than in a cloister. It is a life often understandably
placed under the sign of affliction and difficulty. For the pattern of
the life of the Son of God on earth is invariably renewed, in some

way or another, in the lives of lesser sons and daughters. 'To discern what the will of God is, is to discern what is the direction of the divine dynamism which establishes in us the law of the spirit that makes us the sons of God. In his obedience to the will of God the Christian is thus sovereignly free – if by this liberty one understands an interior consent to one's being and one's becoming.'[43] To say this is not to describe a life which is marked by instability and impulse. The stability it has is determined by the continuous application of the criterion of what promotes the common growth in love. In prayer, and in honesty with oneself, nothing is seen in isolation from this larger context in which purposes greater than we can glimpse are being worked out. This is exactly why, as we have seen, St Paul and the spiritual masters of the later tradition think that every thought and proposal have to be put to the test which the common life will provide. We grow, indeed, by making our choices in this way.

All this may be splendid to describe and praise, but how does it work out in practice? And how is it to be achieved when we are living it out with the long result of time behind us – whether the result be in our own life or that of the world? It will probably cheer us to bear in mind one or two of the counsels of that great old man Barsanuphius, which often seem to mirror so clearly the apostolic thought which he had evidently so long meditated. Writing to a sick brother, discouraged by his inability to do what he thinks he should, Barsanuphius says:

> As for helplessness, and the fact of being at one time thus, and another time otherwise – well, that is what the road is like. One goes a bit on level country and then one comes to cliffs and hills and mountains, and then one finds oneself back again on the right road. And because we are told 'in everything give thanks, we are debtors', let thanksgiving go before everything whether it is eating or drinking or sleeping. Think about the words of the apostle: 'Whether you eat or drink or whatever you do . . .' Hold fast to this in everything, and the God of thanksgiving will look after you.[44]

Anyone who reads this astonishing collection of desert letters with the attention they deserve will be amazed at the range and comprehensiveness of their allusions to Holy Scripture, and by the overriding sense of a spiritual life evolving in liberty.

Knock and it will be opened to you. Ask the good God to send
you the Holy Spirit, the Comforter. When he comes he teaches
us everything, and opens to us all mysteries. Beg to be directed
by him. He leaves neither error nor agitation in the heart, neither
boredom nor lassitude in the spirit. He enlightens the eyes,
strengthens the heart, raises the spirit. Cleave to him, believe in
him, love him . . . Do not be timid . . .[45]

In common with other great spiritual masters, Barsanuphius
teaches that 'every thought in which the calm of humility does not
predominate is not according to God, but is manifestly the
righteousness of evil. For our Lord comes with calm. But all that
the enemy does comes with disturbance and stirring of anger.'

And, if one had to choose a theme on which Barsanuphius seems
to have gone out of his way to find every conceivable quickening
text, it is one which comes earlier in the letter just quoted, and
again and again in others:

'Do not give yourself any fixed rule. Be obedient and humble
and, every day, demand an account of yourself. The prophet
referred to this business of "every day", when he said "And I said:
*Now*, I begin." And Moses: "And *now*, Israel." Keep yourself, too,
in the "now".'[46] Do these words need any special date attached to
them?

# 12

## EPILOGUE

'Keeping the now', as those who seriously try it discover, demands a number of fairly exacting virtues. Not the least of these is that of somehow contriving to get inside the limitations of circumstance, inner and outer, and thus to begin something today, with no certainty of what the result may be. In this, the making of books is not unlike the making of gardens, and indeed the care of both has not infrequently gone together. With Grimald as his teacher, Walafrid Strabo had been happy at St Gall in the early ninth century, where there was a growing library that was to be of more importance in the continuity of European culture than its earliest makers can have guessed. If there is to be a flowering summer, the ground must be prepared and the seed planted, of which perhaps only others will see the result. It was natural that Walafrid, himself afterwards to be abbot of his own monastery of Reichenau, should dedicate his book *On the Care of Gardens* to his old teacher abbot Grimald. He pictures him sitting 'in the green darkness of the apple trees' as the boys, 'your little laughing boys', from what sounds as if it must have been the most humane of schools,[1] are gathering the 'huge apples' in the orchard.[2]

H. E. Bates, a not inconsiderable gardener himself, was reflecting on the making of gardens when he died in 1974 and some of the things he said, many forgotten gardeners might perhaps also have said in their own way. Mentioning how his own garden started from 'a very unpromising piece of farmyard full of docks, nettles, thistles and just about every other noxious weed common to farmyards', he tells how it is still evolving. 'A garden should never stand still. It should never be a monument to complacency . . . Change, I tell myself, is not decay; change is resuscitation, a new view.'[3] It was in this belief that this present book was written as some kind of setting for its predecessor, *Asking the Fathers*. An old rose can reveal unsuspected beauties in a new garden, show a capacity to 'fit' that not everyone might have guessed. I can think of others who might have demonstrated this better than I. But then, like Andrei Sinyavsky, that most quietly companionable and therefore nearly unquotable writer: 'I always imagine there is some book which absolutely must be read, only I can never find out which one it is . . .' [4] Perhaps it sometimes has to be a book one is foolish enough to try to write oneself.

Sinyavsky confesses that in the almost timeless days in prison he thought of books 'constantly'. And among the thoughts which came is one that does not make the old monastic libraries seem so very far away. He writes:

> A book has something of the 'magic cap', or the 'magic tablecloth'. This peculiar property of books was well understood by the old calligraphic scribes who were sensitive to the need of words to flower into pictures or to transform themselves into leafy trees hung with toys. Letters leapt out at you with a roar from the beautiful pathways of the ornamental initial, quite distinct from the undergrowth of the text, and the book was read slowly, with delicious pauses.

This sounds like a discreet and telling counsel, the very condition of the slow evolution of a true culture. He continues even more interestingly:

> The art of the calligraphic scribe cannot be brought back. But we can help the book's age-old longing to be arcane and impenetrable by making its verbal texture so dense that it fairly dances before the reader's eyes, and, catching his breath, he sees little green leaves and the pretty muzzles of red fox cubs running out on to the page from under the black, charred tree stumps of the printer's words. [5]

This aim of writing something that it is not only useful to read 'with delicious pauses', but to which one likes often to return can, of course, also be the enemy of the making of books, as it nearly became in Gogol's case. On this Sinyavsky is at his own most delicious in a book on Gogol newly translated into French. With one of those reversals of expectation which one has even seen him bring off in a television interview, the book begins with the epilogue. During the course of this he says:

> Gogol dreamed of writing a book the reading of which would make the world of perfection come into flower before one's very eyes, a book which would have established, on an earth renewed, an everlasting humanity, liberated from sin. In the imagined

light of this book everything he had produced before in the form of fugitive literary exercises lost all its value, seemed to be inconsistent, noxious, crying out to be revised or suppressed. Gogol never wrote this great book, for it is given to no one to write it, but he was nevertheless led on and penetrated by it . . . Not to write, but to save; not to portray, but to prophesy in the hope of the transfiguration of the world by the power of the living word . . .[6]

What a conflict indeed, and one often not unconnected with another, of which Gogol himself had written:

It seems to everyone today that he could do so much good if only he held the position and place of his neighbour, and that it is his job alone that hinders him. This is the cause of all the troubles. Just now, we ought all to reflect on the possibility of doing some good just where we are. Believe me, it is not for nothing that God wants everyone to stay just where he is now placed.[7]

This could sound like a very reactionary passivity – to which, in any case, Gogol himself never lived up – but it also embodies an old-fashioned wisdom which gardeners and book-collectors some-times learn. It is the wisdom of taking another look round the property, seeing whether it is really true that *everything* has to be rooted out before any improvement can be expected. *Some* new things get old quicker than well-established old things that renew themselves, if they are allowed to do so. It may be as well to make it a rule, on waking, to attend to the diverse messages of the new day. Elizabeth Bishop does it hauntingly, hearing a little black dog, just let out by its owner, bouncing and rushing among the fallen leaves:

Obviously, he has no sense of shame.
He and the bird know everything is answered,
all taken care of,
no need to ask again.
— Yesterday brought to today so lightly!
(A yesterday I find it almost impossible to lift.)[8]

# NOTES

## Chapter 1
## THE DEMANDS OF LOVE

1  Psalm 11. I accept the RSV view that the whole of the suggestions of the first three verses really express temptations of thought and should be treated as one. This possibility is also admitted in the Jewish: *Soncino* Book of Psalms (London 1965). For the first verse I adopt the RSV marginal reading, but in the passage as a whole I do not quote exclusively from the RSV.

2  *SC* 92, pars. 124–6 (pp. 380–84).

3  *RB*, cap. 58.

4  Ephesians 4.23 (Wand).

5  *The Wisdom of the Desert Fathers*, trans. Sister Benedicta Ward, Fairacres, (Oxford 1975), intro., p. xii.

6  For the sake of conciseness I should like at this point to make my own some words from a note to the brilliant lectures of Professor R. J. Z. Werblowsky, *Beyond Tradition and Modernity* (London 1976), p. 129: 'This phenomenon of convergence cannot be exorcized by an invocation of the spectre of "syncretism". Quite apart from the fact that one man's syncretism is another man's ecumenism, one has to take into account that the nature of syncretisms too is subject to developments and changes. It is certainly not a matter of "religions" joining forces against the enemy forces of materialism and atheism (since the contrast has become meaningless in the religious sensibility of many), but rather of the sense of a common responsibility for elucidating and preserving whatever dimensions of religiosity and/or spirituality attach to the human condition.'

7  J. Needham, *Science and Civilisation in China*, vol. 1, preface, p. 9 (Cambridge 1954; several times reprinted). To this unique pioneer study we shall return.

8  *AF*, pp. 128–9.

9  T. S. Eliot, *Notes towards a Definition of Culture*, paperback edn (London 1962), pp. 28, 58, 19 and 32 respectively.

10  *AF*, p. 5.

11  D. Staniloae, 'L'Accueil de la tradition dans le monde d'aujourd'hui' in *Irénikon*, tome XLVII (1974), pp. 451–66. The quotations are from pp. 451, 452, 452–3 and 459–60 respectively.

12  Archimandrite Sophrony, *The Undistorted Image* (London 1958), p. 51. It is, of course, the hope of many of us that a few traditional monastic cases will

survive, in spite of everything. But the prognostic for big institutes does not seem good.

13   1 John 3.20.

14   K. Lorenz, *Civilized Man's Eight Deadly Sins*, paperback edn (London 1974), p. 48.

15   F. E. L. Priestley, *Language and Structure in Tennyson's Poetry* (London 1973), p. 171.

16   For a very balanced and convincing view of Arnold's position, see A. E. Dyson, *Between Two Worlds* (London 1972), ch. 3, 'The Last Enchantments'.

17   Charles Tennyson, *Six Tennyson Essays* (London reprint 1972), p. 119.

18   C. Ricks, *Tennyson* (London 1972), p. 221.

19   T. S. Eliot, *In Memoriam* (1936), conveniently accessible in J. D. Hunt, *Tennyson: In Memoriam* (London 1970), p. 135, cited in Ricks, op. cit., p. 225.

20   T. S. Eliot, *The Social Function of Poetry*, a lecture originally given to the British-Norwegian Institute in 1943 and most easily available in *On Poetry and Poets*, paperback edn (London 1971), p. 25.

21   An interesting case for the survival of religious sensibility forms the bulk of the essay 'Can the Church survive?', in David Martin's *Tracts Against the Times* (London 1973), pp. 171ff.

22   C. Ricks, *The Poems of Tennyson* (London 1969), p. 1350.

23   E. Berridge, *The Barretts at Hope End* (London 1974), p. 175.

24   1 John 4.1.

25   N. Afanasieff, *L'Église du Saint-Esprit* (Paris 1975), p. 173.

26   Dostoevsky, *The Brothers Karamazov*, Penguin edn (1958), vol. 1, pp. 376–7.

27   O. Clément, *Dialogues avec le patriarche Athénagoras* (Paris 1969), pp. 584, 138.

28   Sermon 26, par. 4 (*SC* 22 bis, p. 144). With the exception of this first text, all the others cited and many more will be found in A. Squire, 'Universal Compassion in Leo the Great', in *Studia Patristica*, vol. XIII (Berlin 1975), pp. 280–85.

29   O. Clément, op. cit., p. 461.

30   S. Hynes, *The Auden Generation* (London 1976), p. 323. As someone brought up in a very literary and politically conscious circle in this period, I have noticed only one error of judgement in this fascinating book. Having insisted that *The Brown Book of the Hitler Terror* of 1933 'must have been highly influential in creating the general English attitude towards German fascism' (p. 130), Professor Hynes admits in a note that he can find only one reference to it and *that* in a poem of Herbert Reed. I cannot be the only Englishman who first heard of this book through Professor Hynes!

31   O. Sirén, *Kinas Kunst under tre Årtusende*, Book 2 (Stockholm 1943), p. 330. William Cohn, *Chinese Painting* (London 1948) gives three snatches of this scroll in his plates 94–6.

32　Hesychasm is the name given to a school of monastic training which emphasizes the virtues disposing to physical and spiritual tranquillity. Primarily associated with the monasteries of Mount Athos in the fourteenth century, whose gifted theological defender is discussed in chapter ten of this book, it has its roots in a much older past, going back to the Syrian deserts. Although it derives its name from the recurring Greek word for 'quiet', it would be erroneous to confuse it with teaching of the kind later associated with European 'quietism'.

33　Wilhelm and Jung, *The Secret of the Golden Flower*, revised edn (London 1962), pp. 90–91.

34　Jacques Leclercq, *Le Jeur de l'homme* (Paris 1976), p. 158.

35　F. Jeanson, *La Foi d'un incroyant* (Paris 1963).

36　Psalm 46.4.

37　I. Hausherr, *Les Leçons d'un contemplatif* (Paris 1960), p. 85, no. 60, and p. 159, no. 125. The author of the texts is Evagrius.

# Chapter 2
# DETERMINED LIVES

1　David McLellan, *Marx* (London 1975), pp. 71–2. The major book is D. McLellan, *Karl Marx, His Life and Thought* (London and New York 1973).

2　Michel Foucault, *Les Mots et les Choses* (Paris 1966), p. 274.

3　V. S. Pritchett, *A Cab at the Door* (London 1968). The references are to pp. 185, 43, 201–2 and 185–6 respectively.

4　For Norway the facts, based on government statistics, are admirably represented in a diagram by my friend Noralv Veggeland, *Regional Ubalanse* (Oslo 1976), p. 21. (In Norwegian.) For France the situation with ample bibliographies is well reflected in J.-P. Houssel, *Histoire des paysans français* (Rouanne 1976). The figures show that between 1955 and 1970 one more farm was given up every ten minutes, and this tendency is continuing with a marked accentuation south of the Loire. Cf. pp. 463–7. I have myself direct experience of the same phenomenon in Belgium where I was a village parish priest from 1965 to 1967. At that time every family owned a few acres of land and from two to twelve cows. Today, in this area of Ardennes tourism, only two families still own any land.

5　*Hymns Ancient and Modern*, no. 573, v. 3.

6　G. Lichtheim, *A Short History of Socialism* (London 1970), pp. 34, 72. In this chapter I follow Lichtheim in using the word socialism, not as a party label, but 'as the designation of a historically conditioned response to a particular challenge' (p. x).

7　*The Eighteenth Brumaire of Louis Bonaparte*, par. 2. The complete text, here cited in translation, may be conveniently found in the appendix to E. Fischer, *Marx in his Own Words*, Pelican edn (1973), p. 168.

8   'When tired of economics, Marx relaxed by reading Thucydides and the
    classical authors that were "ever new". He read all Aeschylus in the original
    every year. He was one of the last Renaissance men.' McLellan, op. cit., p. 8.

9   K. Polanyi, *The Great Transformation* (Boston 1957), p.39. Quoted in
    Lichtheim, op. cit., p. 10.

10  Lichtheim, op. cit., pp. 67, 69, 70.

11  M. Merleau-Ponty, 'Marxism and Philosophy', Eng. trans. in *Pheno-
    menology, Language and Sociology*, ed. J. O'Neill (London 1974), p. 179.
    The original will be found in Merleau-Ponty, *Sens et Non-Sens* (Geneva
    1965), p. 230.

12  Trans. E. Fischer, op. cit., pp. 170–71.

13  The phrase with sufficient of the context to explain the point is quoted by
    Merleau-Ponty, op. cit., p. 182.

14  Lichtheim, op. cit., p. 76. But honesty requires one to note the remark of
    Lichtheim in an essay on 'The interpretation of Marx's thought', written in
    1967 and republished in Lichtheim, *From Marx to Hegel* (London 1971), p.
    67: 'The dialectical materialism put forward [by Engels] has only the
    remotest connection with Marx's own viewpoint, though it is a biographical
    fact of some importance that Marx raised no objection . . .'

15  K. Marx, *Capital*, ch. 4, sect. 3. Everyman edn, reprinted (London 1972), pp.
    154–5, with a valuable footnote citing Hegel. A moving example in a work of
    fiction that is certainly based on fact will be found in the circumstances
    leading up to the dismissal of the stonemason Thomas Hearne in Flora
    Thompson's *Still Glides the Stream*, ch. 2. Paperback edn (Oxford 1976), pp.
    26–30.

16  One discussion by Erich Fromm, *Marx's Concept of Man* (New York 1976)
    offers the substantial advantage of a large selection of Marx's early writings in
    translation at the end.

17  Preface to the first German edition of *Capital* (Everyman edn, pp. xlvii–li),
    cited independently in E. Fischer, op. cit., pp. 172–6.

18  J. A. Schumpeter, *History of Economic Analysis* (Oxford and New York
    1954), p. 438 with note 7, and pp. 439, 441 and 885 respectively.

19  Preface to Marx's 'Contribution to the Critique of Hegel's Philosophy of
    Law', in Karl Marx, *Collected Works* (London 1975), pp. 175–6.

20  V. Gardavsky, *God is not yet dead* (London 1973), pp. 169–70.

21  For Marx himself, see the useful passage quoted in Fischer, op. cit., p. 21.

22  Gardavsky, op. cit., p. 172.

23  Same work, same edn as note 19 (p. 182): 'To be radical is to grasp the root of
    the matter. But for man the root is man himself.'

24  *The Twentieth-century Mind*, eds. C. B. Cox and A. E. Dyson (Oxford 1972),
    vol. 2, p. 156.

25  N. Berdyaev, *Les Sources et les Sens du communisme russe* (Paris 1963), p. 262.

26  N. Berdyaev, *Christianisme, Marxisme*, (Paris 1975), pp. 36, 37–8.

27  *Les Sources*, as note 25. Pp. 208, 209–10 and 224 respectively.

28   Richard Pipes, *Russia under the Old Régime* (London 1974), pp. 317–18. In this fine book the author is aware that the chapter on the Church is inadequate. But nothing less than a study as well-documented would be likely to refute the author's main positions.

29   *Les Sources*, as notes 25 and 27, pp. 233–6.

30   Lichtheim, op. cit., pp. 263, 266.

31   Maxim Gorky, *My Childhood*, trans. and introduced by R. Wilks (London 1966), p. 8. I take the view of Andrew Field, *The Complexion of Russian Literature* (London 1971), p. 275: 'It is not at all unlikely that he died at Stalin's request.'

32   F. M. Borras, *Maxim Gorky the Writer*, cited in R. F. Christian, *Tolstoy* (Cambridge 1969), p. 256.

33   K. Clark, *Civilisation* (London 1969), pp. 344, 347.

34   Maxim Gorky, *On Literature* (Moscow, no date, but recent), pp. 214, 231, 291.

35   As note 34, pp. 296, 308, 325; and the conclusion, pp. 347–8.

36   Maxim Gorky, *My Universities* (Moscow, no date, but recent), pp. 343–4.

37   Maxim Gorky, *My Apprenticeship*, trans. R. Wilks (London 1974), pp. 98, 122, 126.

38   *My Childhood*, as note 31, p. 20.

39   *My Apprenticeship*, p. 60.

40   *My Childhood*, pp. 60, 101, 164.

41   *My Universities*, pp. 365, 465–6.

42   A. Field, op. cit. (London 1971), p. 225.

43   *Solitude et communication*, 'Rencontres internationales de Genève, 1975' (Neuchâtel 1975), pp. 165, 167.

# Chapter 3

# SMOKE

1   'In the age of the common man Gorky's *Childhood* perhaps commands a wider audience than Tolstoy's, and there is no doubt that some readers of Tolstoy's book feel a certain impatience with its over-conscious literariness …' See R. F. Christian, *Tolstoy* (Cambridge 1969), pp. 36–7. The whole passage should be read in the light of the two books it discusses. Certainly my own experience confirms Professor Christian's suspicion.

2   G. Steiner, *Tolstoy or Dostoevsky*, revised edn (1967), pp. 235–6.

3   Dostoevsky, *Crime and Punishment*, Book 3: 1 and 5, D. Magarshack trans. Penguin edn (1966), pp. 219 and 272–3 respectively.

4   Op. cit., p. 262. In his defence speech referred to at the end of the previous chapter, it was Shakespeare that Sinyavsky chose as his example of how difficult it can be to 'place' a writer.

5   *Crime and Punishment*, Book 1, 5, p. 72 and *My Apprenticeship*, ch. 16, p. 293.

6   R. Freeborn, *Turgenev, A Study* (Oxford 1963), p. 47.

7   I. Turgenev, *The Portrait Game*, ed. M. Mainwaring (London 1973), intro. p. 21. A charming and useful companion to the reading of Turgenev.

8   R. Pipes, *Russia under the Old Régime* (London 1974), pp. 252, 271, 275.

9   See the two letters from that period cited in A. Lehning, *Michel Bakounine et les autres* (Paris 1976), pp. 81, 84.

10  Freeborn, op. cit., p. 2.

11  M. Bakunin, *Selected Writings*, ed. A. Lehning (London 1973), pp. 31ff.

12  I cite the translation by R. Freeborn, *Rudin* (London 1975), pp. 62–3.

13  Freeborn's note on this in his translation, p. 183, is not satisfactory. It neither gives the reference to Bede, *Ecclesiastical History*, Book 2, ch. 13, nor does it notice how Turgenev has transformed the original.

14  *Rudin*, pp. 89, 91, 144, 146.

15  Ibid., pp. 156–9.

16  Ibid., pp. 166, 177–8.

17  Quoted in S. Hynes, *The Auden Generation* (London 1976), p. 190.

18  For a valuable glimpse of the situation in retrospect, see P. Toynbee, *The Distant Drum* (London 1976), where those fighting on both sides in the Spanish Civil War witness to the living importance of Spanish anarchism.

19  For the interest of Marx see the sketch by D. McLellan cited in chapter three (op. cit., pp. 15–18) and that of Turgenev: Freeborn, *Turgenev*, p. 16.

20  The introduction to Freeborn's *Rudin* was reasonably criticized by Aileen Kelly (*TLS*, 6 June 1975) for its strained attempt to link Turgenev's ideas with those of Carlyle's *Heroes and Hero-Worship*.

21  S. Hynes, op. cit., p. 250.

22  *Rudin*, pp. 157–7, 176.

23  McLellan, op. cit., p. 22.

24  *Selected Writings* (as note 11), p. 270.

25  *Rudin*, p. 157.

26  Freeborn, *Turgenev*, p. 38.

27  Pipes, op. cit., p. 271.

28  Freeborn, *Turgenev*, p. 69, n. 1.

29  Rosemary Edmonds, introduction to Turgenev, *Fathers and Sons* (London 1965), p. 11. This is the translation I cite.

30  *Fathers and Sons*, pp. 17, 19, 30–31.

31  Ibid., pp. 32, 39–45, 58.

32  Ibid., pp. 60–61, 66–71.

33  Ibid., pp. 92, 96, 102, 106, 116, 125.

34  Ibid., pp. 144, 163, 196, 210–13.

35  Ibid., pp. 225, 230–32, 237.

36  A. E. Housman, *Collected Poems* (London 1966), p. 103.

37  C. Ricks, 'The Nature of Housman's Poetry', essay reprinted in *A. E. Housman: A Collection of Critical Essays*, ed. C. Ricks (London 1968), pp. 120–21.

38  Constance Garnett trans., reissued (London 1970), p. 204. My italics.

39  Intro. Everyman edn, *Capital* (London 1972), p. xiii.

40  Ibid., p. lxxi.

41  *Fathers and Sons*, p. 30.

42  Ibid., pp. 122, 125.

43  Freeborn, *Turgenev*, pp. 183, 186.

44  Turgenev, *Smoke*. Everyman trans. by N. Duddington, reissued (London 1970), pp. 225–6; and see p. 228.

# Chapter 4

# WATCHMEN

1  'Many serious scholars still accept a petrine authorship of 1 Peter, at least in the sense that Peter stands behind the letter with Silvanus as his amanuensis or secretary.' See *Peter in the New Testament*, eds. R. E. Brown *et al.* (London 1974), p. 16.

2  J. W. C. Wand, *The New Testament Letters* (Oxford 1946), p. 173. For a useful note on *sobriety* and being *sober* in the NT, see William Barclay, *The New Testament*, vol. 11 (London 1969), p. 330.

3  *Poems in Prose*, no. LXXVIII, Russian and English text, ed. A. Mazon (Oxford 1951), pp. 202–3.

4  W. Barclay's happy translation of Matthew 5.45. It seems right to interpret the apparently unorthodox *words* of Gorky's grandmother in the light of this text. Her instinct is consistently evangelical and patristic.

5  For a fuller discussion, see the passages on this notion in *AF*, pp. 18–19, 54–5, 160–4.

6  In *Librum Regum* 1, Lib. v, vv. 19–20 (*PL*, 79, col. 374C). Although this text was not corrected by Gregory himself, there is no doubt of his authorship: see the introduction to the edn of *Corpus Christianorum*, vol. 144.

7  *Epistola Aurea*, 80, ed. J. Déchanet (Paris 1975), pp. 206–7.

8  Barsanuphe et Jean de Gaza, *Correspondance*, letter 86 (Solesmes 1972), p. 81.

9  Simone Weil, *Oppression and Liberty* (London 1958; reprinted 1972), pp. 164–5.

10  *Republic* 492–3 (ref. not given in previous trans.). In Eng. trans., *Plato Complete* (Princeton 1973), especially p. 729.

11  Philippians 2. 6–8, cited by Simone Weil, op. cit., p. 166.

12  R. Garaudy, *The Alternative Future*, Penguin edn (London 1976), p. 88.

13  IIa, IIae, Q.81, articles 5, 7.

14  Op. cit., pp. 108–9.

15  J. Bronowski, *The Ascent of Man* (London and New York 1973), p. 306.

16  Op. cit., pp. 308–9, 348–9, 334, 353.

17  J. Needham, *Science and Civilisation in China*, vol. 1, p. 9.

18  J. Hamburger, *L'Homme et les hommes* (Paris 1976), pp. 63–4, 97, 113, 124–5.

19  Ibid., pp. 143, 152 ff.

20  Letter 154, ed. cit., pp. 135–6.

21  R. Maurin, *Les Techniques du bonheur* (Paris 1976), p. 122.

22  A. Cottrell, *Portrait of Nature* (London 1975), pp. 230–31.

23  K. Rahner, 'Science as a "Confession"?', no. 25 in *Theological Investigations*, vol. 3 (London 1967), p. 389.

24  Reprinted in E. Faure, *Colloque d'Épernay* (Paris 1977), p. 147. The report of the discussion following this talk is a frightening reminder of how remote even a select audience can be from the thoughts of the speaker.

25  R. Dawkins, *The Selfish Gene* (Oxford 1976), pp. 3, 150, 203 ff.

26  Hamburger, op. cit., pp. 148–50.

27  Op. cit., pp. 4, 208.

28  Interestingly enough, by the summer of 1978, a hundred English doctors had committed themselves publicly to suggesting that instruction in Transcendental Meditation should be given as part of the National Health Service. The report (*Daily Telegraph*, 31 August 1978) does not make it clear how far they were interested in more than therapy. As a result, the question programme 'Tuesday Call' at 9.05 a.m. on BBC Radio 4 on 5 September 1978 took up this subject and produced a number of sensible questions sensibly answered by the Anglican Peter Dewey and psychologist Peter Russell.

29  Ia pars., Q. 105, art. 5.

30  Op. cit., p. 390.

31  A comment on this familiar verse from P. L. Travers, 'The Shortest Stories in the World', *TLS*, 15 July 1977, p. 857.


# Chapter 5
## CHANGE

1  Song of Solomon, 3.3 and 5.7, with ref to 5.2.

2  A rare example of a contemporary who seems to have these gifts is the French-speaking Arab scholar, Samir Amin. His *L'Accumulation à l'échelle mondiale* (Paris and Sfan Dakar 1970), with its *post face* of 1971, is available in paperback (Paris 1976).

3  Ia pars., Q. 1, art. 8.

4  In relation to A. Cottrell's *Portrait of Nature*, quoted in the previous chapter, it should be noted that his concluding words suggest that he expects that we

shall one day 'find' God along the same line of inquiry as that of other scientific discoveries. No theologian has ever believed this.

5 *PG* 45, cols. 145–73.

6 *De Gen. ad Litt.*, II, 17, par. 37 (*PL* 34, col. 279).

7 IIa, IIae, Q. 95, art. 5, corp. and *ad 2um*.

8 Ia pars., Q. 116, art. 4.

9 *De Consol.*, Lib. IV, 6 (Loeb edn, ll. 74–5).

10 Op. cit., cols. 169–70 B.

11 The *I Ching* or *Book of Changes*, trans. R. Wilhelm, English version C. F. Baynes, 2 vols. (London 1951), now available in 1 vol. A new trans., John Blofeld, *The Book of Changes*, 2nd edn (London 1968), is notable.

12 See *Asking the Fathers*, p. 8.

13 A. Waley, *Three Ways of Thought in Ancient China* (London 1939, reprinted 1946), p. 17. I refer to this below as *TTC*.

14 J. Needham, *Science and Civilisation in China*, vol. 2 (Cambridge 1956, often reprinted), pp. 307–8. All subsequent references to Needham are to this volume.

15 H. Wilhelm, *Change*, Eng. trans. C. F. Baynes, paperback edn (London 1975).

16 Edn cit., pp. 16–22, 34.

17 M. Granet, *La Pensée chinoise* (original edn, Paris 1934; latest edn, here cited, Paris 1968).

18 Needham's most eloquent praise of Granet's volume as 'a work of genius' occurs at the beginning of section 13 of his great work, pp. 216–17. His own explicit study of Taoism occurs in section 10, pp. 33–164.

19 Op. cit., p. 75.

20 Needham, pp. 36–7. Needham's trans. of *TTC* 51 is nearly identical with Waley's in A. Waley, *The Way and Its Power* (London 1934). Any subsequent reference to Waley, *TTC* means this edn.

21 Pp. 38, 40, 47 (my italics).

22 Needham, pp. 56–7. See Blofeld's note on this word in his trans. of *The Book of Changes*, oracle 20, which he calls 'looking down'.

23 Needham, p. 57 and Waley, *TTC* 43.

24 Needham, pp. 58, 62. The lines I quote from *TTC* are identical with Waley's version of chs. 28 and 7 respectively.

25 Needham, pp. 68–9.

26 Needham, pp. 273–4 and Granet, pp. 116–18.

27 Needham, pp. 276–7 and Granet, p. 123.

28 Granet, p. 272 and Needham, pp. 280–81, 293. Needham once uses 'interdependence' on p. 289. His note b. on p. 291 is, as far as I can see, his only favourable reference to the work of C. G. Jung, whose name does not even appear in the index, though it is chiefly through Jung that the *I Ching* is now widely known.

29    Needham, pp. 304–7, 310. Jungian users of the *I Ching* seem to have taken their revenge on Needham by never referring to his work!

30    Needham, pp. 322, 336.

31    H. Maspero, *Le Taoisme et les religions chinoises* (Paris 1971), pp.314–17. On the breathing techniques, see the text quoted by Needham, p. 333.

32    A. Waley, *Three Ways* (as note 13 above), p. 20.

33    Needham, p. 124.

34    Needham, pp. 62, 152.

35    J. P. de Caussade, *Self-abandonment to Divine Providence*, 1.1,5, trans. A. Thorold (London 1959), p. 9; and cf. *Asking the Fathers*, ch. 19.

36    Blofeld trans. (as note 11 above), p. 7.

37    11a, 11ae, Q. 167, art. 1.

38    (As note 35 above), 1.2,4 (p. 25).

39    *Docta ignorantia*, Ep. 130 'Ad Probam', cap. 15, par. 28: *PL* 33, 505.

40    James 4.7, *RB* prologue; de Caussade, 1.1,5 (p. 9).


# Chapter 6

# LEVIATHAN

1    C. G. Jung, *Memories, dreams, reflections* (London 1963), pp. 70, 55–7.

2    L. van der Post, *Jung and the Story of Our Time* (London 1976), mentions, however, the case of a nun who was helped by the book and subsequent correspondence with Jung. It is difficult for me not to agree (p. 221) that Victor White's article (*Blackfriars*, March 1955) was a good deal more unfriendly in tone and implication than Jung might have expected it to be.

3    *Memories*, pp. 325–6.

4    Richard Kehoe in the now defunct *Dominican Studies* v (1952), pp. 228–31.

5    R. Gordis, *The Book of God and Man* (Chicago and London 1965). Hereafter referred to as R. G. It will also be a pleasure occasionally to quote, where it is superior, the version of an old teacher Dr A. Guillaume, posthumously published as *Studies in the Book of Job*, ed. J. Macdonald (Leiden 1968), hereafter referred to as A.G.

6    R.G., pp. 219–24, 227.

7    G. von Rad, *Wisdom in Israel* (London 1972), p. 53. Hereafter referred to as G.V.

8    G.V., p. 4. I follow the argument of this book closely, though normally only give references where I cite verbatim.

9    R.G., p. 224.

10    G.V., pp. 38–40 (italics mine).

11    G.V., p.55, quoting Job 32.6ff.

12   G.V., pp. 66–8.

13   G.V., p. 73 (italics mine).

14   G.V., pp. 99–101.

15   Job 26.14 (RSV).

16   Job 40.17 (A.G. trans.). The Eng. trans. by von Rad (p. 118) gives the impossible view that the tail 'hangs down', which cannot be right for a cedar.

17   Job 41.15. (R.G. trans., where the verse is 41.7).

18   Job 28 is discussed in G.V., ch. 9, 'The Self-revelation of Creation'.

19   R.G., pp. 67–75.

20   Job 3.26 and 5.23 (R.G.).

21   Job 6.12 and 7.18 (R.G.).

22   Job 9.32–3 (R.G.).

23   Job 11.6 (R.G.).

24   Job 13.12 (A.G.).

25   Job 13.16 (R.G.).

26   Job 15.25 (R.G.).

27   Job 16.2 (A.G.).

28   Job 16.9, 12, 21 (R.G.).

29   Job 19.22, 29 (R.G.).

30   Job 21.9, 29 (R.G.).

31   Job 21.34 (A.G.).

32   Job 23.3, 6 (R.G.).

33   Job 27.5 (R.G.).

34   Job 30.26 (A.G.).

35   Job 31.35 (R.G.).

36   Job 33.14; 36.23; 37.13 (R.G.).

37   R.G., p. 287.

38   Job 38.2 (R.G.).

39   Job 40.8 (RSV).

40   Job 39.17 (R.G.).

41   Job 41.26 (R.G.).

42   R.G., p. 297.

43   G.V., p. 209, note 25: 'It will never be possible to provide an entirely satisfactory link, from the literary point of view, between the Job narrative and the poetic dialogue . . .'

44   See texts and discussion in G.V., pp. 200 ff.

45   Job 14.19; 19.10.

46   Cf. G.V., pp. 203, 207.

47   G.V., pp. 211–15, 217.

48   G.V., pp. 220–21.

49  Rupert of Deutz, *De operibus Spiritus Sancti*, Lib. 2, 29 (1638D), *SC* edn (Paris 1967), p. 292.

50  C. G. Jung, *Collected Works*, vol. 11, 2nd edn (London 1969), p. 408.

51  The *Bhagavad-Gita*, ch. 11, vv. 19, 23. Ed. and trans. R. C. Zaehner (Oxford 1973).

52  Job 41.6, 14 (R.G.).

53  Amos 3.6b.

54  Isaiah 45.7.

55  G.V., pp. 203–6.

56  Undoubtedly the best study of this subject is H.-I. Marrou, 'Un Ange déchu, un ange pourtant', originally written in 1948 for the volume of *Études carmélitaines* on Satan, and now made available again in the excellent *mélanges* by H.-I. Marrou, *Patristique et humanisme* (Paris 1976), pp. 393–408.

57  As note 4 above, pp. 230–31.

58  G.V., pp. 296–7.

59  G.V., p. 303.

60  Revelation 2.17 (RSV).

61  John Chrysostom, *On the Incomprehensibility of God*, critical text, *SC* 28 bis (Paris 1970).

62  Trans. of 1 Corinthians 2.9 (Wand).

63  *PG* 90, cols. 1184B–C.


## Chapter 7
## REMEMBERING THE SAINTS

1  St John of the Cross, *Dark Night of the Soul*, ch. 12, par. 3. *Collected Works*, ed. E. Allison Peers, revised edn (London 1953), p. 364.

2  E. Allison Peers, *Spirit of Flame*, 7th edn (London 1947), p. 100.

3  Quoted in Crisogono de Jesus, *St John of the Cross* (London 1958), p. 49.

4  Cf. Jean le Solitaire, *Aux Sources de la tradition du Carmel* (Paris 1953), especially pp. 244, 164 ff. and the valuable note on St Teresa, p. 251, note 1.

5  St Teresa of Avila, *Foundations*, ch. 14. *Collected Works*, ed. E. Allison Peers (London 1946), vol. 3, p. 67.

6  This verse trans. by Roy Campbell, Penguin edn (London 1960), p. 31.

7  Here I deliberately quote Peers' prose trans. (edn as note 1 above), p. 365. With regard to the biographical facts, Crisogono is fuller, but Peers' assessment of John's literary development in *Spirit of Flame*, pp. 40–45, is more convincing.

8  This cannot have been the *Flos* of Ribadeneira, which did not appear from Madrid until 1599, after John's death.

9  *PG* 47, cols. 451–2 D. On the debated question of the orthodoxy of these

impressive homilies, see the sensible remarks by Robert Murray, *Symbols of Church and Kingdom* (Cambridge 1975), especially p. 35: 'Messalianism was probably no sect but a "movement", characteristic of Syrian asceticism which laid too much stress on the experience of the Spirit for the liking of ecclesiastics in the institutional Church.'

10   *Piété Confiante*, ed. F. Klein (Paris 1905), p. 114. Reprinted 1948.

11   Judith 8.22. (Vulgate text, from which I translate. The Latin is still in use in the latest edn of the breviary.)

12   Hebrews 11 and 12.

13   Acts 2.44–6; cf. 4.34–5.

14   A. Squire, *Asking the Fathers* (London 1973), p. 111 and *passim* on Anthony.

15   *Sent.*, Lib. III, cap. 10 (*PL* 83, col. 682).

16   Closing paragraphs of Homily 33, *SC* 28 bis, pp. 216 ff, starting at line 353.

17   Palladius, *Dialogue on the Life of St John Chrysostom*, 38. Eng. trans. H. Moore (London 1921), p. 96.

18   See the essays in John Hick, *The Myth of God Incarnate* (London 1977).

19   Excellent review of modern studies of Maximus in opening pages of L. Thunberg, *Microcosm and Mediator* (Lund 1965).

20   Cf. A. Riou, *Le Monde et l'église selon Maxime* (Paris 1973), especially ch. 2.

21   This point is made with admirable clarity in a review of *The Myth of God Incarnate* by H. McCabe, in *New Blackfriars*, August 1977, pp. 350–57.

22   Facts and texts discussed in J. M. Garrigues, *Maxime le Confesseur* (Paris 1976).

23   The two texts of Maximus referred to in this paragraph are discussed in Riou, op. cit., pp. 65, 79.

24   A complete translation of Cuthbert's letter on the death of Bede is most easily accessible in the introduction by L. Sherley-Price to his Penguin translation of Bede's *History of the English Church* (London 1955), pp. 18–21.

25   Sherley-Price trans., pp. 329, 19.

26   R. Southern, 'A Benedictine Library in a Disordered World', in *Downside Review* July 1976, pp. 163–77, citing especially pp. 170, 175.

27   It is thirty years since I read Mabillon's *Traité des études monastiques* in the Bodleian Library copy at Oxford, and I have had some cause to remember the phrase: 'C'est la plus pénible de toutes les vies'.

28   There are some lines in Willbrord's own hand in the manuscript. See W. Levison, *England the Continent in the Eighth Century* (Oxford 1946), p. 65.

29   Good short study in G. W. Greenaway, *St Boniface* (London 1955), ch. 3.

30   It is *possible* that the book survives. See C. H. Talbot, *Anglo-Saxon Missionaries in Germany* (London 1954), p. 58, note 1.

31   Portrait and text in J.-C. Margolin, *Érasme*, 2nd edn (Paris 1977), pp. 152–3.

32   K. Clark, *Civilisation* (London 1969), p. 143. The picture is illustration 97.

33   Robert Bolt, *Three Plays*, paperback edn (London 1967), p. 94.

34   R. W. Chambers, *Thomas More* (London 1935; paperback edn 1976), p. 189.

35 *Cambridge History of the Bible*, vol. 2 (Cambridge 1969), p. 496.

36 Chambers, op. cit., pp. 72–3, 106–7.

37 Bolt, op cit., p. 96. (Italics are Bolt's.)

38 Chambers, op. cit., p. 25.

39 *Utopia*, Book 2, 'Of the Religions in Utopia'. Everyman edn, modernized spelling (London 1951), p. 122.

40 Discussion with reproductions in Margolin, op. cit., pp. 11–17.

41 Sir Thomas More, *Conscience Decides* (London 1971), pp. 56, 48, 55.

42 *Dialogue of Comfort against Tribulation*, Book 3, ch. 27. Ed. F. Manley (Yale 1977), p. 322.

43 There is still no properly scientific study of the documents relating to St Seraphim of Sarov. English readers will find the account and selection of texts in G. Fedotov (London 1952) very useful. I am here sometimes dependent on a valuable study in I. Kologrivov, *Essai sur la sainteté en Russie* (Bruges 1953), pp. 418–40.

44 All the texts cited, and not easily accessible elsewhere, will be found in *Ascètes russes*, eds. Tyszkiewicz and Belpaire (Namur 1957), pp. 65–85.

45 Op. cit., ch. 1.

46 All citations from the conversation with Motovilov are given in the translation by Fedotov, op. cit., pp. 265–79.

47 This study originally in English by Professor Gordon C. Zahn was published in New York under the title, *In Solitary Witness*. I have used the charming German edn of this book, with photographs not in the original, and published under the title G. C. Zahn, *Er folgte seinem Gewissen* (Graz 1967); and my citations are from this book.

48 Psalm 34.19–20.

## Chapter 8
## SOUL-KEEPERS

1 Ecclesiasticus (Sirach) 44.9–11 (RSV, Catholic Version).

2 This text is admirably placed in relation to biblical tradition by G. von Rad, *Wisdom in Israel* (London 1972), pp. 257 ff.

3 A. de Saint-Exupéry, *Terre des hommes* (Paris 1939). I deliberately name this book by its French title meaning 'Earth of men', which better expresses Saint-Exupéry's underlying concerns than *Wind, Sand and Stars*, the title of a good English translation by L. Galantière (London 1939). All the points referred to occur in the last section of the book and are directly translated from the French.

4 Luc Estang, *Saint-Exupéry par lui-même* (Paris 1956): a good reference book, with pictures, it illustrates the last log on p. 189.

5 'Lettre au Général X', in A. de Saint-Exupéry, *Un Sens à la vie* (Paris 1956), p. 230.

6 To me personally, the story told by Andrei Sinyavsky in the communication
referred to at the end of chapter two of this book, which turns precisely on
friendship, is all the more impressive for Sinyavsky's unwillingness to say
much about Russian prisons. Of the right-wing prisons of Chile, we have at
least two very different accounts by those with direct experience, which
confirm each other in their main lines: Hernán Valdés, *Diary of a Chilean
Concentration Camp* (London 1975), and Sheila Cassidy, *Audacity to Believe*
(London 1977). Sheila Cassidy begins spontaneously to talk of a 'bond of
friendship' when she describes how her fellow prisoners helped her after the
ordeal of torture.

7 Peig Sayers, *An Old Woman's Reflections*, paperback edn (Oxford 1978), p.
129.

8 R. Gibson, *The Land without a Name* (London 1975). His earlier book was
called *The Quest of Alain-Fournier* (London 1953).

9 Here again I prefer the French title as emphasizing Meaulnes as the central
character. An English translation appeared under the title *The Lost Domain*,
trans. F. Davison (Oxford 1959).

10 Gibson, op. cit., pp. 34, 284.

11 Gibson, pp. 299, 303–4.

12 Both cited in Gibson, p. 173.

13 Both cited in Gibson, pp. 129, 218. (In a private exchange of letters,
Professor Gibson has agreed with me that the second of these two letters to
Bichet might have been given greater prominence in his study.)

14 John 11.50; 18.14.

15 Bolt, edn cit., ch. 7, p. 208.

16 J.-C. Margolin, *Érasme* (Paris 1977), p. 154.

17 Conference 16.

18 R. W. Southern, *Medieval Humanism* (Oxford 1970), p. 34.

19 Walter Daniel's *Vita Ailredi*, ed. F. M. Powicke (London 1959), p. 60.

20 My references to this work are to the Latin edn in *PL* 195 as being the most
generally accessible. There is unfortunately no satisfactory English translation of this work in print. Its style presents formidable difficulties for a
language so un-Latin as English.

21 The Loeb edn of the Latin with Eng. trans. by W. A. Falconer (London
1923), often reprinted, is easily accessible.

22 References to prologue of *Spiritual Friendship* and *Mirror*, Book 1, 34.

23 Aelred, 662C and Cicero, par. 20.

24 See ch. 7 above, under Anthony the Great and cf. Aelred 664C.

25 663B.

26 *Ipsius animae custos* 663C.

27 Par. 32.

28 665D.

29 *Sequitur marsupium* 666A.

30  666B commenting on John 15.16–17.

31  667D. In this same paragraph equality is said to be *amicitiae proprium*.

32  671D.

33  675A and Cicero, par. 37.

34  676C.

35  *Pernecessarium* 688B.

36  *Maxime consistit* 691B.

37  There is a short entry on the word 'anmchara' in D. Pochin Mould, *Ireland of the Saints* (London 1953), p. 96. Since this word, meaning 'soul-friend', is used in connection with an entry on the life of St Comgall in the eighth-century *Martyrology of Oengus*, Bradshaw Society edn (London 1905), it may be presumed that its usage is even older.

38  *Living Flame of Love*, 3rd strophe, 8.

39  701B–702A.

40  St John Climacus, *Ladder of Divine Ascent*, trans. L. Moore and M. Heppell (London 1955), Step 26, 13, p. 203.

41  The study by Paul Evdokimov, *Sacrement de l'amour* (latest edn Paris 1977) cites *passim* a number of important texts by Chrysostom on marriage.

42  *PG* 63, 201–2.

43  Galatians 3.28. Cf. *Asking the Fathers* (London 1973), pp. 115–16.

44  *SC* critical text Sermons, 1 (Paris 1970), p. 198, par. 5.

45  Isaiah Berlin, *Russian Thinkers* (London 1978), 'Fathers and Children', pp. 261–305.


# Chapter 9
## 'AND WAS MADE MAN'

1  Luke 22.63–23. 11.

2  Cell 7. Illustrated in plate XLVI, *L'opera completa dell' Angelico*, with excellent bibliography and critical notes: U. Baldini (Milan 1970).

3  Cells 6 and 8 respectively (plates XLV and XLVII).

4  Presuming the San Marco pictures belong to the 1440s.

5  We now for the first time possess a critical edition of both the short and long texts of this book: E. Colledge and J. Walsh, *A Book of Showings to the Anchoress Julian of Norwich* (Toronto 1978). I have used the same editors' modern version of their text, *Julian of Norwich Showings* (New York 1978). My own brief comments always refer to the long version.

6  Chs. 2, 3.

7  Chs. 4, 5.

8  Ch. 34.

9  Colossians 2.2. (Wand).

10   Chs. 4, 6.

11   John 10.33.

12   Pliny the Younger, Letters x, 96–7. Eng. trans. in H. Bettenson, *Documents of the Christian Church* (Oxford, various edns since 1943), section 1.

13   The *Summa contra Gentiles* (written *c.*1258–60). I use the Leonine edn of 1934 and here discuss Lib. IV, cap. 1. The verse of Job 26.14 I cite in the Douai version as rendering the Latin Thomas had.

14   Lib. I, cap. 4.

15   Ibid., cap. 5.

16   Lib. IV, cap. 1 *ad fin.*

17   See Athanasius, *Against the Arians* 1, 30–34, cited in M. Wiles and M. Santer, *Documents in Early Christian Thought* (Cambridge 1975), no. 7.

18   'The employment of *homoousios* by Athanasius to express substantial identity was a new development in the Greek language.' First sentence of ch. XI in G. L. Prestige, *God in Patristic Thought* (London 1952).

19   Useful discussion in M. Wiles, *The Making of Christian Doctrine* (Cambridge 1967), 3. Scripture as a source of doctrine.

20   *Contra Gent.*, Lib. IV, cap. 54, quoting 1 Corinthians 1.25.

21   *Summa Theologica*, IIIa pars. Q. 1, art. 1, *ad 1um* and art. 2.

22   See Th. Camelot, 'Le Christ, sacrement de Dieu in Mélanges de Lubac', in *L'Homme devant Dieu* (Paris 1963), pp. 355–63.

23   Leo, 1st sermon for Christmas in Léon le Grand, *Sermons*, 1, *SC* 22 bis (Paris 1964), par. 3 quotes 2 Peter 1.4.

24   I cite texts of Irenaeus, Athanasius, and Gregory of Nyssa in *Asking the Fathers*, pp. 23–4. William of St Thierry is clearly working with this notion in *Epistola Aurea*, par. 263, *SC* 223 (Paris 1975), p. 354.

25   IIIa pars., Q. 1, art. 3.

26   Ibid., Q. 2, art. 6.

27   M. Wiles, *Making* (as note 19 above), p. 106.

28   For the definition in Greek and Latin, see Denziger, *Enchiridion Symbolorum*, 33rd edn (Rome 1965), pars. 301, 302. *Theotokos* is quoted in the prooemium, par. 300.

29   I quote the trans. by Wiles and Santer, *Documents*, 14, pars. 4–9.

30   *De Incarn.* 12. (I quote Robertson's trans. in E. Hardy, C. Richardson, *Christology of the Later Fathers* (London 1954), p. 67. Athanasius's Greek gives 'training' rather than school, in this phrase.

31   G. von Rad, *Old Testament Theology*, 2 vols. (original German edn 1957, 1960). I am using the English trans. in the London edn (1975), and first quoting vol. II, p. viii.

32   Ibid., p. 320.

33   Pp. 324, 329, 335.

34   Pp. 342–3.

35   P. 353.

36   Romans 15.4, cited p. 361.

37   P. 363.

38   Hebrews 11.13, cited p. 374.

39   Isaiah 8.17.

40   Isaiah 45.15. It may be noted that this and following verses have been used as
     a Canticle at Lauds on Fridays in the Roman Breviary until recently, and are
     still retained there among the psalms of the first week. The opening cry of
     Psalm 22 is: 'My God, my God, why hast thou forsaken me?'

41   Vol. II, p. 386.

42   A recent commentator, J. L. Houlden, *Paul's Letters from Prison* (London
     1970; I use the 1977 edn) has carefully discussed the problems in an
     introduction to Colossians, and concludes: 'Our own view is that Colossians
     is a single, coherent piece of writing; we see no adequate reason to dismember
     it, just as we see no adequate reason to doubt that it was written by Paul' (p.
     138).

43   Colossians 1.15–19; 2.9.

44   Antirrhetic III, *PG* 99, 396B. The word I have translated 'bounded' means
     literally 'that which can be circumscribed or drawn around'.

45   Ibid., 406C.

46   *Adv. Haer.* IV, 20, 7. I have quoted the context in discussing man and Christ
     as image of God in *AF*, p. 23.

47   *Spiritual Canticle*, Stanza 5, pars 3, 4; trans. E. Allison Peers, 3rd edn (Image
     Book edn, New York 1961), pp. 70–71.

48   Stanza 5, pars. 2–4, pp. 75–6.

49   Stanza 27, par. 1, pp. 178–9.

50   Stanza 36, par. 13; and Stanza 37, par. 2, pp. 461–3.

# Chapter 10
# 'THAT MAN MIGHT BE MADE GOD'

1   This translates literally the notion as St Thomas picked it up from what he
    believed to be a sermon of Augustine cited in 111a, pars. Q. 1, art. 2. It
    is also often offered in translations of Athanasius, *De Incarn.*, 54, which
    more literally means 'he was humanized that we might be deified'. It is
    no personal reproach to the often able men who taught me as a theological
    student that I never remember anyone even mentioning this phrase in St
    Thomas, much less attempting to explain what it might mean. They only
    represented the school in which they had been trained. Silences of this kind
    are, of course, not peculiar to Catholic colleges. Even M. Wiles, in a good
    brief explanation of what the Fathers *did* mean by the phrase actually writes
    that they did not mean the words 'to be taken with full seriousness'. (M. Wiles,
    *Making*, pp. 107–8.) His intention in writing thus is clarified by his explana-
    tion, but the phrase nevertheless has the effect of minimizing how seriously
    they *did* take the notion. It could more justly be written that, since the end of

the thirteenth century, western theology by and large has not taken the major convictions of the Fathers with full seriousness. The need to remedy this situation in a satisfactory way is still an urgent one.

2   R. Poirier, *Robert Frost, the Work of Knowing* (New York and Oxford 1977), pp. 302–3; and cf. p. 299.

3   Conveniently accessible in *Complete Poems of Robert Frost*, paperback edn, (London 1967), p. 18.

4   Luke 2.15, Douai trans., italics mine.

5   Pp. 169–73.

6   Hebrews 2.14a and 4.15b.

7   The views of St Thomas on the human knowledge of Christ, for instance, go well beyond what anyone is required to believe to remain perfectly orthodox, and he is no exception in this matter.

8   *De Civ. Dei*, 14,5; *PL* 41, col. 408. I quote these sentences at the end of a discussion on the Christian attitude to the body in *AF*, ch. 5.

9   There is unfortunately still only one major modern study of Gregory: J. Meyendorff, *Introduction à l'étude de Grégoire Palamas* (Paris 1959); English version, *A Study of Gregory Palamas* (London 1964). The study I offer here is based almost exclusively on a slow reading of Meyendorff's 2-vol. edn of Gregory's *Triads*, G. Palamas, *Défense des saints hésychastes*, 2 vols (Louvain 1959). It is much to be hoped that we shall sooner or later have a similar critical edn of at least Gregory's homilies for, as the late C. Ernst says, Gregory 'holds a position in the East not unlike that which has been held by St Thomas Aquinas in the Catholic West': *Theology of Grace* (Dublin 1974), p. 51.

10   *Tr.* I, 1, line 19.

11   *Tr.* I, 3, 13 and cf. 12.

12   1 Corinthians 1.30, quoted by Gregory several times in the course of the *Triads*.

13   The phrases quoted are part of the long final sentence of *Tr.* I, 1, 5. The whole of *Tr.* I, 1 is relevant, but especially 4 and 5.

14   *Tr.* I, 3, 34.

15   2 Corinthians 4.6 and 7a.

16   *Tr.* I, 2, 2. Meyendorff translates *prosopon* as 'person' rather than 'face' in both the text of Paul and Gregory's interpretation of it, a defensible course.

17   In his short introduction to vol. 30 (*The Gospel of Grace*) of the new English translation of the *Summa Theologiae* of St Thomas Aquinas (London 1972), C. Ernst writes that 'it is only fair to say that he does not develop what might be called the "Christomorphic" potentialities of grace' (p. xxii). This is exactly what Gregory Palamas does.

18   *Tr.* I, 3, 49.

19   Romans 10.9.

20   *Tr.* II, 3, 43, last sentence.

21   *Tr.* II, 3, 46, quoting 1 John 1.2, 5; Ephesians 5.8; and 1 John 3.2.

22   *Tr.* I, 3, 15.

23   *Tr.* I, 3, 34, last sentence.

24   *Tr.* II, 1, 11, oblique reference to Romans 2.13.

25   *Tr.* I, 2, 3, 4, and cf. *passim* under 'Heart' in *AF*.

26   *Tr.* II, 1, 31.

27   *Tr.* I, 3, 18, 19.

28   *Tr.* II, 3, 52.

29   *Tr.* II, 3, 66, opening sentences.

30   *Tr.* I, 3, 22. A perfectly natural interpretation of Gregory the Great's own words in *Dial.*, Book 2, ch. 35: 'While that outward light irradiated his bodily eyes there was an inward light in his mind', etc.

31   *Tr.* II, 3, 52, final phrase.

32   Cf. *Tr.* I, 3, 18, 42.

33   *Tr.* II, 3, 73.

34   *Tr.* III, 1, 28.

35   *Tr.* III, 1, 33, recalling Basil *De Spir. Sanct.*, 36.

36   *Tr.* II, 2, 19, 20, alluding, of course, to Romans 12.1.

37   *Tr.* III, 3, 5, alluding to Romans 5.6. The phrase 'school of God' is to be found in *Tr.* I, 1, 7.

38   I cite a relevant phrase from Leo's Ember Saturday sermon 51, par. 3, in *AF*, p. 33.

39   See two vols., *Writings from the Philochalia on Prayer of the Heart* (London 1951), and *Early Fathers from the Philochalia* (London 1954), both by E. Kadloubovsky and G. E. H. Palmer. There is also the handy and charming J. Gouillard, *Petite Philochalie de la priere du coeur* (Paris 1953) now in paperback, with its useful appendix on the 'memory of God' in Islamic tradition. A new translation of the *Philochalia* by Philip Sherrard is being prepared for publication.

40   *Writings from the Philochalia* under Simeon, no. 120 (p. 126). I have been unable to trace this passage in the new critical edns of Simeon so far published.

41   Ibid., no. 100 (p. 120). This appears in Simeon's *Cent.* 3, no. 65, Greek critical edn, *SC* 51 (Paris 1957), pp. 100–101.

42   A. J. Wensinck, *Mystic treatises of Isaac of Nineveh* (Amsterdam 1923; Wiesbaden reprint 1969), ch. 74, p. 341.

43   Allusion to Matthew 5.44–5 in William Barclay's translation.

44   *Showings*, ch. 32.

45   Ibid., ch. 28.

46   Last sentence of ch. 33.

47   IIIa, par. Q. 8, art. 3, citing 1 Timothy 4.10, 'saviour of all men'; and 1 John 2.2, 'also for the sins of the whole world'.

48   I take *De Veritate*, Q. 14, art. 11 to belong to the period 1256–1259.

49   Hebrews 11.6.

50 Op. cit., *ad 1um.*

51 Acts 10.1 ff.

52 *Showings*, ch. 32, edn cit., pp. 231–2.

# Chapter 11
# THE LONG RESULT OF TIME

1 1 John 4.20.

2 For this reason, in spite of the damage done to the cylinder by the heating-system at Aldworth, we can still hear his voice chanting out a passage of *Maud*, which he recorded for Edison in 1890, the only famous English character to accept.

3 C. Ricks, *Tennyson* (London and New York 1972), p. 165.

4 *Locksley Hall*, ll. 11, 12. (Ricks edn, which usefully refers in its note to *The Day-Dream*.)

5 *The Day-Dream*, 'L'Envoi', 1, ll. 7–12. (Ricks edn, p. 632).

6 P. Henderson, *Tennyson: Poet and Prophet* (London 1978), p. 150.

7 *To Speed the Plough; Mechanisation comes to the Farm* (London 1977).

8 Op. cit., p. 193.

9 Ibid., pp. 193, 197–8.

10 Ibid., p. 205.

11 Ibid., p. 210.

12 D. Morris, *The Human Zoo* (London 1969). I cite the paperback edn of 1971.

13 Ibid., pp. 200, 209, 213.

14 Both phrases are from Morris, p. 211.

15 Luke 7.24.

16 Twelfth century. Plates with details in K. Weitzmann, *Icons from South Eastern Europe and Sinai* (London 1968). Of the fifteenth-century Lazarus at Pantanassa, G. Mathew mentions, in a phrase his old students will hear him saying, 'the quick unwinding of the sere cloth'; *Byzantine Aesthetics* (London 1963), p. 155.

17 M. F. Wiles, *The Spiritual Gospel* (Cambridge 1960), p. 1.

18 P. 25.

19 C. H. Dodd, *The Interpretation of the Fourth Gospel* (Cambridge 1953). I cite the paperback edn of 1968.

20 P. 363.

21 P. 366.

22 Pp. 147–9.

23 P. 368.

24 St Thomas Aquinas, *Summa Theologiae*, vol. 30, trans. C. Ernst (London 1971), p. xxiii. I cite this translation and its notes, but the references may be found in any text according to the usual convention.

25  1a, 11ae Q. 106, art. 1.

26  Note f, p. 5.

27  Q. 106, 1 *ad rum* and *2um*.

28  Ibid., *ad 3um*.

29  Ibid., art 2, last sentence. Note b, p. 8.

30  Ibid., art. 4.

31  Q. 108, art. 1; St Thomas is quoting John 1. 14, 16, 17.

32  Ibid., *ad 1um*, quoting Romans 14.17.

33  Q. 109, art. 1 *ad 1um*.

34  M. F. Wiles, *The Divine Apostle* (Cambridge 1967), Epilogue.

35  I am here chiefly dependent on G. Therrien, *Le Discernement dans les écrits pauliniens* (Paris 1973), a full study of *dokimazein* with an excellent bibliography to date of publication. Non-scriptural quotations refer to this book.

36  Thessalonians 5.19–22 (especially pp. 72–9).

37  P. 75.

38  Galatians 6.2–5.

39  Benedict makes the contrast with the 'bitter zeal' which separates from God as well as from everyone else.

40  The sentences of chief importance are Romans 12.2 and 14.22–3.

41  These are mentioned in Romans 5.3–5.

42  Philippians 1.9–11 (especially pp. 165ff).

43  P. 284. Therrien is certainly right to criticize Cullmann for his underestimation of the ecclesiastical dimension of this subject in Paul's thought (cf. especially p. 304).

44  Solesme's edn of the correspondence cited in ch. 4, note 8. Here I cite letter 507 (p. 337) where Barsanuphius is citing 1 Thessalonians 5.18; Romans 8.12; and 1 Corinthians 10.31.

45  Letter 196, p. 160, citing Matthew 7.7.

46  Both quotes from letter 21, pp. 26–7. Also available in critical Greek text in D. J. Chitty, *Patrologia Orientalis*, tome XXXI, fasc. 3. Barsanuphius is citing Deuteronomy 4 and Psalm 76.10 in Septuagint and Vulgate readings (77 in Vulgate numbering). The point is not dependent on whether this is what the Hebrew here really means. Barsanuphius has collected many more texts of the same import in other places, where there is no doubt about the sense.

# Chapter 12
## EPILOGUE

1  Anyone who has read J. M. Clark, *The Abbey of St Gall as a Centre of Literature and Art* (Cambridge 1926) will recall how lively a picture of the school there can be constructed from the surviving documents.

2  All the phrases quoted are from Helen Waddell's translation of Strabo's

dedication in her *Medieval Latin Lyrics* (originally London 1925; I have used the Penguin edn of 1952, p. 127).

3    H. E. Bates, *A Fountain of Flowers* (London 1974), p. 9.

4    A. Tertz (Andrei Sinyavsky), *A Voice from the Chorus*, trans. K. Fitzlyon (London 1976), p. 8.

5    Both quotations, ibid., p. 15.

6    A. Tertz, *Dans l'ombre de Gogol*, trans. G. Nivat (Paris 1978), p. 26.

7    Cited ibid., p. 14.

8    Elizabeth Bishop, 'Five Flights Up', in *Geography III* (London 1977), p. 50.

# BIBLIOGRAPHICAL NOTE

It is unfortunately not possible to give a bibliography, in the conventional sense, for this book or its predecessor *Asking the Fathers*. Had it been so, probably neither would ever have been attempted, for both deserved to be done by an abler man. Those who have been patient enough to read the present book with any attention will, I hope, have seen that, while I think it necessary to evaluate various evolutionary theories of the human situation, I do not think it possible for a Christian of orthodox belief to commit himself to some view of an *inevitable* consummation of his expectations in a form that can be tangibly envisaged or communicated. On the contrary, it seems to me that a consummation of this kind is expressly denied by the weight of Scripture and tradition. What *can* be affirmed is that a hidden consummation is certainly at work, and that it will embrace all that is genuinely human and true. Thus it is very probably hidden for the most part in humble, human tasks, successively assumed in faith. If this book has a basic theoretical thesis, it is best suggested by the words of Professor Marrou which I have cited on the title page. They occur in a witty, imaginary address to soldiers returning from the war, printed in Geneva in June 1945, and reminding them that the real war they will have to fight is only just beginning. This text has recently been reprinted (no. 15) in a collection of his own writings put together by his many admirers and friends in H.-I. Marrou, *Crise de notre temps et réflexion chrétienne* (Paris 1978). It impressively displays the lifetime concern of a profoundly believing scholar with the relations between Christianity and culture. As he says in another piece on the responsibility of the thinking man, written in 1962 (no. 16): 'The Church has been in a state of crisis at least since the Tuesday after the first day of Pentecost. I name the Tuesday relatively . . .' (p. 215). And he sees an element in this crisis as being the need that someone should assume the task of representing the absolute value of the truth. His astringent and informed mind does not lightly compromise with evasions in matters either of faith or learning. Specialist though he was in the

235

Graeco-Latin humanities, he was able as early as 1930 fairly to assess why these could no longer easily function as the sole basis of modern culture (no. 17). Nor, though a practising churchman, does he spare the clergy the inadequacies of the theological training they often receive and give (e.g. no. 42). As a historian he is able pertinently to draw attention to the factors which led to the relative over-clericalization of Christianity in the West (no. 33), with effects that almost everyone today deplores. Like many of the Fathers, to whom he devoted most of his scholarly energies, Marrou challenges again and again those 'timorous souls, who confuse orthodoxy with laziness of spirit and, to avoid error or the risk of error, gladly renounce thinking, and would like everyone else to renounce it with them' (p. 341). There are, in fact, few pieces in this fascinating anthology that are without some bearing on the questions discussed in this present book in the spirit of its first chapter.

Apart from the indications given in my apparatus and directly related to the text, there are just a few chapters on which I should like to make an additional bibliographical comment. Anyone not already persuaded of the importance of something other than a distant and dismissive attitude to Marx and Marxism, discussed in chapter 2, would do well to take a day off and read a short study, not written by a communist, which begins with the resounding and fairly incontestable sentence: 'No thinker in the nineteenth century has had so direct, deliberate, and powerful an influence upon mankind as Karl Marx.' Isaiah Berlin's *Karl Marx*, originally written in 1939, and now issued in a fourth edition (Oxford 1978) is spirited, honest, and gripping enough to wake them from their sleep, and the appended 'Guide to further reading' by Terrell Carver will be invaluable to any student wishing to find his way about the extensive related literature.

The question of the *I Ching* or *Book of Changes*, discussed in my chapter five, is an altogether more difficult matter. I have found the seven lectures by Helmut Wilhelm, now published together in English under the title *Heaven, Earth and Man in the Book of Changes* (Washington University Press 1977) of absorbing interest and value. But I do not see how it could be recommended to those who have little or no acquaintance with the *I Ching* or the world of ancient Chinese philosophy in which it moves. For them, much of it will scarcely be intelligible. It would, however, surprise me if those in whom these interests have already been awakened do not find it so illuminating that they would have wished that this follower in the spirit if not always, and then, always expressly, the letter of his father, had given us rather more.

I am aware that my chapter nine can hardly hope to have avoided exposing me to criticism from various directions in the present climate of discussion on the subject of the incarnation. On only one matter, at the beginning of my attempt to display the Chalcedonian position, should I like to add an additional comment. I happen to believe that it is true to say that 'the primitive, undivided Christian tradition has from the first prayed to Christ as to God' (p. 160). But I am perfectly well aware how difficult it is to interpret the early evidence. I do not imagine myself to be saying more than that it is in the first liturgical formulas that the later theological clarifications are already implicitly embodied. It does not seem to me, for instance, wholly impossible that the enactment of the Synod of Hippo as late as 393 that 'at the altar prayer is always addressed to the Father' (Canon 21, Mansi iii, 922) reflects the tradition of an older time when the relation between the Father and the Son was still under discussion. For this same reason I, like the reviewer in the *Times Literary Supplement* (7 January 1977), found that the modest book of Martin Hengel, *The Son of God* (London 1976) 'comes like a breath of fresh air in an overcrowded room'. Professor Hengel does, it seems to me, successfully help us to find our way into a period of greater obscurity in these matters. Not only does he strike a number of accurately aimed blows at the foundations of the theories of a number of scholars who have only increased our obscurities. He insists upon the importance of liturgical texts such as that of Philippians 2.6ff., with which his study begins, in the evolution of early Christology. As he says in the course of a particularly concentrated page, replete with references: 'It is understandable that bold christological sketches were not at first presented in the form of speculative prose, but in hymns inspired by the spirit; the language most appropriate to God's "inexpressible grace"' (p. 76). Whatever reserves may be felt about this developed form of Professor Hengel's inaugural lecture at Tübingen in 1973, one sentence in his preface deserves to be pondered by all who engage in these studies: 'The historian misunderstands the true nature of New Testament Christology unless he grasps its theological concern and its inner consistency, while a dogmatic approach which does not take seriously the historical course of Christology during the first decades of primitive Christianity is in danger of becoming no more than abstract speculation.' Of considerable importance in the same field is C. F. D. Moule, *The Origin of Christology* (Cambridge, 1977).

# INDEX